ADVENTURES IN CHRISTIAN FELLOWSHIP: THE LIGHTRIDER STORY

ADVENTURES IN CHRISTIAN FELLOWSHIP: THE *LIGHTRIDER* STORY

An American Bus Driver's Perspective on God and Country

To God Be the Glory

MIKE MANGANELLO

ADVENTURES IN CHRISTIAN FELLOWSHIP: THE LIGHTRIDER STORY

Copyright © 2026 by Lightrider, Inc.

All rights reserved. Permission granted to duplicate less than 3,000 words provided acknowledgment is given.

ISBN: 978-1-970950-00-7 (hardcover)
ISBN: 978-1-970950-01-4 (ebook)

Published by Lightrider Ministries, Upland, IN. (www.lightrider.org)

Lightrider is a longtime member of ADF Church & Ministry Alliance (www.adfchurchalliance.org)

This book is a work of nonfiction. The author has made every effort to ensure that the accuracy of the information in this book was correct as of publication and disclaim any liability to any party for any loss, damage, or disruption caused by errors or omissions, whether such errors or omissions result from negligence, accident, or any other cause. Neither the author nor the publisher nor any other person(s) associated with this book may be held liable for any damages that may result from any of the ideas made by the author in this book. Furthermore, any internet addresses (websites, blogs, etc.), telephone numbers, or the like in this book are offered only as a resource. They are not intended in any way to be or imply an endorsement by the publisher.

All Scripture quotations, unless otherwise marked, are taken from the Holy Bible, New International Version®, NIV®. Copyright © 1973, 1978, 1984, 2011 by Biblica, Inc.™ Used by Permission of Zondervan. All rights reserved worldwide. www.zondervan.com The "NIV" and "New International Version" are trademarks registered in the United States. Patent and Trademark Office by Biblica, Inc.™

Scripture quotations marked ESV are from the ESV® Bible (The Holy Bible, English Standard Version®), copyright © 2001 by Crossway, a publishing ministry of Good News Publishers. Used by permission. All rights reserved.

Scripture quotations marked NKJV are taken from the New King James Version®. Copyright © 1982 by Thomas Nelson. Used by permission. All rights reserved.

Scripture quotations marked NASB are taken from the New American Standard Bible®. Copyright © 1960, 1962, 1963, 1968, 1971, 1972, 1973, 1975, 1977, 1995 by The Lockman Foundation. Used with permission. All rights reserved.

Scripture quotations marked BSB are taken from the Berean Standard Bible®. The Holy Bible, Berean Standard Bible, BSB. Copyright © 2016, 2020 by Bible Hub. Used by permission. All rights reserved worldwide.

Photos restored and/or digitized by Dan R. Boyd.

Drone photos by Vinnie Manganello.

Printed in the USA.

Dedication

Hindsight is a great tool for revealing the reality of God's hand in directing, providing for, and protecting families, ministries, and indeed Our Republic. That's why an accurate knowledge of history is so important, yea essential, and why some American history has been included in this narrative.

To say that God's been gracious to Lightrider would be like saying that they get snow in Buffalo! We have been deluged, nay buried, by His faithfulness, provision, protection, and love. Indeed, we serve a Gracious, with a capital G, God.

America, too, and the Church in America, have been beneficiaries of His boundless grace. Chapter 26 acknowledges and offers gratitude to God for His hand in America's founding, growth, and conduct. It's also a plea, a prayer, that He bring revival on this land, enabling His promise ". . . [If] my people, who are called by my name, will humble themselves and pray and seek my face and turn from their wicked ways, then will I hear from Heaven and will forgive their sin and heal their land" (II Chronicles 7:14). May America be a Nineveh, not a Sodom . . .

Scripture tells us that it takes two things to defeat the evil one: the blood of the Lamb and the testimony of the saints (Christians) (Revelation 12:11 ESV). This book is the latter. It seeks to thank and glorify the God in Whom we trust for His miracles by the mile, getting and keeping Lightrider Ministries plying the "endless ribbon" of American highway these past 39 years, as well as prospering our nation, providing those highways while preserving freedom essential for such plying. It is a factual account of Lightrider's story, a story still unfolding, with an emphasis on situations, places, and people rich with what some might call God Sightings, God's Provision—or Miracles, if you will. But you, the reader, be the judge.

This author's duty in this is found in Deuteronomy 4:9 (NASB): ". . . keep your soul diligently, so that you do not forget the things which your eyes have seen and they do not depart from your heart all the days of your life; but make them known to your sons and your grandsons." (Thank you, Sam Cocking, who happened by the office as this dedication was being written, calling to mind that verse.) Hence, this book is dedicated to my family—my wife, Debbie Manganello; our daughter, Danielle Fromer; our son-in-law, Michael; and their son, our grandson, Orrin.

"Even when I'm old and gray, do not forsake me, O God, until I proclaim Your power to the next generation, Your might to all who are to come" (Psalm 71:18 BSB).

In loving memory of
Thelma, Esther, & Glenn Surguine

"The guiding principle and
prayer of this Nation has been,
is now, and shall ever be
'In God We Trust.'"

President John F. Kennedy at a breakfast for
International Christian Leadership
9 February 1961
As recorded in "American Minute"
by William Federer (page 333)

Contents

Foreword ix

Preface xi

Introduction xiii

About That Bus Driver xv

1 Heeding the Call 1

2 Getting Underway 5

3 Immediate Need Met with Answered Prayer. 9

4 Miracles by the Mile—Lightrider's First Mobile Retreat 11

5 Kids to California—More Miracles on Mobile Retreat Number Two 17

6 A Significant Speed Bump Encountered Early On. 21

7 God Provides a Co-Pilot via a Personal Miracle or Two 25

8 Random Grace in Adversity, Again and Again and 29

9 Miracles or Highway Happenstance 37

10 More Tranny Travails. 41

11 God's Grace, Great Golf, and Good Gravy 45

12 Lightrider's Livery—Throwing Lightrider's Hat into the Cultural Fray 49

13 Deer Season; Bicycle Beneficence; Mercy on the Mountain;
    A Trucker's Life Spared; an Icy Tale of Two Coaches; Nuclear Threat; &
    a Couple of Coast-to-Coast-with-the-Holy-Ghost Highlights. 51

14 A Word or Two or Three Thousand Five Hundred Twenty Five of Testimony. 65

15 Observing Tradition Remembers Forgotten Truth 71

16 Lightrider's Miracle Bus 75

17	A Girl's Life Saved by the Hand of God	81
18	Left Behind	87
19	Recycling God's Love	93
20	Lightrider's Ministry Report—25 Years OTR	95
21	The RedBarn—Connecting Kids to Christ	97
22	We Interrupt Our Sojourn with Great News	101
23	A Proverbial Poke, with Love—Calling on Disney to Repent	103
24	The GrayBarn—A Sanctuary for Seniors	109
25	Task Force Upland—Preparing to Weather the Storm	117
26	God & Country Forum—Dialoguing the Biblical Heritage of Our American Republic	119
27	The Dan Plan—Lightrider's Transition to Today	125
28	Wandering Wheels and the Mobile Retreat	127
29	The Lightrider Experience—Blueprint for Fellowship	131
30	O Canada—Nice Neighbor to the North	137
31	Manufacturing a Redefined Motor Coach a New Way—in the USA	145
32	Snapshots and Short Stories	155
33	Adventures in Christian Fellowship—Five Takeaways	187
Appendix 1	House Resolutions 397 and 443; NAE Insight Briefings '94 and '96; Scripture, Quotes, and General Facts With Regard to America's Biblical Heritage	195
Appendix 2	Details—The H1213 and the H1213 Project	217

Foreword

My intention during the many years talking and dreaming about writing this book was to ask my friend Jay Kesler—co-worker in the vineyard, former President of Taylor University, and Lightrider board member since 2010—to write this foreword.

Sadly, about six years ago, Jay suffered a physical event in his body that has made such a request impossible.

Speaking with Janie, Jay's sweet wife, shortly before she began walking the streets of gold, she opined that Jay would have without a doubt been happy to have penned such an honor for me.

Hence, the following is an endorsement by Jay of Lightrider Ministries published in an early Lightrider brochure, followed by his thoughts about our dreams of creating a specialty vehicle to transport seniors:

"I am very enthusiastic about the Mobile Retreat Ministry. I have spent a lifetime in youth work demonstrating the effectiveness of removing young people from their familiar surroundings and involving them in retreat experiences. Through fellowship, new experiences, stress, and concentrated focused teaching, wonderful things happen in their lives. Results with young people can be duplicated with adults using the same principles. The addition of the mobile element adds a further dimension that greatly increases the adventure and effectiveness. I'm excited about this concept.

Jay with Bernese mountain dog friend Bennett at Lightrider's Senior Men's Fellowship.

The Lightrider Staff are experienced leaders with a proven track record in this ministry. I recommend this ministry to any who want to minister in a creative way."

Dr. Jay Kesler, President, Taylor University

Jay also wrote this:

"Lightrider has developed the H1213, a new concept in motor coaches. Their step-less vehicle will open the door to mobile retreats for a much wider age range, enabling them to duplicate those same wonderful things in the lives of senior adults that have worked so well with the younger generations. Our elderly will be able to come aboard with their kids, grandkids, and great-grands, allowing adventures that comprise the entire family. Youth reaching out to the elderly will be able to plan outings for retirement communities that actually get everyone out and about. The potential of the H1213 to increase the depth of ministry opportunity for the church is tremendous!"

(See Chapter 31 and Appendix 2 for details about the H1213 and the plan to manufacture it right here in Upland, IN.)

Preface

It's been said that life is like a tapestry. A tapestry viewed from the front reveals a picture or image, clearly recognizable. Viewed from the back, however, a disorganized, knotted mass of colors and threads displays no discernable order, much less a recognizable picture or image.

This writing is a verbal tapestry of, primarily, my life with and for Christ in ministry at Wandering Wheels and Lightrider Ministries—basically His plan for my life being lived out. Reading it described in sequences of events is like viewing a tapestry from behind, as it is the joining of these sequences that reveals an image of that life's plan, or more accurately God's plan for that life. "For I know the plans I have for you, declares the Lord, plans to prosper you and not to harm you, plans to give you hope and a future" (Jeremiah 29:11 NIV).

I'm reminded of a prank we played on groups of kids during many a seemingly interminable, 18-hour day at the Magic Kingdom at Disney World. Long lines and heat sometimes forced us to come up with activities to keep kids occupied. One such was visiting Cinderella's Gift Shop in the castle. We'd show one of the nice suits of armor for sale to our gaggle of teens, pointing out a few of its artistic features. Then we'd pick an individual, a girl usually, and point out the intricate artistry of the tapestry used like an apron or breach cloth on the suit of armor, mentioning the incredible work visible from the back of the tapestry. Inevitably, the girl would lift a corner of the tapestry to get a peek at the back, whereupon we'd begin to exclaim, "Pervert, pervert!" (See Chapter 23 for more Disney intrigue.)

But I digress.

Introduction

Those employed in the transportation industry know that buses are the vehicles that transport passengers within cities, while highway or over-the-road (OTR) travel happens aboard motor coaches. However, the average dude or dudette, whether riding in the city or traveling over the road, sees the guy or gal in the front seat with a steering wheel in his or her grip as the "bus driver." Hence, our broader use of that term in this writing.

Dinah Shore used to croon about seeing the USA in your Chevrolet, but checking the scene from the driver's seat of a motor coach hauling souls adds serious depth to such observation. People, more than geography, are what make a nation.

FAT FOR FREE

A common custom in retail America very popular with bus drivers is the feeding of said drivers for free when stopping at restaurants with herds of travelers. It's tough to moderate one's eating when the cost is removed, especially at Mickey D's, where well-trained staff always ask, "Do you want fries with that?" or "Shall I supersize your order?" Who wants to hold up the line by making hollow excuses?

Is it any wonder coach operators tend toward the corpulent? Being fat for free is an honest estate, though it might be said that such is the result of insidious marketing blandishments. After all, billboards advertising

restaurants frequently have notices saying, "Buses Welcome—Drivers Eat Free."

Of course other factors contribute to the corpulent coach drivers' pudgy persona like getting the munchies while driving and popping fat pills or fat capsules, a.k.a. plain and peanut M&Ms, to mitigate the need. I actually developed the habit of chewing on soda straws as an effort to slow the growth of my girth.

It is suggested that those unfamiliar with Lightrider (LtR) might begin sojourning with us by gaining an understanding of the whys and wherefores of mobile retreats, pioneered by Wandering Wheels (Wheels), polished somewhat by LtR, and found in Chapters 28 and 29.

Observations expressed here were made while bicycling and or driving a motor coach with Wheels, no longer in service, and/or LtR, still in service though presently operating without a motor coach.

Actual names have been used out of gratitude and to add veracity to the narrative while providing touch points for the potential thousands of readers who participated in the ministries of Wheels and/or LtR. Each of these ministries prospered, largely in part because of the efforts of His legions of helpers acting in concert, one with another, from time to time, contributing their God-given gifts, talentsm and love to the ministry mix.

Hence, as a practical matter and given the limits of this aging author's recall, a relatively small fraction of actual names of "team members," participants, and contributors have been recognized in this narrative. My sincere apology, given in advance, to those myriad friends, neighbors, and men and women of God who, too, gave to these two ministries and have gone unrecognized in this narrative. Please understand and forgive.

My apologies, too, to those mentioned by name who were not contacted for permission for such mention, whether because they couldn't be found or I simply forgot to get in touch—so sorry.

The Alumni Office at Taylor has been a big help in my finding many of those I have managed to contact. Thank you, TU!

One last concern as we, you (the reader) and I, begin: In this day and age, as in the very beginning of this Republic, mention of anything having to do with government, Church, faith, or the intersection of the three may cause offense. As Patrick Henry observed, "If I were to propose opening a window on a sultry day, there are those who . . . would say that it is treachery and sedition."[1]

Please know that my intention is to illuminate, not to offend. These words of Paul, quoted by Gary Hamrick at Cornerstone Chapel (online) apply: "For am I now seeking the approval of man, or of God? . . . If I were still trying to please man, I would not be a servant of Christ" (Galatians 1:10 ESV). "So have I become your enemy by telling you the truth?" (Galatians 4:16 NASB).

---

[1] This quote learned from watching *Story of a Patriot* at Colonial Williamsburg with dozens of Wheels and LtR groups (confirmed August 17, 2025, with GPT-4o mini).

About That Bus Driver

The author, Michael Glenn Manganello, was born on Groundhog Day 1948 along with a womb mate—not Punxsutawney Phil, rather a twin brother, Stephen Clark, 12 minutes his junior, to Master Sergeant Arthur and Mrs. Esther Manganello at the Camp Stoneman Army Hospital in Pittsburg, Contra Costa County, California, a military brat right from the get-go. One other sibling, Richard Lawrence, a brother, two years older and—once the trio was fully grown—three inches taller, rounded out the family.

Arthur, from Worcester, Massachusetts, had met and married Esther Surguine from Lewis, Colorado, in Honolulu, Territory of Hawaii, on 27 December 1942, having been courting at the time of the Japanese attack on Pearl Harbor on Sunday, 7 December 1941. Art and Esther had been out to dinner on the Saturday evening prior to the attack. Later that evening Art hitched a ride back to his quarters at Hickam Field, adjacent to Pearl Harbor, with Esther's roommate's beau, a young US Navy ensign stationed aboard the USS *Arizona,* which, just a few hours hence, would become his final duty station.

At age 11, in 1958, following 10 years of life in Concord, California, and a year and a half at Camp Chaffee in Fort Smith, Arkansas, Mike with his mom and two brothers sailed from Seattle, Washington, aboard the MSTS *MM Patrick* to Naha Port on the island of Okinawa, an American protectorate at the time, joining his father Arthur who had had remote duty with the US Army, HQ USARYIS (United States Army Ryukyus Islands), Fort Buckner, since 1957. It had been a 17-day voyage across the Pacific with stops at Yokohama, Japan, and Pusan, Korea.

Mike lived with his family on Okinawa for 10 years. During this time the family traveled back and forth to the Continental USA, calling on extended family in California and Massachusetts on four separate occasions, enabling Mike and his brothers to visit all 50 of the United States and most of the provinces of Canada before leaving high school.

Following graduation from Kubasaki High School, an American Overseas Dependent School, and taking two years of off-campus college classes with the University of Maryland, Mike departed "the Rock" in 1968 to matriculate on campus at the University of Maryland, College Park, Maryland.

Being drafted shortly after graduation from U of M, Mike was inducted into the US Army at Fort Holabird, Baltimore, Maryland, doing Basic Training and Advanced Individual Training (AIT) at Fort Knox, Kentucky. Following two months serving as a guinea pig at Ireland Army Community Hospital doing medical research, he was assigned duty at the Intelligence Directorate (J2), HQ USECOM (United States European Command), Patch Barracks, Vaihingen, near Stuttgart, Germany.

Honorably discharged in September 1973, Mike moved to Upland, Indiana, where he has resided ever since. Mike served the Lord with Wandering Wheels, formerly of Taylor University, for 15 years prior to co-founding Lightrider Inc. in 1987, where he continues to serve. He married Debbie, who had a 12-year-old, redheaded daughter, Danielle, on 4 May 1991 in Conway, South Carolina.

ONE

Heeding the Call

During the last five of my 15 years at Wandering Wheels, a dream of using a double-decker highway coach as a mega Possum (what we called our sleeper buses at Wheels) consumed my imagination and prayers. Seeing such a coach in San Francisco while on a Possum trip had been my inspiration. It was not a clunky old city double-decker bus like you might see in London, but a magnificent motor coach built for the highway rather than city streets.

One Sunday in late August 1987 while attending Upland Evangelical Mennonite Church (UEMC), Upland, IN, God spoke to me. Not in an audible voice, but as an idea that came to me, put forward after five years of dreaming and scheming, talking and praying over this double-decker. Jim Mathis was preaching about Jesus calling His disciples when it occurred to me that God wanted me to quit vacillating and get with it on the oars. "What about my Visa bill and the mortgage on my trailer," I responded, almost out loud, "if I quit my job to live my dream?" God's idea came to me at that moment. If my boss at Wandering Wheels, Coach Bob Davenport, the founder and director, would keep paying me to lead Possum trips but allow me to use the time between those trips to start a new bus ministry, this just might happen.

On Monday, I hauled my 39-year-old self upstairs to Coach's office and asked him. Tuesday morning I was sitting at the dining table in my trailer thanking God and wondering what to call a double-decker bus ministry. God had given me a dream and had pushed me out of my comfort zone to begin accomplishing it. This part-time employment at full-time pay arrangement endured until June 1988, when we took the first Lightrider on a test drive to Cincinnati for a nice supper at the Boathouse at the Montgomery Inn prior to our first paying, mobile retreat a week later. I never missed a single Visa or mortgage payment during those months, or ever since for that matter. Indeed, Lightrider has never failed to pay a bill. God is good.

One night during this LtR start-up, I headed to bed in my trailer at about midnight. Seeing my Bible on the dining table, I realized that I had not read it that day. Opening it randomly, running my finger down the page, I stopped at Proverbs 16:3, "Commit your works to the Lord and your plans will be established." Talk about an "encouraging word."

Naming the ministry was an important challenge. A rerun on TV of *Knight Rider*, an adventure series about an automobile with an animated personality, gave me the idea for Light Rider. Sure, we were planning to ride at night, but night is darkness and we were carrying His light. When the logo came off the page of an artist friend, Snowball (Paul King), I noticed that the "t" in *Light* became a cross in the center of the name when the two words were united, so *LIGHTRIDER* seemed to be a Divine endorsement of that name. We even got a monogram: LtR.

In the fall of 1987 Jim Mathis, then pastor of UEMC, along with some elders of the church, laid hands on Bob Walker and me, sending us out as home missionaries. UEMC, which became Upland Community Church (UCC) some years ago, continues to support LtR monthly. Jim Mathis served on the LtR board, as did his successor at UEMC, Jerry Cline.

Church members Dick and Marsha Becker obtained Public Passenger Chauffeur's Licenses, enabling them to drive for LtR. Dick served on the LtR board too. Geoff Schwartz did some driving for us as well. Both applied their skilled hands in constructing our buildings, converting various double-deckers into tools for ministry and pouring yards of concrete as needed. Many in our church have helped to keep LtR "On the road to revival" these 39 years and counting.

God has used my church family to keep LtR in the fight and me in the faith. Seeing His hand in every aspect of our ministry continues to motivate our mission of proclaiming the message of Jesus Christ, encouraging individual faith in Christ and strengthening Christian relationships through fellowship.

Five local businesses were invaluable in helping us get first the Possums and then each of the three Lightriders set up to take His Light on to the road.

UPLAND HARDWARE

Gregg Ballinger, proprietor, was an invaluable helper when we found on one project or another that we had designed ourselves into a corner. For instance, we had fabricated a "chuck box" for preparing meals while on mobile retreats that was to be hung on the side of Possum Two. Gregg's idea of cutting a hockey puck in half to make "rubber bumpers" to protect the bus's paint job greased that project into a very successful conclusion.

CHRIST INC.

Christ Inc., just seven miles east of town, distributed accessories to truck stops nationwide, like laminated truck atlases with low clearances marked on all state and US highways in the lower 48, essential information for frequently operating a double-decker coach off the usual trade routes.

Reflective triangles, flares, headlight bulbs, spools of wire, tire thumpers—you name it, if it was used aboard a semi or motor coach, they had it and usually gave it to us or sold it to us at cost. We had to get to know their resident attack Lab, Colonel, but once he got to know us we were in.

Our bunk design at Lightrider, for safety, eliminated the vertical steel supports used on the Possum in favor of nylon webbing used in seat belts, of which Christ's was well stocked. My brother Rick, a mechanical engineer, encouraged this design change, informing me that the closed-cell foam with which we padded steel uprights in the Possum would be as nothing when, Heaven forbid, stopping collision-propelled bodies.

ICKES' RV SURPLUS SUPPLY INC.

In Montpellier, just 13 miles beyond Christ's, Ickes' has indeed been a Godsend. Offering, at surplus prices, a plethora of rivets, nuts, bolts, rolls of vinyl, seat cushions of all sizes, RV toilet valves, chemicals, and the like, as well as ideas to help our shade-tree mechanical selves put together the devices, bunks, chuck boxes, and other stuff essential for operating mobile retreats. For the last few decades, Randy Bonewit and his brother Wendell, along with Wendell's pretty freckle-faced wife, Brenda, have cheerfully helped, encouraged, and instructed us in all things RV, enabling Wheels and LtR to convert and outfit buses and coaches into safe, comfortable venues for fellowship.

JENNERJAHN MACHINE, INC.

Jennerjahn in Mathews, IN, came online helping to keep LtR on the road (OTR) by making an essential yet unavailable part for our first double-decker. Brian Jennerjahn, the dad, engineered and manufactured this mambo bushing, part of the drive-axle suspension. Brian's son, Chris (see Chapter 9), worked with their engineer Roger Vogel on a proposal for engineering and manufacturing a mechanized overhead luggage-handling system for LtR's concept coach for senior travel, the LowRider (see Chapter 31).

We had a wonderful mobile retreat out West, with Roger's family aiming to tick off at least one item, seeing Hover Dam, from Roger's father-in-law's bucket list. But, again, I digress.

UPLAND TIRE

Before Upland Tire opened, Mike Pearson was doing maintenance for LtR while we were garaged on Main Street in Judge Porter's big red barn. When Pearson opened Upland Tire, he had one of the five bays equipped with a 14-foot door so that he could get our double-decker inside for maintenance. Mike brought friendship, skill, integrity, and maintenance availability to LtR, enabling us to prosper.

TWO

Getting Underway

Finding, funding, and outfitting that first Lightrider proved to be nothing short of miraculous. Miracles have been a necessity that we've witnessed frequently during these 39-plus years in His service.

September 1987. Borrowing a car from a good friend, Chip Wehling, to check out a Neoplan double-decker in use by Imperial Travel of Lafayette, IN, 80 miles west, was my next move. Despite my having had 15 years' bus-driving experience, crusty old Bob Calloway, the CEO at Imperial, wouldn't let me drive. But as a passenger able to go upstairs during the ride, the prime benefits of the double-decker experience, the peaceful quiet and the beautiful view became mine, something I would have missed had I been belted into the driver's seat downstairs.

Having forgotten my wallet, a real rarity for me, necessitated my bumming five bucks from Bob to buy a Whopper for lunch, my first experience at fundraising. Although Calloway had promised to keep his eyes open for an available, suitable, used double-decker, I wondered if my ostensibly penurious estate might dissuade him from keeping that promise.

However, in November of 1987, Bob Calloway made good on his promise. He called on a Friday to say he had found just the right double-decker for us—a lightly used, 1974 Neoplan Skyliner with low mileage, no rust, and, though built in Germany for the Los Angles Rapid Transit District (LARTD), a US engine and drive train. For just $75,000 we could drive it home from Los Angeles. My offering $300 and an old Lincoln as a down payment got a chuckle and a no from Calloway, though that was all we'd managed to raise at the time. He did accept my request for a day to check with a local Christian family, Leland and LaRita Boren, for whom I had done odd jobs for a year just after mustering out of the US Army back in 1973. The work had been a wonderful mix of odd jobs around their farm and home or chores at their business, Avis Industrial, then in downtown Upland, like disking fields, helping to birth calves, driving a forklift—a real learning experience.

One morning, on arriving at their home, I saw their black cat, one of many, curled up on the garage floor. It was a fun cat, so I snuck up on its sleeping self and gave it a nudge with my toe. It did not stir—it was stiff as a board, not sleeping but, in fact, quite dead.

Walking into the house to report this sad circumstance to LaRita, I found her in her office. Opening my mouth to say, "The black cat is dead," at the same moment Lori, about nine at the time, one of their three kids, entered the office from the other side, I said instead,

"The ebony feline has expired." Lori's eyes got big and she exclaimed, "The black cat is dead?" She began to cry . . .

So, Saturday morning after my call with Bob Calloway, over coffee in the Borens' kitchen, Leland and LaRita listened to a very hastily thrown-together business plan/proposal/plea. Leland, playing devil's advocate, laughed at my admittedly simplistic, incomplete plan to accomplish such a far-fetched dream. LaRita, however, asked how much Lightrider needed. When told, she offered to give Lightrider half: $37,500!

My father, a retired Army finance officer visiting from Massachusetts that weekend, was very skeptical about my faith, Christians in general, and, in particular, my feeble plan. He was the first to hear about this wonderful provision from God, and it caused him pause, let me tell you.

Thirty-seven-five big ones was a lot of dough to my poor, trailer-dwelling, 39-year-old self. Taking a walk that evening, seeking help with the burden that someone had bet big bucks on my dream, I chanced to pass a gigantic American flag that had recently been unfurled under lights at Avis Industrial just across the highway from Taylor University. That flag reminded me that our founders, trusting the same God as me, putting their lives, their fortunes, and their sacred honor on the line, got this Republic underway. Getting a bus on the road carries quite some responsibility, to be sure, but all I was risking was my pride. God was providing not just the funding, but was bolstering my faith too.

On Monday morning Lightrider offered Calloway $30,000 up front if he'd grant us six months, interest free, to come up with the rest. Impressed that we had raised 30 grand overnight, he said that he would trust us for the rest. Bob Walker, my good friend and partner in this venture, and I flew to Los Angeles—he from Naples, Florida, where he lived and worked, me from Indianapolis. We met Max Majewski, an entrepreneur who had bought at public auction two Neoplan Skyliners from LARTD, one to sell for funding in order to convert the other into a motor home. Max had advertised the one for sale in *National Bus Trader* (*NBT*) for $45,000. Hence, crusty old Calloway was risking only $15,000 on this Whopper-eating stranger from Upland. Larry Plachno, founder and editor of *NBT*, would become a friend in ministry and all things motor coach.

Bob and I, excited that God was directing our steps, took ownership for Lightrider of what had been Unit 9900, used in the Park & Ride system of the LARTD. We pointed her east for the 2,143-mile journey to Upland, taking the first physical step to fulfilling the mission of our ministry, blessed with fair weather the whole way. Unit 9900 performed nicely during this first step of becoming a tool for ministry. We did, though, break a security mirror jutting down from the ceiling of a gas station overhang with the top of our double-decker, an unnoticed harbinger of what would later be seen as a blessing in the rough. We parked our proud, new-to-us, would-be Lightrider at our church in Upland. It rained cats and dogs that night. Our Neoplan Skyliner leaked from every seam, window, and door—it looked like a rainforest inside. This was going to take some work.

Bob and I had received estimates from a factory in northern Indiana to fabricate the steel bunks needed to convert our seated city bus to a sleeper highway coach. But that company contacted us saying that their new company policy was that no contracts under a million dollars would be considered. Our project would have been only a few thousand. We had been left in the lurch, or so it seemed.

That same night, however, I ran a Possum trip that stopped at a Mickey D's in Muncie to pick up a staff member, a Ball State student who had volunteered. The couple that had brought her to the Mickey D's knew a steel fabricator in Muncie by the name of Dick Craw, who, hearing of our need, offered to help. Dick of Craw Steel later went on to do all of the steel fabrication work we needed, at or below his cost. What would have been a few thousand became a few hundred. God is good.

For nearly six months God brought to us everything needed to convert Unit 9900 from a double-decker transit bus seating 80 into the recreational coach sleeping 30 that would be called the Lightrider: steel fabricator Dick Craw to make the bunks; upholsterers Dane and Doris Rodman, in Jonesboro, to string webbing onto the steel bunk frames and to sew the cushions with foam rubber donated by Foamex in Fort Wayne (Art and Millie Sivits of Grabill Missionary Church connected us there); He also provided parking for the Skyliner at Virgil Coral's farm, along with tools and willing, skilled volunteers; office space (thank you, Doc Oliver) needing only to be moved into; friends in Hessen Cassel, brothers Carl and Ray Sorg, who, in the dead of winter, dug a hole under the coach parked in their farmyard, enabling them to crawl underneath to install a holding tank for the toilet they'd mounted; and even a nonprofit charter (thank you, Jim Mathis) needing only a name change from EMC Bus Company to Lightrider, Inc. All these people and things appeared just in time through unexpected meetings, overheard conversations, new acquaintances met at McDonald's, and old friends. God's fingerprints were all over it!

Coral's farmyard was alive with farm critters, including peacocks and turkeys. One morning Bob and I arrived to work on the LtR. When we climbed out of the car, a juvenile turkey, being pursued by two comparatively massive peacocks, scurried right over to Bob, jumped up into Bob's arms, and laid his little head down on Bob's shoulder. It was the picture of domestic tranquility—a trusting little life protected. The peacocks lost interest, wandering off . . . But I digress.

Now we come to the funding miracle. Three days prior to the deadline for getting the $45,000 to Imperial Travel, I drove out to Ron Keller's home for what proved to be a providential meeting. Ron, then Registrar at Taylor, was a Lightrider board member who had picked up some parts for the bunks being fabricated at Craw Steel in Muncie. Because his wife, Judy, had taken his car with the parts in the trunk to run an errand, Ron and I had an unexpected chance to chat.

Ron asked about the 45 grand. Still totally clueless about where it was coming from, yet somehow still convinced that He would get it to us in time, all I could do was shake my head. He asked if we'd consider borrowing it. "Who would loan $45,000 for 15 years to a nonprofit start-up to purchase a 14-year-old bus?" I asked. "The Christian Service Foundation," of which Ron was President, was his reply. This foundation required a co-signature from a Mennonite Church.

That very evening was the quarterly business meeting of my church, which just happened to be Upland Evangelical Mennonite Church. After two and a half hours of haggling over the mission's budget and such, a motion to adjourn came to the floor. I stood, desperate for a hearing, and, amid a cacophony of groans, asked the full congregation assembled there if they would vote to give the church council authority to co-sign for a loan to start a bus ministry. Lightrider got unanimous approval ("unanimous"—a word that had never before been used in a sentence with the UEMC congregation).

The following evening, two days before the deadline to raise the $45,000 for Imperial, was the church council meeting, where 14 men heard my proposal and a testimony of what God had already done. Again, He brought unanimous approval.

The next day the Christian Service Foundation cut Lightrider a check and I drove to Fort Wayne to pick it up, prior to calling Bob Calloway to invite him to lunch the following day. He was going to be paid the full amount on the exact day it was due. He would be hearing, in person, the testimony of just how God had orchestrated this miracle. We picked up that lunch tab too, so Calloway even got paid back for the Whopper he had so graciously provided me on the day we had met. God is good.

THREE

Immediate Need Met with Answered Prayer

Nostalgia Night at Taylor University: the author with Taylor University Prof Maryland McQueen and Goliath, his car.

At this time, my car, a 55 Chevy Belair Sport Coup, the first car I had ever bought, was undergoing a very lengthy but much-needed body restoration, a big favor from a new friend, Bill Thompson (a reverend and member of LtR's board). Needing a car in the interim, I had asked the men at a Thursday prayer breakfast for the Christian Businessmen's

Committee (CBMC) to pray that God would bring Lightrider some wheels for "company" use. Two days later, on Saturday morning, snuggled into the crushed, green velvet of an overstuffed bucket seat, I drove a magnificent 1977 Lincoln Town Car home from Marshall, MI—it was so long you could land aircraft on the hood! (Sorry, no picture available.)

Did Lightrider really need a Lincoln? God must have thought so. The car had a trailer hitch. A donated stake and rail trailer made that Lincoln into a virtual pickup truck—we could haul parts and supplies yet accommodate a gaggle of donors in style when the occasion called for it.

One of the prayer warriors that Thursday morning, good friend and longtime roomie Tom Gearhart, who would serve a long while on the LtR board, had a friend, Gary Dobbertine, a widower of two years, who, in donating his late wife's car to Lightrider, had at last found a Kingdom use for it. God is good.

That old Lincoln served LtR for many years. But, in the spirit of full disclosure, it suffered a little adolescent abuse along the way. One evening, returning from a dinner out with a couple, Bruce and Linda Sebastian, donors and friends, the question of the car's mechanical prowess came up while at a stop sign in Upland—could this beast actually burn rubber? My idiot self, rising to the challenge, using an old technique from my high-school days, put the automatic transmission into neutral, then floored the gas while shifting the tranny back into drive. My expectation of wild fishtailing with squealing, smoking tires didn't happen. In fact, the car did not move forward an inch; instead, it began rolling backward. The drive shaft broke at the rear axle and began beating against the floorboards like the devil himself. Linda couldn't have left the car any faster had it been equipped with ejection seats.

Being a car guy, it was readily apparent to me what had happened. The only upside of the experience was that the incident would not have to be reported to a stunned, angry father. But I digress.

FOUR

Miracles by the Mile—Lightrider's First Mobile Retreat

The LtR at the National Archives on Pennsylvania Avenue, Washington, DC, on a later retreat.

Lightrider's very first mobile retreat on 5–11 July 1988 was with an adult Sunday-school class, the Bridge Builders, of the Grabill Missionary Church, Grabill, IN. Our itinerary: Mystic Seaport, CT; New York City; Washington DC; Williamsburg, VA; and DC again before returning to Grabill. That was some retreat, and God's merciful hand was very evident, repeatedly. After many minor mechanical foibles with the compressed air system and air conditioning, we made it to Mystic, though a bit late.

Arriving in NYC the following day, Bob Walker, the other Lightrider co-founder, dropped me with the 26 Grabill Gobblers to see Manhattan, as my dad used to say, *shanks mare* (on foot). Meanwhile Bob took the Lightrider to a friend's bus garage in Newton, New Jersey, for repairs. This friend was an old buddy from Wandering Wheels, Larry Kleindienst, aka Spare Parts. His family had a bus ministry, King's Coach.

Sure enough, right on time, at 11 p.m., the welcome sight of the Lightrider coming down the avenue to pick us up after a wonderful day, finishing with a late supper at the Plaza Hotel, greatly cheered our group. Our weary but grateful selves boarded the Lightrider for the overnight jaunt of 210 miles down to DC.

Minutes later, at about midnight, west bound on the NYC approach to the George Washington Bridge, crossing the Hudson River into New Jersey, the Lightrider lost all power, mechanical and electrical. We rolled to a stop, blocking the travel lane (there was no shoulder). Realizing the danger to our passengers, our being dark and stalled in a heavy flow of semi trucks supplying the city by night, but being new to this vehicle, it took me a moment to figure out how to open the door, given the power failure. Finding the manual release, fumbling with the reflective triangles, I finally managed to get out and rush to the rear of the Lightrider. What a relief to discover a large city truck with a flashing yellow light had already been stationed there, providing visual warning and physical protection from harm—a semi could not have hit us even if its driver had been asleep at the wheel.

Seeing smoke coming from the battery compartment, I lifted the cover. An electrical solenoid had broken loose and fallen onto the positive battery terminal, shorting out the electrical system and shutting everything down.

While I tried to decide what to do next, a massive wrecker backed up to the front of the Lightrider. We'd been wondering how our broke selves could pay for a tow. We'd had to ask this, our first group, to pay for this retreat in cash so we could buy fuel on the retreat. Welcome words were painted across the back of that tow truck, "No charge for this service." The New York City Port Authority wasn't about to let Lightrider, or anyone else for that matter, obstruct traffic on their bridge.

Passengers and all, that wrecker easily lifted the front of our stricken coach, towing us west across the bridge into New Jersey, where the young driver pulled onto the shoulder to remove his hook. Not wanting to be stranded on the side of the road, Bob and I begged the driver to at least take us to the next exit, even trying to bribe him.

As God would have it, the Port Authority supervisor happened by in his car and authorized the driver to take us to an all-night diner in Fort Lee, NJ. Our passengers were safe, had restrooms, coffee, and pie. With the windows propped open for ventilation, it being a wonderfully cool evening for July in the Big Apple, with a gentle breeze too, all were quickly snoozing away in the bunks we had set up for them. One of the passengers, John Carpenter, an electrician from Magnavox in Fort Wayne, with me holding a flashlight, had us on the road and underway by dawn's early light.

Had we broken down five minutes earlier, we'd have been a coach load of strangers stranded in downtown Harlem. Five minutes later, and we'd have been on the side of the road in rural New Jersey, having to charter a bus and hire a tow truck. God is good.

Arriving in DC a bit late but having had a great day there visiting many of the major sites together, we departed the metro area late evening heading south toward Virginia on I-95. At about midnight, we pulled into a rest area to allow the passengers to change into their Batman outfits or what have you for another evening sleeping aboard.

Trouble appeared in the form of yellow headlights—ours, a sign that the generators wasn't putting out enough juice. What to do? I sat on our front bumper, asking God that question. Just as I finished my prayer, two empty motor coaches from Fellowship of Christians in Action out of Titusville, Florida (Rudy Moeberg, FCA's founder and director, was a good friend), pulled in and parked in front of us. The two drivers walked back to check out our double-decker.

Hearing of our dilemma, one of them suggested that they escort us south, one coach in front, one in back, as far as the big Speedwell and Briscoe 76 Truck Stop just north of Richmond, VA. If our batteries died and the lights went out, we'd be safe until we got there (diesels run fine without charged batteries). If our batteries stayed charged and the lights stayed on, we'd depart the convoy just south of the 76, blinking a thank-you with our running lights, then heading east on I-64 for Williamsburg, our next destination.

But die our batteries did, necessitating our spending that night and the entire next day in the 76's parking lot while a local mechanic endeavored to find and repair our charging problem.

He was unable to do so. Fortunately, a good friend of ours, Jim Bennett, pastor of Immanuel Baptist Church in Richmond, allowed us to come over just before dark and spend the night in their air-conditioned, carpeted Sunday-school rooms—what a blessing.

As the sun came up, we departed—not for Williamsburg, but for home, driving like we were possessed to get there before dark, after which having no headlights would again be a major problem. We made it to Grabill in the dusky dark.

Bob and I spent the night with a couple of our passengers, Don and Yvonne Clark, who would become great friends, helpmates to us in ministry. We got a start at first light for Upland, just an hour and a half away, having had a wonderful retreat with wonderful people, experiencing one God sighting after another. In 50 years of doing these mobile retreats, I've never, ever seen two empty FCA buses together anywhere. What a Godsend!

The venerable Grabill Gobblers, a well-reasoned nickname earned by their penchant for serious nibbling while riding—usually peanuts with candy corn—continued from Lightrider's eventful maiden voyage to frequent fellowship with us aboard the Lightrider while checking

The Grabill Gobblers aboard the Durango and Silverton narrow-gauge railroad in Colorado.

out the four corners of God's North American creation. From Alaska, Newfoundland, and Labrador, to Catalina Island and Key West, God has kept us in His sight, prodding and protecting with His hand from time to time.

By May of 1993 the Gobblers had become seasoned Lightriders. A couple of them, Donna and Ron Cleven, wrote the following poem, which pretty well describes the experiences they'd had aboard the Lightrider:

T'WAS THE NIGHT BEFORE LIGHTRIDER

T'was the night before Lightrider, and all
  through the house
We hunted for clothing—me and my spouse;
With sleeping bags hung on the railing
  to air,
We hoped last trip's odors wouldn't be there!
The two of us snuggled together in bed,
Knowing three non-private nights lay
  ahead.
The next day to Clark's we went in a flutter,
To board the big bus and stash all our
  clutter.
When out on the highway there arose such
  a clatter,
We sprang from our seats to see what was
  the matter.
From out of the engine—a light like a flash,
Bob stomped on the brakes and Mike hit
  the dash!
The Ritz crackers and popcorn and Pepsi
  did flow,
And dripped through the ceiling to Cal's
  bunk below.
When what to our wondering eyes should
  appear,
But a bright neon sign saying
  "NO RESTROOMS HERE!"

Then our little bus driver, so lively and
  quick,
Whipped out the "ralph" bucket 'cause
  we all looked sick.
Relief finally came—we were no longer
  stalled,
It was back on the bus and our numbers
  we called.
Now Marilyn, now Calvin, now Diane and
  Jim,
On Claudia, on Jerry, on Donna and him.
To McDonald's or Wendy's or maybe the
  mall.
Now stash away, stash away, stash away all.
With dry heaves behind, and tummies
  content
We put on our jammies and to bed we went.
So on down the highway the Lightriders flew
With a bus full of Bridge Builders, and both
  of us, too.
All of a sudden there was noise on the floor
As he rushed down the steps to that small
  bathroom door.
As we poked out our heads and were
  looking around
Down from his bunk Jerry came with
  a bound.
He was dressed all in plaid from his head
  to his toe,
And his feet were both lighted with slippers
  that glow!
A bundle of clothes he had thrown
  in his sack,
And they looked like they came from the
  flea market rack!
On the bus, how we giggle; we all are
  so happy.
We play games like Uno, and some take
  a "nappy."
Then Mike grabs the PA while sipping
  a Coke

And proceeds to tell us that same old dumb
  joke!
The stump of a straw he held tight in his lips
As he shouted out orders, suggestions, and
  tips.
"Now, Sweet Thing do this," and "Sweet
  thing do that."
"Bob-a-loo, find the T-shirts, you know
  where they're at!"
Through cities and mountains and each
  destination
We always come home with a good
  education.
We've walked and we've talked and we've
  fellowshipped well,
But by this time our clothes are beginning
  to smell!
Well, we've had a great time and seen lots
  of sights,
And been blessed in our hearts by
  devotions at night.
We grew close to each other, and God was
  so near.
And that's why the Lightrider trips are
  so dear.
We've had lots of fun making memories
  with you . . .
The eight of us planning and thinking this
  through.
So bring all your pictures, t'will be a delight
When we get back together on reunion night!

These Gobblers were a faithful, fun bunch. One time, Don Clark, a frequent flyer with LtR, managed to secret onto the Lightrider a large, ugly, rubber rat with its nose clamped in a rat trap. He put it inside the lavatory located downstairs in this, our first Lightrider. Then, during our orientation meeting being held upstairs as we departed Grabill, he spoke up saying that it looked like someone had had an accident in the lavatory.

Sweet Thing—as Debbie had become known to this group—alarmed by such news, immediately got up and ran downstairs to check out the situation. Upon opening the lavatory door, expecting to find a puddle of ralphing or worse on the floor, she saw instead this huge, ugly rat, nose clamped in a trap. She shrieked, not unlike a stuck pig. The automated rubber rat, equipped to respond to sound, began violently thumping about. Debbie shrieked even louder. Her audible anxiety, easily heard upstairs, had the group wondering and I alarmed—had she fallen on the stairs?

Don had gotten us but good! At this writing, Debbie may have forgiven him. We all had a good laugh, though I was thankful that Debbie hadn't had a heart attack. Unbeknown to me and or the group, that very morning while getting the LtR into fighting trim for this retreat, Debbie had discovered a nest of baby rats in the glove compartment. Her first thought on seeing this mad thumper was: "It's the mama!" Don gave the rambunctious rubber rat to LtR, where the critter's enthusiastic thumping managed to cause multiple future passengers at least pause, if not actual cardiac concern.

Another time, while driving, needing help with something, I got on the PA requesting that Sweet Thing come downstairs to the flight deck. Six ladies showed up . . .

"As ambassadors of Christ, we are to share His love with the world. As Christians, it is essential that we maintain close bonds with the body of Christ, the Church, sharing the burdens and benefits of that body. We trust His Spirit to guide and direct all areas of our lives."[2]

---

[2] From LtR's Doctrinal Statement.

At LtR, Christian fellowship is our shtick. There's nothing quite like shaking and baking (should the AC fail), caring and sharing, for a few days together on a double-decker running down the highway for cementing relationships.

Christian fellowship is a major ingredient, essential though frequently missing, in maintaining while sharing one's faith through thick and thin: "... whether living in plenty or in want, I can do all things through Him who gives me strength" (Philippians 4:12–13). Fellowship is an excellent venue in which to grow such strength.

FIVE

Kids to California—More Miracles on Mobile Retreat Number Two

18 July–2 August 1988

Mount Rushmore in South Dakota was to be seen en route to California on this first mobile retreat with kids but had to be forgone. This shot was from a visit several years down the road.

17

God's provision and protection that first fateful Lightrider retreat, so essential in getting us home safely, proved to be a harbinger of His modus operandi for the second. This time it was to be 30 kids from Mississinewa Middle School, Gas City, IN, on a 16-day sojourn out West, departing just eight days after the Grabill Gobblers had arrived home.

We'd planned on driving overnight to Mount Rushmore, SD, then on to Teton National Park for hiking and on to Jackson, WY, for whitewater rafting on the Snake River. Continuing the drive west, we'd visit Salt Lake City, UT, swim in the Great Salt Lake, and arrive in San Francisco by day five. Then, having added bikes to LtR's ministry arsenal, which we'd dubbed Wheels West, we'd bicycle south across the Golden Gate, taking the Pacific Coast Highway 400 miles to Azusa, CA. After spending day 13 at Disneyland, we'd reboard the Lightrider, heading east toward home, seeing the Grand Canyon; Colorado Springs, CO; and the St. Louis Arch along the way—an ambitious itinerary to be sure.

But having personally accrued 39,000 miles touring on a bicycle and better than a quarter million miles driving a Possum, having two Wandering Wheels veterans, Bob Walker and Kelly Koons staffing, this ought to be a piece of baklava, right? No such luck.

On day one, after less than 500 miles, our air compressor, an engine component essential for operating the air brakes, failed just east of Des Moines, IA. Though it would take us three days to get across this state, God provided everything we needed: parts, a mechanic, and a preacher, Richard Grimm. Abandoning his wife, Pam, Richard spent two of those three days with his old church bus keeping our kids entertained at water parks, bowling alleys, and shopping malls. This simple man of God came out of the woodwork, repurposing what could have been hours and hours of shear boredom—spiced up with heat, dust, flies, and such—into days of fun and fellowship. God is good.

By day four we'd made it as far as Cheyenne, WY, where once again our not-so-trusty Lightrider faltered. Thankfully, we had altered course, forgoing Rushmore, the Tetons, and Jackson, shortening our route while staying closer to the trade route where parts, should they be needed, might be more available. Renting a car, I drove 102 miles to Denver to pick up an obscure part, a Williams slave cylinder for the pneumatic throttle linkage that an hour on the phone in these pre-internet days had managed to locate.

Returning to Cheyenne, expecting forlorn kids hanging around our stalled steed, I found instead a cheering throng. The Beach Boys were in town for a festival, Frontier Days, an annual event in Cheyenne. Bob and Kelly had parlayed the money not spent on the whitewater raft trip into concert tickets. Local church moms had chauffeured, in a fleet of private cars, Lightrider's group to the fairgrounds. Our kids were standing in the very front row, screaming, clapping, and swooning as Brian Wilson and the Beach Boys crooned their magic harmonies from a rodeo stage. After that, whatever was to befall our journey, we could do no wrong. God is good.

Continuing west, encountering more mountain grades, the Lightrider continued repeatedly overheating. Every few miles, all night long, we'd have to stop to pour gallons of water into our steaming radiator—it felt like a never-ending old Gabby Hayes movie set in Death Valley. Limping into Rawlins, WY, we were delighted to find a Cummins garage (the Lightrider had a

Cummins engine). But when the service manager realized that it was a VT903, a particular Cummins model that he despised, he refused to work on the Lightrider, kicking us out to cross the high desert on our own.

Sure enough, as we ventured farther and farther west on I-80 across the Great Divide Basin, overheating got the best of our engine, which seized up, putting us once again on the side of the highway. Every half hour for the next three, sweltering hours we attempted to start the engine, but it failed to even turn over.

Finally, desperate to get these uncomplaining kids to shelter, food, and water, we began flagging down passing 18-wheelers. Putting three or four kids aboard each of the westbound rigs that would stop, which was just about every one of them, we requested that their drivers drop them at Little America, a truck stop we knew to be up ahead. I'm getting misty-eyed recalling how these "Knights of the Highway" so willingly came to our aid.

Bob and I, now alone with our seemingly fatally stricken steed, once again took to our knees, crying out to God for His help. We tried once again to start the engine. Not just turning over, something it had failed to do for the past three hours, it roared to life! God is good.

Upon catching up with our group at Little America, we decided it best to charter a coach, sending Kelly with them to San Francisco to begin the bicycle portion of this adventure. Meanwhile, Bob and I proceeded to drive the Lightrider the remaining 150 miles to Salt Lake City and Cummins Intermountain, the largest Cummins garage in the country.

Now late afternoon, still east of Salt Lake, figuring that we would have enough time for supper and still arrive at Cummins before they closed at 5 p.m., we stopped at a Mickey D's. Getting our food to go, we climbed aboard to continue on our way, only to find that the throttle no longer worked—the same problem we'd had back in Cheyenne.

While I went back inside the MacDonald's to find a pay phone—these were pre–cell phone days—to call our Indiana prayer warriors, Bob decided to do some praying on his own. "If you don't show me how to fix this problem right now, I'm heading home, leaving this beast and its problems right here." He then went around back of the Lightrider, opened the engine compartment, and heard air leaking from the slave cylinder we'd installed the night before. Tightening the fitting of the air line feeding that cylinder a turn or two was all it took. By the time I returned from making my call, Bob had the throttle working. We got to the Cummins garage right before closing. God is good.

As Kelly and the kids arrived in San Francisco to begin their bike trip down the coast, the mechanics at Cummins Intermountain pulled and rebuilt the Lightrider engine. Bob and I would drive it up the Parleys Canyon grade just east of the city, checking to see if it would overheat, which it did, time and again.

After several days of this, the mechanics were tiring of the project, hoping we'd accept their work and leave. We didn't know whether we should just accept it and head out into the desert again—we were, understandably, a bit gun-shy. So we prayed and asked God for an answer right then. As we finished praying, a mechanic went to shut the idling engine down to check something, but it would not shut down. An injector had fouled, meaning the Lightrider wasn't going anywhere that night. No clearer, more timely answer could be given. God is good.

Finishing their bike trip, and then following a full day at Disneyland, our wandering group boarded yet another charter coach, arriving in Salt Lake City hoping to board the Lightrider for our return to Indiana. No dice; the engine, though freshly rebuilt and in good operating condition, was still not able to pull the Parleys Canyon grade without heating up.

Kelly called his father-in-law, Don Soderquist, then the number two man at Walmart, who was able to get us a corporate rate on Delta. Bob, Kelly, and I then stood at the Delta ticketing counter, maxing out our personal Visas purchasing airline tickets, flying our kids safely home on the sixteenth day as scheduled. God is good.

"Great is Thy Faithfulness, O God my Father . . . Morning by morning new mercies I see: All I have needed Thy hand hath provided . . ."[3]

---

[3] Thomas O. Chisholm, "Great Is Thy Faithfulness," 1923, public domain.

SIX

A Significant Speed Bump Encountered Early On

Bridge encounter in Acadia National Park, many years down the road from the events in this chapter. The road had been resurfaced since our last visit to Acadia, but the change in vertical clearance had not been noted on the highway signage.

About a year into our "Adventure in Christian Fellowship," it became apparent that this 1974 Neoplan Skyliner, former Unit 9900 of LARTD, could not cut the mustard. Overheating, sundry breakdowns, and such were actually the least of our worries. This double-decker, the first one in America with US components, was in reality a prototype vehicle not intended for highway use. It had been made for the Park & Ride system in LA whose routes evidently had no bridges below 14 feet. Our trusty steed was 13 feet nine and a half inches in height, three and a half inches higher than the 13 feet six inch lowest maximum legal vehicle height limit in the lower 48 states and Canada!

The first indication that our Lightrider was indeed not street legal had been chains dragging on the roof while attempting to enter the Massachusetts Turn Pike en route to Nova Scotia in June of 1989. We were refused entry, forcing us to conduct ourselves along highways and byways parallel to the Mass Pike. Every over-the-road (OTR) driver knows that low bridges proliferate on surface roads; as do intersections with signal lights and stop signs. Our over-height condition placed us in a very dangerous and sluggish situation, to say nothing of being illegal.

Once back home, we called Bob Calloway, from whom we'd bought the coach. He told us to check with Neoplan USA, for whom Calloway was a dealer. Annemarie Chenoweth, President of Neoplan USA, a stern, intractable woman who insisted that we'd bought the coach "as is," said that we were stuck with it, or words to that effect. It seemed that our best, indeed only conceivable option was to make our Lightrider a home for fish, kinda like the present plan befalling another aging steed of that day, the SS *United States*. But I digress.

God, however, had another option up His sleeve; an option we never even thought possible. When some of our frequent travelers, all of whom had been aboard the Lightrider multiple times, and with me on Possum trips at Wandering Wheels, heard of our dilemma, many of them deluged Annemarie with letters pleading for help.

Several of these travelers were corporate presidents, university professors, men and women of the business world. Christians all, their letters were kind, well-reasoned queries, void of hyperbole or vitriol, expressing strong endorsement of Bob and me as men given to strengthening America while advancing God's Kingdom. As such, Lightrider was an important, yea essential effort in a foundering culture. Any help Neoplan USA tendered would only cast a positive light on Neoplan.

Those gracious letters fell upon deaf ears, or rather were viewed by Annemarie's blind eyes. However, Bob Lee, Vice-Chairman of Neoplan in Germany, parent company of Neoplan USA, somehow, no doubt the Lord's doing, got wind of our dilemma. Lee had been the engineer who, back in 1974, had designed and built Unit 9900 for LARTD. Now, in the fall of 1989, Vice-Chairman Bob Lee invited Bob and me to meet with him in Atlanta, GA, as he would be in country for a massive motor coach show. We hopped into our previously God-provided Lincoln Town Car to make the 10-hour drive.

Entering the luxurious hospitality suite at Bob Lee's hotel in Atlanta, we found Bob anxious to help dissolve Lightrider's dilemma. Annemarie was there, too, no doubt present, without pretense, by command.

It was a short meeting, Bob Lee having already decided on a course of action. After discussing the situation for a bit, he laid out his plan, workable if our prototype pony could make it to Neoplan USA's manufacturing facility in Lamar, CO. Two things were proposed, both to be at Neoplan's expense.

First, Neoplan mechanics would cut our Skyliner in half, horizontally, just below the upstairs windows, removing 3.5 vertical inches of the walls, and then they'd weld it all back together again.

Second, the engine cooling system, which had been engineered for stop-and-go city driving at less than highway speeds, would be replaced with a much larger system, engineered for sustained highway speeds over long distances, pulling mountain grades, and the like. And if there were other changes or improvements we desired, they would be accomplished for us at cost.

Delighted with this chance to save our steed from not only becoming a home for fish, but to become the highway-capable, legal double-decker with which to continue our purposeful sojourn, we gratefully accepted. With the improvements we requested, like installing glass windows to replace the yellowing, scarred-up Lexan originals, the project was to take three weeks and cost Lightrider $26,000. Such a deal!

Such a deal, instead, took five months, costing LtR $48,000. Such a nightmare! How could any one-horse operation survive five months without that one horse—to say nothing of the 48-grand ransom? But once again, God had our six—or, as some might say in the military, given the nighttime reference, our eighteen hundred. He paid the bill and put us in touch with a horse or two, keeping LtR on the road and in the fight during the rebuild.

The first such steed was a handsome Neoplan Jetliner, a single-decked motor coach loaned to LtR by a Neoplan maintenance operation in Honey Brook, PA. This seated coach, which had to be picked up in Honey Brook, allowed us to keep our obligation to transport the Taylor University Art Department from our town of Upland, IN, to New York City in January 1990. With Bob Walker being stuck in Lamar pressuring Neoplan to get done fixing our Skyliner, Craig Moore, a friend and Director of the TU Art Department, having an Indiana Public Passenger Chauffeur's license, filling in for Bob, helped me with the overnight drive. The students had to sleep upright in the bus seats rather than stretch out in the bunks on the Lightrider, but did so with little complaint. Halfway to New York a blizzard set in, but that's another story.

For the duration of the five months, with Bob stuck in Colorado, we managed to borrow a single-decked sleeper coach from Rudy Moeberg's Fellowship of Christians in Action, the same outfit whose pair of empty coaches had provided us with a way forward back on our very first retreat when plagued with generator failure. With this FCA coach, LtR was able to stay on track with our mobile retreat calendar, meeting every obligation up until the very end of this oddball odyssey.

We had one retreat with kids from Beulah Missionary Church of Elkhart, IN, that was scheduled the week before we believed our faithful Skyliner would finally be back on duty. By then, we had had to return the FCA coach because it was needed back in Titusville, FL. Just before having to make the call, disappointing those kids who had spent a year raising money for our planned adventure, telling them we had to cancel their retreat because we didn't have a coach with which to conduct it, God again intervened.

We got a call from the group. It seemed that some of the kids in the group had won the State Swim Meet and were headed to the regionals. Could LtR, on the following weekend, conduct a retreat with adults from their church instead of taking the kids as scheduled? Our calendar was open that following weekend, so we were quite happy to make the adjustment.

In fact, in all 33 of LtR's years conducting mobile retreats we never once had to cancel a retreat because of mechanical failure, or for any other reason (although we did delay one for two days once because the AC was on the blink). And we at LtR always managed to get our groups home on schedule. Given the number of breakdowns encountered, that too was miraculous. Groups occasionally had to cancel their plans with LtR, but LtR never had to cancel a retreat from our end. God is good.

That first Lightrider did yeoman duty for 15 years and 850,000 miles, serving over 11,000 people on 361 mobile retreats over 2,092 days on the road. That's over five and a half years OTR! She did squawk a bit while accomplishing all this. We had had to replace her engine six times, and she was on her third engine when we got her.

We'd name the engines after the cities where engine failure had occurred, like the Denver engine, Jackson engine, Nashville engine, and so on. Each time God provided the funds, church buses, or charter coaches, whatever we needed. Each replacement engine put in by LtR, after the Salt Lake engine, was a Diesel Recon donated by Cummins Engine Company, regardless of miles or warranty, LtR only having to pay for the labor of the R&R (removal and replacement). When Lightrider's Miracle Bus (see Chapter 16) replaced her in 2002, she was donated to a sister ministry, Eagle Wings.

"What God proposes He provides for . . ."

SEVEN

God Provides a Co-Pilot via a Personal Miracle or Two

Let's digress for just a bit. In 1990, at the age of 42, my endomorphic self had become well adjusted to—yea content with—the single life. My constantly on-the-road lifestyle might even had been seen as a mandate for such. God, however, had other plans.

Word came to me from family in South Carolina that their daughter Donna, my cousin, was to be married. Weddings are a great time of family reunion. Checking the LtR calendar revealed my availability to attend. Checking with a travel agent netted my penurious self a super-saver, non-refundable round trip airline ticket for a very affordable 99 bucks—Indy non-stop to Myrtle Beach, SC—Great Honking Beak!

Then came the rub. A volunteer scheduled to drive a LtR retreat with Girl Scouts traveling to a camp in Minnesota during the time of the wedding had a conflict and could not take the wheel for this group. My partner Bob said he could run the retreat by himself, but we both knew that it would not be legal for one driver, given the distance, requiring me to drive this retreat. Getting mad at God is always pointless, but it made me sore having to miss out on such a family event, to say nothing of losing 99 bucks on the non-refundable ticket.

Debbie Manganello, aka Sweet Thing, caught in action.

Then God's plan kicked into high gear. It seems Bob's friend Ross Giordana, having a Public Passenger Chauffeur's License, had moved from Florida to Wisconsin. This enabled

Bob to drive the Girls Scouts as far as Wisconsin, where Rob jumped on board to continue the drive to their camp in Minnesota.

My previously sore self, looking down out the plane's windows to the colorful, early fall Tennessee mountains below, en route to the wedding, found myself begging God's forgiveness at my recalcitrant attitude toward His merciful, gracious Self. One negative thought did come to mind, though: my recollection that there was a sister or some such that had been introduced to me on a visit some eight years previously. All I remembered was that my single, confirmed old bachelor self was not interested.

Arriving at my cousin's home in Florence, the first person encountered in their driveway was none other than the aforementioned single woman. God Himself must have opened my jaded eyes as I not only recognized her but recalled her name, Debbie. My interest was immediate!

What took place next is mostly hearsay as our smitten selves, not unlike infatuated teenagers, bumbled our way through the wedding preparations and clean-up. My cousin Dave was married to Debbie's sister Linda. Their daughter, Donna, the bride, was Debbie's niece and my cousin. The groom, Chris, no relation, was, coincidentally, from Contra Costa County, California, where I had been born and raised.

After the wedding the family gathered at Dave and Linda's place. Debbie and I spent hours talking while floating in the pool on a queen-sized float. Debbie's daughter Danielle (Debbie had been widowed for nine years), sensing our interest in one another, kept trying to drown me by splashing vigorously. Family members, alert to our mutual interest, managed to distract Danielle.

Later, when the family decided to go out for a bite, they just let us float on what they had dubbed the "Love Boat"—that was the only meal we have ever missed. In fact, we were unaware that we'd been left.

On returning home to Indiana, having such strong interest in Debbie, wanting to go back to see her sometime down the road, checking with the travel agent became a priority. What was found was a last round-trip ticket available at the 99-buck non-refundable price, for two days hence. It had to be purchased right then, without even a chance to check with Debbie. My Visa bill was growing along with my passion.

Calling Debbie got not her but her answering machine. Getting on the plane, not knowing if Debbie was available or even if she wanted to see me so soon was a concern. Having called my cousin, Dave, after getting Debbie's machine, knowing he would meet me at the Myrtle Beach terminal, was scant comfort.

Back then at Myrtle Beach airport one deplaned commercial aircraft via an open-air stairway followed by a short walk to the terminal building. This terminal had large windows that were like mirrors reflecting the Southern heat but blocking any view into the building. Was Debbie waiting inside or just Cousin Dave?

Upon entry, there—striking a pose in a pretty little sundress—was Dave, er, I mean Sweet Thing. Returning home from this weekend visit, I called my friend Tim Burkholder, a professor at Taylor University, who, known as Diamond Tim, sold engagement rings. Tim would meet me immediately at his office on campus. "The Wedding Song" played on my car radio while making the two-minute drive. It had been exactly two weeks since my meeting Debbie at Donna's wedding.

Two weeks later, Debbie and I were staffing a weekend—Friday afternoon through Monday early morning—LtR Retreat to DC and Annapolis, MD, with a Sunday-school class of adults from Rolling Meadows, IL. The group, quickly realizing Debbie and I were both single and interested, made sure that every restaurant meal had us sitting side by side.

At 9 p.m. Sunday, while motoring down the Pennsylvania Turnpike en route home on our double-decker, one of the passengers, Ken, a large garbage-truck driver sitting by me upstairs, asked what my intensions were for Debbie. "Let's find out," I said. Getting on the PA, I asked Debbie to come upstairs. We had a little stool in the open area between the horseshoe-shaped passenger seating area for Debbie. Taking a knee, and waxing a bit eloquently, I asked Debbie to be my wife. She sat there, smiling, but without speaking. Ken, thinking this was a turn-down, began to weep. I asked her whether she had understood the question. She finally spoke up, smiling broadly, saying "Yes!"

Bob, who was driving, heard screaming and laughter from upstairs so he pulled over on the shoulder and came upstairs to find out what was happening. We later stopped at a Howard Johnson's (28 flavors of ice cream and one flavor of food) to call Danielle with the news.

Danielle was staying with Debbie's sister, Ada, back in South Carolina while Debbie was staffing this LtR Retreat. But Danielle would have no part of our getting married, threatening to tie herself to a pine tree. Ada said not to worry about Danielle, that she'd come around, which she did, blessing our marriage if I would accept her cat.

We chose a date for the following May, allowing Danielle to finish that school year. Ken and his wife came to the wedding. God had blessed me with a wonderful wife and co-pilot along with a red-headed stepchild . . . with cat—a white, long-haired Persian named Princess.

Arriving back in Rolling Meadows as scheduled at about 7 a.m. Monday, we said goodbye to our group as they got off the Lightrider.

To a person, they all remarked that though they had been in the same Sunday-school class for decades, they had not known one another like they did now, after this weekend retreat fellowshipping one with another. It's marvelous what a quality time of fellowship can achieve.

That group, incidentally, prior to our return, had made a beautiful card with Rhett Butler and Scarlet O'Hara of *Gone with the Wind* fame on the front and $149 inside which they'd surreptitiously collected for us. That paid the Visa charge for a very nice copper weather vane with a sailboat that I'd purchased at the Annapolis waterfront. That weather vane graces the peak of the porch of our double wide to this day. The inscription in the card sums up the event pretty well: "It all began on a bus; with the twenty six of us; and to that add a little heaven, with precious number '27' [Debbie, aka Sweet Thing]. On September 23, Mike got down on bended knee. He called Debbie to his side, and asked her 'Will you be my bride?' With the Father looking from above, He blessed these two with mutual love. Twenty-six Lightriders all in tears, praying God's blessing on all their years."

Debbie and I were not the only couple to get engaged on the Lightrider. Years later, another couple—Uplanders Tom and Marlene Clester—asked and answered this same question while aboard. Mick and Jane Roush are yet another LtR couple.

One last aside if you please . . . Taylor University was presenting me an award, Chamber of Service Distinguished Friend, at a little banquet on campus. Debbie was in Indiana for a visit so was able to attend. When asked to speak, I said, "One of the greatest fears us aging endomorphs have is getting invited to such a soiree and having to find a date. I went overboard and got a fiancée . . ." There was gasping, followed by laughter and applause—Upland was delighted with the news. In this case, I did the proposing, though God did the prompting and providing . . .

Debbie became an indispensable part of my life—and Lightrider Ministries' too. God had pulled off a few more miracles getting us together. Danielle, aka The Child, added a wonderful dimension to my life as well, being as she was a force drawing Debbie and I always closer to each other and to the Lord. Even Princess added interest and a bit of humor. She was actually an attack cat! She acquired a habit of lurking near the front door when Danielle was arriving home from school. She'd then sneak out, jump up, and grab Danielle from behind around the thigh with all four legs, scaring the hoodoo out of Danielle, if not the actual doodoo.

At this writing, Debbie and I are approaching our 34th wedding anniversary as she enters her third year of recovery following a fierce bout with a malady, Legionnaires' disease, which almost took her life. Four weeks in the ICU, three weeks in long-term acute care, followed by three months in physical rehab—it was indeed a year of miracles, attested to with pictures in the issue of LtR's *Good News Gazette*, included in Chapter 32. We learned the meaning of and became dependent upon "His new mercies every morning." God is good.

"Because He lives, I can face tomorrow. Because He lives, all fear is gone. Because I know He holds the future, and life is worth the living just because He lives." These words are from *Because He Lives* by Bill and Gloria Gaither.

Today, 11 September 2025, tweaking this chapter, which was written five months ago, the verse above continues to comfort. Yesterday Charlie Kirk, founder at age 18 of Turning Point USA, was assassinated in Utah, adding pathos to this 24th anniversary of 9/11; pathos with hope and determination; America, by God's grace, will continue the healing process presently being accelerated by the widespread revival being witnessed on dozens of our university campuses.

EIGHT

Random Grace in Adversity, Again and Again and . . .

The early Lightrider at Garden of the Gods outside of Colorado Springs, CO.

It's been said by someone recently that God spreads His grace around like a four-year-old spreads peanut butter—all over the place. Lightrider has frequently and gratefully experienced this—God's grace, not the peanut butter.

This book recalls quite a bit of adversity, mostly mechanical troubles and mostly not life threatening, PTL! God's grace seems to abound most during adversity—certainly, it is more easily recognized. No doubt this is why, as they say, there are no atheists in foxholes, because when the shooting starts and trouble comes knocking, it's then that God's grace takes on a bit more visibility. His grace day to day may go unnoticed and may be considered unremarkable, but shame on us. His grace in times of trouble or times of tranquility is most definitely needed, even if less appreciated.

In July 2001, while attempting the steep climb to the Flying W Ranch in Colorado Springs, CO, our venerable old 1974 Neoplan Skyliner kept overheating, requiring us to pull over and fast idle the engine in order to cool it down.

Just starting the third of four long westward retreats that summer, an intermittent overheating problem, despite valiant efforts of our mechanics, Mike Pearson and Steve Kuhn back home, was getting worse. At times we could not even get around town without pulling over to cool our engine. How could we get over 10,850-foot Wolf Creek pass en route to our missions work in Chinle, AZ, with youth leader Elizabeth Montalvo's happy group of high-school kids from Christ the Savior Lutheran Church of Fishers, IN? How could we look to returning to the altitude and heat of the Southwest on our next retreat, a 12-day round trip to California with a Baptist church from Wyandotte, MI, knowing we had just three days at home to find and correct our problem?

A new radiator would take 12 weeks for delivery—we had only three days. A specially built replacement radiator from Bowden's in Muncie would take a week to construct—we only had three days.

As our kids got off the Lightrider in the parking lot of the Flying W Ranch, a chuck wagon-style restaurant with a live Western Music band, my mood was becoming a little despondent. My twin, Steve, chatted with me about it for a bit—we were considering chartering a bus to get our group to Arizona while one of us limped our ailing Skyliner to the Neoplan factory, which happened to be just a couple of hours away. But it was the weekend and there was no way to get ahold of anyone at Neoplan to see if there was anything they could do to help even if we did manage to get our sickly steed there.

So we prayed, asking God to direct our steps, as we are instructed in Proverbs 3:5-6: "Trust in the Lord with all your heart and do not lean on your own understanding. In all your ways acknowledge Him, and He will make your paths straight." We decided, following our wonderful evening at the Flying W, to continue west and trust Him to get us safely to Chinle, which He was faithful to accomplish.

Once on site in Chinle, we determined to at least pull out the engine thermostats, though they had been replaced just a few months before. Jeff Rajca, the missionary who we were there to serve, said that there was not a parts store in Chinle where gasket material and such could be found—we'd have to go to Gallup, NM, 120 miles away. He asked what the problem was. He used to drive buses and said that in this area there were two things people did when their buses got older and started overheating under extreme circumstances.

One thing was to install a pump with a switch on the dash so that the driver could soak the radiator with a mist of cool, fresh water whenever the bus was in danger of overheating. The thinking being that nothing overheats in the rain. The second idea was to install a heat-activated electric fan in front of the radiator to increase airflow across it.

Jeff said that he happened to have a freshwater tank in the attic that he thought would work fine for us if we wanted it. As it turned out, the tank could not have been a more perfect fit for us if we had custom ordered it. Working with Jeff's dad, Pastor Ron, who drove to Gallup for the parts, we were able to get a spray system up and running for under a hundred bucks—and it worked! As a kit to do this same job cost over $450, and didn't even include the freshwater tank, we made out like bandits.

Although our intermittent overheating problem failed to surface again en route home from Chinle, we were encouraged to have our "rain simulator" standing by in case of need; we were blessed by God's provision of an affordable solution—a timely answer to our prayers for help and direction. God is good.

Once home, we had new thermostats installed by Mike Pearson at Upland Tire, which proved to be the solution to both the intermittent nature of our overheating and to our overheating under mild driving conditions.

However, on the following retreat, which had been our biggest concern, we did find that our aging radiator was no longer efficient enough to deal with keeping the engine cool under extreme driving conditions like climbing up to Mount Rushmore during a South Dakota heat wave. Yet we were already mechanically equipped to compensate for such situations with our custom-built, God-provided onboard auxiliary rain-maker—which proved to be very effective. And we were emotionally equipped as well, having felt His hand chart our course through this hot spot in our summer's work. His grace in our adversity was indeed felt!

Writing this in a comfortable, cool office, I'm reminded of a poster depicting two sailing ships serenely at anchor in a calm harbor. The caption read, *"Ships are safe in harbor, but that's not what ships are made for."*

Despite our mechanical storms while on the road that summer, we experienced God's grace—grace that would have gone unnoticed had we stayed safe in harbor. Twelve new lives had been written in His Book of Life; physical mountains were "moved" on behalf of two mission organizations; and four churches were strengthened through work, fellowship, and seeing God in His Creation, His people, and His actions. There's no telling what else God accomplished unseen in hearts onboard and along the way. My heart had been blessed, my faith firmed up, and my resolve to stay the fight had been refreshed. Still, it is nice to get back into safe harbor from time to time, if only for a little while.

A quick note: Those kids from Christ the Savior Lutheran were in Chinle to apply a concrete surface to a go-kart track being used by Jeff Rajca as an outreach to Navajo kids on the reservation. The dust on the track would clog the air filters on the go-karts, requiring filter changes every 20 minutes or so. The Navajo kids would lose interest, hence the need to concrete the surface.

Jeff lived in a bread truck beside his parents' house, his energy and means all spent on sharing Jesus with these Navajo children. It takes two things to defeat the evil one: the blood of the Lamb and the testimony of the saints (Revelation 12:11). Jeff's testimony in the arid climate of Arizona was certainly a sterling example to our young saints from green, moist Indiana.

There is a third necessary component in defeating the evil one that we shared frequently with youth groups: courage. Even Paul, the greatest missionary that ever was, asked of his followers in Ephesians 6:19 NIV: "Pray also for me, that whenever I speak, words may be given me so that I will *fearlessly* make known the mystery of the Gospel" (emphasis mine). As observed in the previous chapter, "Because He lives, I can face tomorrow. Because He lives all fear is gone."

On a subsequent retreat with Elisabeth Montalvo and her kids from Christ the Savior Lutheran to Washington, DC, we attended, in

2000, a large national Youth for Christ conference called DC/LA. While the group was at the conference, I had the chore of what we called "guarding the bus." Hence I was at Union Station where coach parking was allowed. There is a wonderful food court in the basement so my "guard duty" wasn't too onerous, though being absent from the group was never my first choice.

God's grace often manifests itself in small bouquets of encouragement, and such was His plan for me that day in the basement of Union Station. I had lined up behind a young lady at a Greek food vendor. The massive chef behind the counter looked past the young lady who had already ordered, asking me, "What are you having?" "The whole chicken deal," I responded. The young lady in front of me, hearing my voice, turned around, beaming, and said, "Mike Manganello?" What a surprise! She had been a kid on a Wheels or LtR retreat some years ago. Presently she was a youth pastor of a church in Iowa in DC, with her own group for the DC/LA thing.

We chatted for a few moments until our orders came up, and then went our separate ways. I found a table in the very crowded court, but all of its chairs had been taken for use elsewhere. So, leaving my "whole chicken deal" on the table, I went looking for a chair. A nearby table, with a crowd of kids chowing down, had an unused chair. Putting my hand on the chair, I asked the girl next to it, "Is this chair taken?" She looked up, smiling big, saying, "Mike Manganello?" She, too, had been on a mobile retreat with me a few years prior; she was now a youth group leader in DC for the DC/LA thing too, and also with a group of her own—from Michigan, if I recall.

Certainly, for two young ladies who had been on two different LtR or Wheels retreats from two different groups to recognize my voice and recall my name, pronouncing it correctly, after more than two years was beyond coincidental.

The fact that in this ginormous food court with hundreds of young people my happening to come upon each of these young women such that they heard and recognized my voice before seeing me seemed likely to have been a set up . . . perchance a Divine set-up. My having been to this place many times with multiple groups, I had a couple of favorite vendors, the Greek place not one of them. In fact, I'd never ordered food there before. On this occasion, it happened to be the one vendor without a long line of hungry patrons.

God was encouraging me with evidence that LtR may have had a bit of influence in the lives of a couple of kids. It made my day, let me tell you.

Speaking of pronouncing my name, my sweet wife, Debbie, shortly after we'd married (Debbie had started her own house-cleaning business, Maid in USA), was leaving a phone message on the answering machine of friend and coworker Tammy Maloney, aka Tammy Whammy: *"Hey, Tammy, this is Debbie Mag . . . Magaranga . . . Oh heck, you know who this is . . ."* And, on hearing that message, Tammy, laughing herself silly, played it over and over for her husband, Vance, and family, then called Debbie and played it back onto our answering machine.

Debbie, a Southern belle from the deep South (Conway, South Carolina), had had a time getting accustomed to a few of our Northern names, customs, and such. Likewise, we'all, up in these parts, had a learning curve as well when it came to understanding some of Debbie's vernacular. In fact, for Debbie's 40th birthday, her best friend and coworker, Laurie Davenport, created a dictionary with 40 of Debbie's expressions and their English meaning. But I digress.

On New Year's Eve weekend in 1994, we'd been skiing Breckenridge west of the Eisenhower tunnel in Colorado with the senior-high youth group from North Suburban Evangelical Free

Church of Deerfield, IL, and Kevin Conklin, youth pastor, TU grad and dear friend.

Climbing the grade on I-70, approaching the Eisenhower Memorial Tunnel, I turned on the driver's light to check the one gauge that wasn't properly illuminated: the oil pressure. It registered zero! No oil pressure! Nada! Great honking beak, what to do? Heavy, fast-moving traffic going home from the slopes surrounded our slow-moving selves. Pulling onto the snow-covered shoulder would put us in a very precarious situation in these pre–cell phone days, so attempting to continue driving until the next exit seemed to me to be our best move. We made it through the tunnel, the summit of the climb, and then downhill, coasting, passed a couple of dark exits to the Idaho Springs exit and pulled into the parking lot of an all-night diner.

Setting the brake and fast idling the engine to cool it down a little, I rushed outside to the rear of the LtR, finding the back end of the coach drenched in black motor oil. I shut down the engine, realizing that it would never turn over again. It seems that a new device we'd installed to lengthen engine life had itself been made with weak components that burst under the heavy load and heat generated during the climb. We were dead in the water. But God's grace had brought us to a safe place with food, restrooms, and phones.

While the post-skiing hungry kids were happy to take advantage of the diner's services, I got on the phone seeking transportation, a charter bus if possible. There was not a bus of any kind available; all were occupied taking folks to the casinos or other New Year's Eve venues.

One of our group's wealthy kids, bored of eating and waiting, decided on a personal course of action. He was going to take a cab the 55 miles on to the Denver International Airport (DIA) in Aurora and find a flight home. I had not considered either of these options, but his plan got me thinking.

Cabs would charge $55 for the trip and could accommodate five passengers. Kevin got on the phone to his church and found a way of getting a special rate for flying the group home to Chicago from one of North Sub's parishioners. We then called for six cabs and bundled our group off to DIA.

Dick and Marsha Becker and their two sons, part of our group, managed to rent a car at DIA to drive home. Sadly, they ended up getting caught in a blizzard in Kansas and had to find a motel for a couple of days.

Arranging to have the LtR towed to a Cummins garage in Denver, Steve Kuhn and I cabbed it with the group to DIA too, and there found haven with relatives of mine in Aurora: my cousin Beverly and her family, the Fellers. Instead of sitting up in a red-eye to Chicago or getting caught in a blizzard, we ended up at a Benihana's having a great, if late, New Year's Eve supper with family—an unmerited blessing, making this my best New Year's Eve in memory. We flew home the next day.

As if all of God's grace in getting us safely off the road and our group safely home were not enough, that's not why I tell this story . . . About a week later I flew back to Aurora with, as I recall, my partner Bob Walker to pick up the LtR with its rebuilt engine for its return to Upland. We ended up spending a couple of days and nights with the Fellers: Cousin Beverly, her husband, Rich (if you can believe it), daughter 11-year-old Megan, and younger son Corey.

When we departed for Upland with the Lightrider, we left, by arrangement, very early in the morning without waking the family. Tucked into a groove on the steering wheel was a note, left there the night before by young Megan. It read, "This may not mean much, or sound rude, but I think your bus breaking down was a blessing in disguise. My faith in God was dying, and from the way you minister, even in your everyday conversations, really restored that wonderful gift God gave me . . ."

Still getting misty recalling that incident, Bob and I just looked at each other, agreeing that note of encouragement and the grace of God that it described was indeed worth the hassle and expense caused by our New Year's Eve's mechanical machinations. God is good.

This is probably a good place in this narrative to share a few bouquets received over the years, comments we published in some of our brochures, comments recounted here as short verbal accounts concerning His grace to Lightrider:

I had such a great weekend and I feel that my being on the trip with all those kids really enhanced the Campus Life Ministry here. Your trips allow these kids to experience things like they've never seen before—and to hear the Gospel and see it lived out in new ways, too.
—Jenny Williams, YFC Fort Wayne

I want you to know how much I appreciate what you are doing as a ministry. You are showing people the beauty of our country,

On a Florida retreat with Kevin Conklin's North Sub-E Free kids, we were blessed by a bagpiper in full kit and kilt at New Smyrna Beach.

Conklin with North Sub kids at Stone Mountain, Georgia.

taking them away for a short time from their daily pressures and all the time showing them that men can love and serve God. You are showing people, especially kids, that men who love God aren't wimps. I'm pleased that two of my children have been exposed to your example.

—*Naomi Clark, mother and passenger,
Leo, Indiana*

It was so much fun for us to get to know you. Your love for our teens and heart for God was clearly seen by all. We are very excited about what God is doing through the Lightrider Ministry.

—*Susan and Jeff Wetherill,
missionaries to the youth of Ireland*

It is indeed rare to find men and ministry that fit together in such perfect symmetry as the Staff and the Lightrider bus ministry. Their breadth of vision, depths of character, and wealth of experience make them men who are perfectly suited for this marvelous ministry.

—*Reverend Jim Bennett, Family Ministry,
Immanuel Baptist Church, Richmond, VA*

God's grace can take many forms, sometimes physical, as demonstrated in these stories, and sometimes spiritual, as borne out in these testimonies. Words of encouragement, though intangible, have been an essential part of God's grace to all of us at Lightrider Ministries.

Devotions beside the Grand Canyon with youth from 1st Baptist Coldwater, MI, on an earlier retreat.

NINE

Miracles or Highway Happenstance

Albuquerque—June/July 2015

We were using our second Lightrider, the one we'd ordered built by Neoplan USA to replace our first double-decker (see Chapter 16). This, yet another breakdown, happened on a retreat with a youth group from Grace UMC in Hartford City, IN. We'd done eight retreats with this church, starting in 2013, each funded by a single donor family: Chris and Christy Jennerjahn, who were trying to get area youth to come to their church with the goal of bringing younger families in to grow into the future.

This retreat took us out West, where we were seeing the "Grand Canyon" of the Yellowstone. I went upstairs in the Lightrider and found 10 kids and one of their leaders playing cards, so I urged them to get off the Lightrider to see this lovely part of God's Creation. After this stop, they had no interest in seeing anymore of Yellowstone so we moved on to the real Grand Canyon in Arizona.

The same adolescent indifference persisted on our arrival at the South Rim of the Grand Canyon, so we stopped only at Desert View, forgoing the many extra miles to be driven if we'd seen more. Hence, our transmission gave out in the parking lot of a Golden Corral at dinner time instead of along the highway in the middle of nowhere. It just happened to be in Albuquerque, near where my daughter Danielle lives with husband Michael and their son, my grandson, Orrin.

Danielle had a good friend, Lorraine McCutcheon, who—along with church staffer, John Nystrom—got her church, Monterey Baptist, to send vans over to the Golden Corral to transport our group back to the church to spend the night there, saving us the expense of a hotel. Another of Danielle's friends, Jacob, was friends with the police who, because of that connection, provided surveillance for the disabled Lightrider overnight in a dangerous area where cars are broken into regularly in broad daylight!

At first light we engaged a tow truck to haul our trusty if ailing steed from the Golden Corral to an Allison Transmission garage, Stewart & Stevenson, in hopes that a minor repair might be all that was needed, enabling us to get our group of travelers home aboard the Lightrider rather than the expensive alternative of chartering a coach. No dice—a major, time-consuming repair would be necessary.

The church fed us breakfast that morning. Then they loaned us their small church bus to drive our group home to Indiana, obviating the need to charter a coach! The youth group leader from Grace, Abigail Poucher, a Christian Ed student at Taylor University, was willing to drive a rental car in convoy, with LtR staff driver Rich Coolman at the wheel of the church bus.

One of Grace's leaders had a contact in Tulsa, OK, at The Heart Church. They opened their church, allowing another overnight stay, sans hotel bill, for our tired travelers. This church, too, provided breakfast for the group the next morning. God is good.

Once the group was on the road toward home, we engaged with figuring out the mechanical problem. Phoning a friend, Tom Bazow, in the motor coach business in Fort Wayne, Excursions, Inc., it was learned that a rebuilt transmission in St. Louis could be at Stewart & Stevenson in Albuquerque within 24 hours, with the core, our broken tranny, on its way back to St. Louis, all for about half the price estimated by Stewart & Stevenson.

However, being an Allison-authorized garage, Stewart & Stevenson was not allowed to install the aftermarket rebuild from St. Louis—we'd have to have the Lightrider towed somewhere else if we went that route. Charles, the service manager, was adamant that the Allison rebuilt tranny would be a better product, and so we decided to go with the Allison. As you will see in the next chapter, Charles was dead wrong.

Debbie and I were able to stay at Danielle's while the logistics worked out. So, instead of a hotel bill adding to the cost of the problem, we were able to be with family.

About a week later, my brother Steve returned Monterey Baptist's church bus to Albuquerque. He arrived in town late so stayed at the Econo Lodge on Central Avenue. Coincidentally, the McDonald's next door to this motel had been the scene of a drug deal gone bad. Jacob, Danielle's friend who had arranged police protection for the broken-down Lightrider at the Golden Corral, was an undercover police officer at the time and had taken seven 45-caliber rounds of friendly fire and lived! But I digress.

Once it was determined that Stewart & Stevenson would make the repairs, Steve, Deb, Orrin, and I rented a car to return to Indiana until repairs were completed. The day we arrived home, I went into atrial fibrillation. What a blessing to be home when this happened instead of during the breakdown. Deb already had her plane ticket for our vacation the end of July, so she and Orrin flew back to New Mexico. A week later I flew out for the previously scheduled part of our vacation, allowing me to drive the repaired Lightrider home.

Rather than piecing together a recollection of that eventful drive home, I've inserted, unaltered, the actual after-action report tendered to the LtR board. This report also provides an update about other circumstances impacting LtR's future at that point in time:

REPORT: RETURN FROM ALBUQUERQUE, AUGUST 2015

Get comfortable—I'd like to share the sit rep (the rest of the story).

Got back to Upland at 05:30 hrs. yesterday (Thursday, 6 Aug) with the LtR, PTL! It was my 3d attempt at leaving ABQ since breaking down there 30 June 2015.

Monday I made it 10 miles before having to be towed back to Stewart & Stevenson (the garage) for repair work on the rebuilt tranny (covered by warranty).

Then again I departed the garage Tuesday am but had to return after just a mile because of a bad drive line vibration, undetected during the garage's test drive following the Monday return. The drive shaft, having been removed for towing, had been incorrectly reinstalled by the tow truck driver when he dropped the LtR at the garage (covered by warranty).

Leaving the 3d time, the LtR managed to escape the seemingly maniacal mechanical malfunction suction of ABQ about 2:30 Tuesday pm.

The LtR ran hot, but cooler than the day we arrived in ABQ, allowing me to reach Weatherford, OK, following a delightful if brief stop at Big Vern's Steakhouse on old Route 66 in Shamrock, TX, by midnight, 8 hours out of ABQ.

Wednesday became a 20-hour marathon. She ran cool all day and into the night. Following a 1-hour stop at Lambert's Café in Ozark, MO, home of "throwed" rolls, 2 fuel stops, a power nap in Rolla, MO, narrowly avoiding a fire truck and emergency vehicles blocking the inside lane around a curve on a hill east of Rolla, 2 hours parked at a semi jackknifing on I44 west of St. Louis, a near head-on with a small car that had evidently flipped around in high-water, innumerable construction zones, incompetent drivers and constant rain from Rolla to Grant County, IN, the Good Lord and a band of Guardian Angels saw us (me and the LtR) home just before dawn Thursday.

Thank you to my daughter and her neighbor Lonny for lodging and transportation during this ABQ adventure. My previously planned week's vacation turned into just a weekend.

Debbie had been in ABQ on week one of her planned 2-week vacation there when I flew in Thursday evening 30 July.

The damage to the exchequer was quite severe, though Charles, the service manager at Stewart & Stevenson, managed to trim about 6 grand from the bill generated by his computer. Though the $24,000 charge was $3,000 higher than the original estimate, in addition to the Allison-rebuilt tranny, it included a rebuilt turbo charger, a new rear main seal in the engine, and sundry other small defects best corrected while the engine and tranny were out of the coach. Though some rust was encountered under the coach, there was nothing reported that could be considered unsafe.

Arriving home with an expired DOT inspection (we had intended to be home 2 July, 29 days ahead of the expiration), we have some work to do before again being street legal. We're having the lower front of the LtR restructured to use flat glass for windshields—both lower windshields are severely cracked—instead of the rare and expensive curved originals. Body work is required to correct badly rusted frame members under the skin. Steve Brinkerhoff has reported alarming symptoms of what could be serious structural defects that are hidden from view. The hoped-for 30 years and 3 million miles of our "new" Lightrider has been soaked by the cold wind of reality. With the current planned repairs, I'm estimating 2 years and a hundred thousand miles of useful life left in our much-less-durable-than-expected steed. That will be 16 years instead of 30 and 730,000 miles instead of 3 million.

The intermittent overheating problem needs to be diagnosed and corrected, probably requiring a rebuilt radiator.

As Jay has observed to Steve Manganello, if it takes 50 grand to get the LtR back into fighting trim, that's a whole lot cheaper than buying another double-decker, scarce parts notwithstanding.

Getting our aging drivers into fighting trim will require replacement rather than repair. Lightrider needs successors real soon if we are to continue youth operations with our soon-to-be-refurbished LtR.

The exchequer is going to need some attention, too, soon and very soon. Though many of our regular small donors have been stepping up to this task, a mighty humbling blessing let me say, we're going to need a lot of dough right away.

I saw two bumper stickers in ABQ. One said "What really doesn't work is prayer," and one that said "Real Men Pray." I for one am going with the second one. Please pray fervent thanksgiving that the LtR has gotten home safely, that the course we've chosen is His, and that He provides the people, the stamina, and the resources to stay the course.

Stay the Fight, Keep the Faith, and above all else guard your heart (Proverbs 4:23).

Mike

That extra day in Albuquerque necessitated by the false start home allowed me to be with Orrin when his name was drawn to attend Estansia Valley Classical Academy. This was a Charter School planted by Hillsdale College, where Tim, the son of our good friend Tom Thiery, was the principal.

Given the 2,000-mile separation between Debbie and my home in Indiana, with our daughter's family near Albuquerque, sharing such a landmark event seemed to be yet another case of God fulfilling Romans 8:28 (NKJV): "And we know that all things work together for good to those who love God, to those who are the called according to His purpose." And "I see His hand of mercy, I hear His voice of cheer, and just the time I need Him, He's always near." (*He Lives*, by Alfred Henry Ackley, 1933)

TEN

More Tranny Travails

Steve Brinkerhoff performing pre-trip maintenance. Despite valiant mechanical efforts at home by professionals and LtR staff alike, machine malfunctions happen, generally at the least opportune time (see Murphy's Law).

A scant seven months after the tranny failure in Albuquerque, we found ourselves in Myrtle Beach, SC, with one of our favorite groups on LtR's Annual Paul E Turner Golf Classic (see Chapter 11). But then our tranny troubles returned. The LtR was losing tranny fluid, lots of it, making a massive puddle in the parking lot at the Caledonia Golf Resort where our group was playing.

To check out the source of the leak, we drove the LtR to a nearby school-bus maintenance facility where, providentially, Debbie's sister Wanza worked. It seemed we needed an Allison garage to make repairs, but the closest was in Columbia, SC, and it was closed on the weekend and would only open Monday morning.

We finished out the golf agenda by pouring gallons of tranny fluid into our machine at regular, short intervals. Some of our group had to fly home from Myrtle Beach as they had work obligations Monday, but we managed to limp the 150 miles to Columbia, where we spent Sunday night sleeping aboard the LtR in the Allison garage parking lot.

Monday morning, that garage had us back on the road toward Indiana in an hour or two, confident that the problem had been corrected. It had not.

We made it to a Flying J truck stop outside of Charleston, WV, where, stopping for fuel and supper, we discovered, to our chagrin, tranny fluid all over the back end of the LtR. Charleston had an Allison garage, but it was closed.

As God would have it, LtR had a friend in town, Jonathan Secrest, a youth pastor. He had connections with a car-rental place so was able to get us a deal on a 15-passenger van. Our group size had dwindled enough as a result of the guys who had flown home, enabling the remnant of our group—golf clubs and all—to only just fit into that van. Jonathan drove the guys the six remaining hours back to Upland and returned a day later to take the van back.

Debbie and I spent the night at a motel near the Allison garage in Charleston to which we'd had the LtR towed. By noon Tuesday morning the LtR had once again been repaired, so Debbie and I headed north to Upland, some 300-plus miles away, believing that our Allison odyssey had ended. It had not. Indeed it was just getting started.

Yet we made it home to Upland without further incident. Then, 10 days later, on a Friday, we headed west with a student ministry from the University of Kentucky, Lexington, en route to Phoenix for a week of service in a soup kitchen. We made it as far as Oklahoma City. Once again, tranny fluid was drenching our stern. Fortunately, OK City had an Allison garage. But it was closed. Then again, it was a nice weekend weather wise, a local church welcoming us to spend the next two nights with them.

Bright and early Monday morning found the LtR parked in front of the overhead door at the OK City Allison garage. Once again, we were taken care of promptly, so were again on the road by about noon, our group of congenial, collegial Christians continuing to roll with the Allison punches without complaint. Really, as great a bunch of kids as I could recall in my then 43 years on the road with kids—and they from a secular university. A few hundred miles farther west, their admirable congeniality would once again face the Allison test.

Stranded on the corner in Winslow, AZ, what a fine sight to see: not a girl in a flatbed Ford but a gaggle of girls and guys in a Neoplan Skyliner glistening under a sheen of tranny fluid—dead in the water yet again! The nearest Allison garage was 66 miles farther west in Flagstaff, AZ.

We prayed and came up with a plan—what, D or F by this time? Skip Phoenix. Charter a coach to at least get our wonderful group of students to the South Rim of the Grand Canyon, the one recreational stop planned on this short-term missions trip. Tow our oily rig close to 300 miles east to Stewart & Stevenson, the Allison Transmission garage in Albuquerque where our Allison Odyssey had begun back in July.

After a day viewing the Grand Canyon, our charter coach would bring these remarkably cheerful students to Albuquerque where we once again would enjoy the hospitality and love of an overnight or two at Monterey Baptist Church, the church that had so graciously cared for Lightrider at the onset of this odyssey eight months prior.

Our group maintained their gracious, humble spirit, actually asking me from time to time how they could be praying for me, more concerned with what I was going through than with their situation.

Hopefully, Stewart & Stevenson in Albuquerque might at last make a permanent repair that would enable us to get our group back to Lexington, Ky. As it happened, the rebuilt tranny that they had installed had to be removed and rebuilt, a week-or-longer proposition, which necessitated chartering another coach to get our group home.

The upside was that I got some time with my daughter's family, who live near Albuquerque. My studly grandson Orrin, eight years old at this time, was a hit with the college girls who invited him to pass the time playing cards and such with them.

The Stewart & Stevenson garage discovered that an update in the transmission design had been poorly instituted at the Allison rebuild facility near Chicago. The very experienced crew of rebuilders used a seal from the original design that did not work well with the output shaft called for in the new design. Fortunately the warranty covered most of the mechanical work spread out from Columbia, SC, through Charleston, WV, Oklahoma City, OK, ending up in Albuquerque, NM. Those great kids and His wonderful churches along the way covered lodging and meals. LtR got stuck with transportation expenses and about $2,000 worth of transmission fluid. God is good.

"While we walk the pilgrim pathway, Clouds will overspread the sky; but when traveling days are over, not a shadow, not a sigh." (*When We All Get to Heaven*, Eliza Hewitt, 1898)

Paul Turner, namesake of the annual Paul E Turner Memorial Myrtle Beach Golf Retreat, with his wife Betty upstairs in the second Lightrider.

ELEVEN

God's Grace, Great Golf, and Good Gravy

After our wedding and her subsequent move to Indiana, my wife, Debbie—one of six daughters and four sons—needed to make it back home to South Carolina each January for a special annual gathering of her sisters with their mom. This gathering originated as an effort by the sisters to grant their mom respite as 24/7 caregiver to their father after he had suffered a debilitating stroke. The sisters would take their mother to the "Beach"—Myrtle Beach, that is—where she was wined and dined, so to speak, for a few days. The brothers and brothers-in-law, meanwhile, would fill in as caregivers for their father.

God provided for our family's unique need in such a unique way. Our niece Shawnna worked to get golf groups lodging and such at a Myrtle Beach Resort, Compass Cove. My brother Steve, an avid golfer, was working as a fight instructor in Marion, IN, near Upland. His boss and friend, Dick Darlington, said, "Since there's not much flying going on this time of the year, why don't we take your brother's bus to Myrtle Beach for some golf?" Steve, working with Shawnna, organized an annual golf retreat to Myrtle Beach and timed it to coincide with Debbie and her sisters caring for their long-suffering Momma. This retreat became known as the Annual Paul E Turner Memorial Golf Retreat.

As explained in Chapters 28 and 29, LtR's usual team on mobile retreats was made up of three drivers and a "Lovely Assistant." On each of these golf retreats I would fill one of the three driver slots while Debbie, aka Sweet Thing, would act as our "Lovely Assistant."

On arriving at the "Beach," Debbie and I would jump ship, leaving the next four days of golfing, devotions, and retreat logistics up to Steve and the number two driver, frequently Buck Simpkins, also an avid golfer. Debbie would enjoy time with her sisters and their Momma while I hung with my cousin Dave Lawson, married to Debbie's sister Linda. If the golfers had any special needs, like mechanical problems with the Lightrider, emergency-room visits or the like, Steve would give me a call to handle those needs. Dave would be my wheel man, getting us to the Lightrider, parts store, hospital, or whereever.

Many friends helped to organize and/or drive the Paul E Turner Memorial Golf Retreat over the years. One such man was John Wheeler. John worked diligently to organize golf games like the Yellow Ball, create pairings, scrambles,

Speaking of Tying on the Feed Bag . . .

Wheeler Youngens at a Sonic in Branson.

and the like. He also provided golf-centric prizes, like special golf balls, gloves, and other paraphernalia. He personally created watercolor paintings depicting the Lightrider in spectacular natural settings to include famous golf courses. He helped to fund these retreats for occasional individuals who might benefit from such help.

Tying on the feed bag was always an important part of the formula. This was done at favorite watering holes like The Carolina Road House, Drunken Jack's, The Original Benjamin's, and the like. Good gravy was always an essential ingredient in this unique recipe for Christian fellowship.

One memorable encounter happened at Drunken Jack's. It seems the hostess's name was Taylor, as proclaimed by her name tag. One of our golfers, Eric Turner, was wearing a shirt with the name Taylor embroidered on the left front—Taylor for Taylor University, located here in LtR's home town, Upland, IN. The coincidence of the two Taylors began a fun relationship between this young lady and the LtR golfers. She, Taylor Suggs, was preparing for a short-term mission trip and so the guys, then and there, decided to take up an offering to help her in her mission. Becoming friends, on subsequent retreats, our group kept up with Taylor and her needs going forward into her marriage and life in general. God's grace, great golf, and good gravy—a winning recipe, that's for sure.

We need to pause our narrative with the news this day, 26 June 2025, that our dear friend John Wheeler has been promoted to Heaven. John's service with LtR goes way beyond the Paul E Turner Memorial Golf Retreats he so loved and helped to make possible.

John took many a family reunion retreat aboard the LtR. A picture of one to Branson, MO, graces my office wall. It shows a gaggle of his grands smiling and waving in a Sonic Drive-in, the LtR parked outside. On that retreat, my brother Steve asked during a devotional if anyone would like to pray. Every hand of every grand shot up; John and his kids, the parents, beamed with pride and shed a tear or two of joy in their youngsters being so enthusiastic about Christ. I get misty thinking about it.

One fond memory of John and his family was the occasion of son Jonathan's return from several months of active duty in Iraq after his Naval Intelligence Reserve unit had been called up. LtR had the privilege of taking the Wheeler family to the Dayton International Airport in the wee hours to meet this uniformed warrior, father of seven, deplaning beneath a replica of the Wright Flyer—misty doesn't begin to cover it. Familial love along with gratitude to God for bringing Jonathan through the dangers of combat, coupled with patriotic pride, it was a special event indeed.

LtR's patriotic livery, described in the following chapter, along with a police escort back home to Springboro, OH, were nice complements to this very American welcome.

John Wheeler was a true servant of God, a pillar of the faith—he was greatly loved and will be greatly missed. But I digress.

We rejoin our narrative in progress . . . For 33 years, in this way, God provided the means for Debbie and me to "work" our way to the "Beach" to meet Debbie's longtime family obligation while getting me some refreshment and recharging with a different part of the family. God is good.

Getting Debbie home in this way could have been a big burden, but was instead an act of God's grace: "Wonderful grace of Jesus, Greater than all my sin; how shall my tongue describe it, where shall its praise begin? Taking away my burden, setting my spirit free; for the wonderful grace of Jesus reaches me." ("Wonderful Grace of Jesus," Haldor Lillenas, 1918)

The first Lightrider, showing our flag and cross together, on Taylor's campus.

TWELVE

Lightrider's Livery—Throwing Lightrider's Hat into the Cultural Fray

The year was 1997. Cultural collapse in the USA was continuing to corrode American values, what Charlton Heston would refer to in his talk to the Harvard Law School Forum on 16 February 1999 titled "Winning the Culture War": "I believe that we are again engaged in a great civil war, a cultural war that's about to hijack your birthright to think and say what resides in your heart. I fear you no longer trust the pulsing lifeblood of liberty inside you . . . the stuff that made this country rise from wilderness into the miracle that it is."

What should or could LtR do? Showing the flag and showing the cross and showing them together came to mind. Steve Kuhn, longtime friend and a big part of LtR, came up with the idea of painting our coach to look like the American Flag—the entire 40-foot long, 13½-foot-tall double-decker.

Have learned recently that the flag flown at Fort McHenry after the British bombardment during the War of 1812 that inspired Francis Scott Key to pen "The Star Spangled Banner" was 40 feet long too, but I digress.

The only cross sported on the Lightrider at the time was the one in the center of our name. We came up with an image of 13 stars in a circle with a cross in the center. It represented America as a new nation with 13 states symbolized by 13 stars. The cross in the center signified that Christian values were central to America when she was founded. In support of this idea, ponder thoughts of some prominent people found on our website www.lightrider.org.

This new livery showed the cross not wrapped in the flag, but together with the flag (see Chapter 15). It seemed like a Divine inspiration to me. The thought of painting any vehicle to look like the flag had never occurred to me. But here it was! Sometime later, I chanced to see the Lightrider running along a country road about a half-mile distant across the runway at Air Marion, Inc. in Marion, IN—what a "fine sight to see." Even at that distance, the American flag was not only clearly discernible, but seemed to invite a salute as well.

Rob McCoy's paint shop in Marion did the stripes and the blue field. We then got the coach home to our new garage in Upland, where Steve Kuhn and his then bride-to-be, Carrie, spent the weekend applying vinyl stars in a very precise pattern to the blue field, completing our new flag motif, a motif of which we continue to be very proud.

Recently, Dennis Prager put out a five-minute video in which he talked about the three essential American values that are engraved on all American coins. Can you name them without looking? Liberty—the freedom to do, or say or to be whatever you want. *E Pluribus Unum*, our unofficial national motto prior to 1956, "out of many one"—out of many colonies one nation, which came to mean out of many cultures, nationalities, and ethnic groups, one people—the American People. Finally, In God We Trust—not just our national motto, but the American way of life, practiced by most Americans from the Pilgrims forward. It's been a hallmark of American life since at least 1811 when Francis Scott Key wrote it into the fourth verse of what would become our national anthem. It's been LtR's hallmark from our get-go too, that's for certain.

My brother Steve proposed a slogan that we painted on the back of our Lightrider: "Strengthening America, One Church at a Time." After all, the Church played a big part in building America. You may recall the "Black Robe Regiment," made up of about 700 church pastors who got the word out about the American Revolution as it was happening. It's not hyperbole to say that without the Church there would be no America today.

And today, 2025, if that same church doesn't get fired up, sounding the alarm from "the church house to the White house," saying "We want God in America again," America's last day will fast approach (from Carman's 1993 impassioned song for our confused nation, "America Again").

Steve Kuhn, a little later and unbeknownst to me, painted a message on the roof of the Lightrider. It was invisible unless the Lightrider was viewed from a vantage point above it. One such vantage point was a frequent stop on LtR retreats that included New York City's World Trade Center Observation Deck. Our groups were part of the average 1.8 million visitors each year from December 1975 when the Twin Towers opened up until that dark, dark day, 11 September 2001, when the towers were brought down; when America was attacked by nothing short of pure evil—evil disguised as agents of a so-called god. Please forgive my digression.

Coach parking in Manhattan has always been in short supply given the amount of coach traffic to that little island. For a time, parking was allowed on the southbound side of West Side Drive, which then bordered the west side of the World Trade Center. When visiting the Top of the World, as the Observation Deck was known, we could look down and show our group of kids the LtR parked far down below in what appeared to be a line of several other miniature coaches.

Kuhn's message, painted in six-foot-tall black letters on the white roof, running most of the length of the Lightrider, was quite easy to read even 1,377 feet up in the sky: "Jesus Loves You!" Another "fine sight to see," let me tell you, and another very important message to get out there during these continuing decades of America's cultural collapse.

THIRTEEN

Deer Season; Bicycle Beneficence; Mercy on the Mountain; A Trucker's Life Spared; an Icy Tale of Two Coaches; Nuclear Threat; & a Couple of Coast-to-Coast-with-the-Holy-Ghost Highlights

The author with Dottie Pierce pulling a grade on the 1975 Wandering Wheels Coast-to-Coast bicycle trip.

DEER SEASON

Sign at an auto body shop: "It's Deer Season. Heads or tails, you lose." Back in the early 1980s, at about midnight en route to Alaska, we were modocking across South Dakota on I-90 in Wandering Wheels' Possum Six with Dale Patten at the wheel. I was standing on the lower step, leaning on the dash looking out the windshield. Suddenly antlers flashed by and we slammed into the rump of a 12-point buck.

The impact broke the curbside headlight, throwing a circuit breaker, shutting off the driver-side headlight, and leaving us doing 70 mph in the pitch black. We're talking dark, like the inside of an Alaskan well-digger's pocket. All we could see was a faint orange hue from the running lights reflecting off the highway just in front of the coach. By the grace of God, Dale managed to keep the coach under control, getting us safely stopped and onto the shoulder. There are 150-or-so human deaths in the US each year from deer strikes.

We located and fixed the short in the curbside headlight socket, and the driver-side headlight came back on, enabling us to continue on our way. A couple of the passengers had walked back along the shoulder until they felt and heard broken glass underfoot—the unfortunate buck was lying dead nearby. Fortunately, his big self was alone, not accompanied by a wrecked coach full of human bucks and buckettes . . . thank you, Lord!

Speaking of deer, we'd had a less dangerous encounter on another retreat, this one when climbing Bear Mountain in Possum Four about 3 a.m. while driving from Jackson, WY, to Salt Lake City, UT, en route to California. We were only doing about 10 mph in first gear on a steep two-lane, nearing the summit.

Several deer were loitering around on a low bluff on the left side of the highway. Recalling the expression, caught like a "deer in the headlights," I thought it might be worth testing that theory with the hand-controlled spotlight on snub-nosed Possum Four to see if the deer would actually "freeze." I hit, with the spotlight, a small doe standing just above the highway on the left. She not only did not freeze, but lunged onto the highway just in front of us. I hit the brakes and slid to a rapid halt. We were so close to the scared little doe that I had to lean forward and look out the bottom of the windshield.

She was running in place, rather like a dog on a waxed floor, repeatedly, frantically glancing up over her right shoulder at me. Her little hooves eventually got enough purchase on the slick asphalt that she made it off the pavement onto the right side of the road. Reaching full traction on the naturally rough surface, she then bounded gracefully into the night, memory no doubt seared by her encounter with a brilliantly lit, extremely noisy behemoth. I, on the other hand, laughed, lamenting that no one else had been awake to see our funny encounter with nature, but very glad the little doe had been spared calamity—and having learned that "deer in the headlights" do not necessarily "freeze."

A few minutes later, at the summit, Bob Walker, roused from sleep by a routine call of nature, asked me to pull over and let him off the coach to appease said need. He stood just out front of the Possum, facing away, proceeding to prosecute his problem. It occurred to me to test his reaction to the spotlight—evidently humans do freeze in the headlights. But, again, I digress.

BICYCLE BENEFICENCE

Let's shift gears to another time and location to learn more about God's hand of protection. The scene: Late seventies or early eighties, spring break in Florida, 50 Taylor University students riding bicycles with Wandering Wheels from Pensacola to Tallahassee. Terry Stuart and Jo Stark, each remarkably pretty coeds, riding side by side on the final leg of the 250-mile sojourn on a quiet, two-lane without shoulder blacktop somewhere between Sopchoppy and Tallahassee.

A couple of things happen simultaneously. A retired guy with his wife in a large automobile towing a long travel trailer is pulling cautiously past the two young ladies. The outside rider, Terry, while attempting to shift gears, experiences chain derailment, which throws her off balance and sends her sideways into Jo. Jo veers left, hitting and falling under the side of the trailer forward of the trailer's twin axles.

The retired guy, bless his heart, seeing the situation in his passenger-side mirror, takes his wife and most everything he owns into the left-side ditch. As God would have it, Jo's sweatshirt is snagged by the trailer's entrance steps, probably saving her life. Still under the trailer, she is dragged into the grassy, shallow ditch, but is kept out from under the trailer wheels.

Driving back-up on this particular spring-break trip, I arrive on the scene in Possum Four, a 35-foot motor coach with a sleeper interior. Phil Summerville, a tall, lanky member of the Wandering Wheels staff, is standing in the road, waving his arms over his head to flag me down. We get Jo out from under the travel trailer and onto one of the bunks in Possum Four, with Terry cradling Jo's head in her lap. Picking up speed en route to the hospital, I happen to look in the inside rearview mirror, learning what it means for one to be writhing in pain. It seems that one of her hands may have been run over by one of the trailer wheels. We pass an oncoming ambulance with its lights flashing and siren screaming heading to the scene, but I'm not stopping until arriving at the hospital.

Mercifully, Jo was okay, no permanent injuries, but she did take on the look of a raccoon with a full band of deep-purple bruising around both her eyes. The week after the trip, back at Taylor, despite her appearance, Jo spoke at a chapel service, wanting to share testimony of His love and protection. She was grateful not to have been killed or seriously injured. But equally important to her was that God had used this horrible, life- and limb-threatening experience to re-energize her love for and desire to serve Him.

Earlier on this spring-break trip I had had a chance to share with the whole group during a devotional time about something special that had happened to me the previous day. I had been in the chow line beside the lovely Terry Stuart at supper that evening. That day, while riding in the Florida sun, she had gotten her lips badly sunburned. She turned and looked at me and said, "My lips are aflame . . ." My then single, young self took that as a compliment.

If we may digress a moment longer: on a summer Wheels' bike trip in Vermont, we chanced to stop by a ski slope at Stowe Mountain to ride the "luge," an alpine slide in a half pipe track, enabling the ski slope profitable use of their chairlift and slope during warm weather. Coach Davenport, always the competitor and going too fast, managed to scrape his leg but good on the concrete track. Later in that day, we stopped at Woodstock, a cute tourist destination. Word passed around that Charles Bronson was at the ice cream shop. I wandered over there to get a look and sure enough he was seated at a table, smaller than life, with a lady friend, chatting. Davenport, dressed in bicycling togs like our large group, entered the shop a bit later. Bronson noticed Coach's scraped up leg and said to his friend, "Looks like the old guy had a spill."

MERCY ON THE MOUNTAIN

More miracles happened aboard Wandering Wheels' Possum One, a Hawaiian Blue sleeper bus constructed with a superior coach body mounted on a Chevrolet school bus chassis. It was January 1975. The youth group was from Stuart UMC of Stuart, Florida. Possum One was in Florida, having transported 30 Taylor kids down for a 1,000-mile bicycle ride around the perimeter of the state, singing as a group about our Savior along the way. We were using Possum One to conduct mobile retreats to the Smoky Mountains with Florida groups while the Taylor kids bicycled. We had just completed a Smokies run with Miami Christian School.

We departed Stuart UMC after supper for the overnight drive, with Rob Shafer, Joe Prilwitz, and I staffing, 30 high-schoolers on board. Arriving at Great Smoky Mountains National Park the next morning, we spent the day hiking in the Smoky Mountains and camping out the next night. The following day we visited Gatlinburg, TN, and saw a couple of sights nearby.

Then God got seriously involved. We had stopped late afternoon at Newfound Gap as we left the area for our return to Stuart. Three kids had wanted to get out to take pictures. I recall, looking out the window, that it was so overcast that those pictures would show only the inside of a cloud. It was the last sight and last thought I remember.

Starting down the highway US 441 toward North Carolina, a 7 percent grade, Rob at the wheel, we hadn't gone far when the brakes gave out. Of the three of us, Rob was the senior driver, having driven in the Rocky Mountains many times. We hit the rear of a Toyota four-wheel drive, sending it off the highway backwards. The driver of the Toyota, despite suffering a fractured skull, hiked back up to the highway, hitchhiked down the road to where God had landed our busted-up Possum, and helped pull kids out of the wreck.

The rest of this story is hearsay because, so I'm told, I hit my head on an overhead bunk when awakened from a nap, getting up rapidly because of all the screaming. Helping Joe get the kids herded to the back of the bus and on the floor, I then knelt behind Rob, encouraging him to clip overhanging boulders and road signs on the right side of the highway and scrape the side of the bus along the cliff wall in an effort to slow us down. Doing that left a trail of blue paint, pieces of the custom-made oak dashboard, broken glass, tennis shoes, and the like for the next two and a quarter miles around dozens of curves—my twin brother, Steve, clocked it when coming down the following day with Possum Two to pick us up.

Rob tells me that at one point the steering seemed to give up and the bus drifted to the left, across the double yellow, headed for a steep drop into the rocky stream paralleling the highway. The hood had popped up, limiting our vision forward to peer through the crack where the hood was hinged to the firewall.

How fast were we going? Possum One was equipped with a five-speed manual transmission and a two-speed electrically shifted rear axle. Evidently, the rear axle had gotten hung up between its two gears, which essentially put the bus into neutral—zero engine braking and the service brakes had faded completely—a fully loaded bus heading down a 7 percent grade. On previous trips, when creeping down that same highway in first gear, if I put in the clutch, it was like hitting the accelerator. God only knows how fast we were going.

Then, on its own, the bus drifted back to the right, back across the double yellow, leaving the pavement, wheels and axles furrowing into the soft, muddy, snow-covered ground, missing several large trees, slowing gradually, then rolling onto the passenger side, coming to a gentle halt. The kids reported feeling no impact. God Himself had landed our crippled, beat-up steed in that perfect spot.

Four of us spent the night in the hospital at Bryson City, NC. There were no permanent injuries, though one of the girls won't get on a bus to this day and I have never recovered memory of the event. Four kids were snatched from the hand of Satan, saved during the screaming, shouting, and praying melee, their pastor having gotten on the bus at the last moment—more of God's grace. Sometime later we'd joke about offering on future retreats a bus wreck . . . for an extra $20,000.

Pictures taken just after the accident show all four wheels smoking—we had just recently had the brakes relined. Smoking brakes mean that they were functioning. Rob, experienced as he was in mountain driving, surely had not faded the brakes. My thinking is that inferior brake lining had been installed. In fact, following the previous retreat with Miami Christian, I had requested that their mechanic have a look at the brakes because they had felt weak to me—but he had found no fault.

With no memory of the event, I'm left only the verbal accounts of the other staff and passengers. I am in one picture wearing shorts and a favorite ski sweater, standing barefoot on the upside of the bus, pulling kids out of a window.

My twin, Steve, and John Bonham had driven Possum Two the 500-or-so miles overnight from Indiana to pick us up at the hospital the following morning to continue our return to Stuart. The nurses, seeing Steve, assumed it was me up and around without their permission or knowledge. Right away, they set after him and he played it to the hilt, having some good fun at their expense. I'm glad that they didn't seek retribution on my innocent, still-in-bed self . . .

How did we make it around all of those slow-speed curves without flipping over at what must have been a terrifying speed, not hitting anymore cars going down the mountain or encountering any uphill traffic, either one? What force carried our broken bus away from the certainly-fatal drop into the rocky stream on the left side of the highway and back over the double yellow to such a perfect place for a crippled bus to land? Seems to me that it had to be the very hand of God Himself—thank you, Lord!

A TRUCKER'S LIFE SPARED

While we're talking mountains and brakes failing, there was an incident in Colorado: on I-70 west of Denver, descending with the Lightrider, loaded with kids, eastbound toward Denver, at least six lanes. We're in the outside lane, geared down a bit, traffic moving past us on the left. Suddenly in my driver-side mirror is a horrifying sight; about a quarter-mile behind us, appearing around a curve, comes a semi with its 18 wheels smoking like a dragster doing the quarter-mile, in my lane, gaining on us like gangbusters.

Knowing that this section of I-70 has runaway truck ramps accessed from the outside lane, while maintaining speed, I got us moved as far left as possible onto the shoulder of the inside lane beside the median, wanting to give the high-balling truck room to get by us to take a runaway ramp if one presented itself. He blasted past us in a flash, all wheels smoking, a state trooper trailing him by 50 yards, both disappearing around a curve up ahead. We—me along with a gaggle of kids who happened to be up front—began to pray fervently that God would save that trucker's life.

As we approached that curve, expecting to see a big hole in the outside guardrail, we instead encountered a swarm of plywood sheets covering the entire eastbound side of I-70, all three lanes.

We slowed, continuing down the highway, and were able to roll right over the spread-out plywood. The semi was stopped on the right-hand shoulder about a quarter-mile farther down the hill, right against the guardrail. The trooper, having stopped close behind the semi, also on the shoulder, had gotten out of her squad car and was running toward it with a fire extinguisher in hand. All of the trailer wheels were on fire.

Evidently, the driver was able to rub his flatbed trailer with its load of plywood against the guardrail, tearing the nylon webbing straps that had been securing the plywood. Once freed from the restraints, the plywood departed the trailer along with its heavy weight, lightening the semi's load enough for the glazed brakes to bring that formerly heavy load to a halt. Either that, or God Himself, parted, like the Red Sea, the webbing . . . Either way, we were relieved to see that man's life spared and felt that God had indeed answered our prayer.

AN ICY TALE OF TWO COACHES

We saw again the hand of God, also in Colorado, in December 1981 while heading to Loveland for a few days of skiing with Dennis Yoder and his group of single adults, mostly from his church in Goshen, Indiana. A few Uplanders were on board too: Donna Porter, Carla Koons, Linda Tittle, and Carolyn "Sparky" Jones, to name a few. This time we were aboard Wandering Wheels' Possum Four, a 1977 35-foot MCI MC-5 that we'd converted into a sleeper coach.

Possum Four was set up with US mechanical components by Motor Coach Industries (MCI) in Pembina, North Dakota, just across the border from Winnipeg, Canada, where it had been manufactured. Wandering Wheels had bought it brand-new (it had been ordered and built for Hare Krishna, who defaulted, making it affordable and available for purchase by Wheels).

My brother Steve had flown to Winnipeg to pick up the coach. Riding in the cab from the airport to the factory, he asked the driver if he knew the name Bob Davenport (founder and director of Wheels). The cabbie asked if he had played for the Winnipeg Blue Bombers. Davenport, following a phone call from Henrietta Mears, world-renowned Christian Educator at First Presbyterian Church of Hollywood (Hollywood Presbyterian), in which she counseled him about the importance of observing the Christian Sabbath, played pro football for the Winnipeg Blue Bombers rather than the Cleveland Browns, for which he had been a first-round draft choice over Jim Brown, because the Canadian Football league did not play ball on Sunday. Amazingly, the cabbie, being a real football fan, was quite familiar with the name Bob Davenport.

Over the years, Wheels (and later LtR) would spend a night at Hollywood Presbyterian, sleeping on the carpeted floor of the nicely air-conditioned youth hall with groups traveling on a very popular 11-day retreat we called a California Run. The night in Hollywood was the only night on those entire retreats spent stopped.

On one such night Kelly Koons and I had chosen to sleep on Possum Four parked outside Hollywood Presbyterian while our third driver, Paul "Snowball" King, slept inside with the group. About 11 p.m., a very pretty young lady knocked on the door of the bus. She said that Tom Hafley, a former Wheels staff guy who had planned to connect with us while in Hollywood, had had an emergency with a kid

Deer Season, Bicycle Beneficence; ... & a Couple of Coast-to-Coast-with-the-Holy-Ghost Highlights

Back row, left to right, Wayne Dalland, Scott Pugsley, Phil Summerville, Mike Manganello, Curt Anderson. Front row, left to right, Mel Callison, Ted Bowers, Dale Patton, Larry Kleindienst a.k.a. Spare Parts, Jim Gore.

at the orphanage where he worked and would not be able to see us. Disappointed, Kelly and I went back to bed.

Not long later, another young lady, this one in chauffeur's uniform, knocked on the bus door. She had double-parked a very long, white Lincoln limousine beside and in front of Possum Four. It seemed that her bosses, in the limo, were interested in our bus and its lively paint job. Would we come out and meet them? "Who are they?" we asked. "The Doobie Brothers," said she. Dressed only in Wheels shorts, but armed with a tire thumper and a 4D-cell flashlight, we approached the back door of the limo, which the lady chauffeur opened. Tom Hafley and another friend from Taylor, Barry Huffman, called out a popular insult of the day, shocking Kelly and me to the max.

We got Snowball up and took a ride down Mulholland Drive in the limo with Tom, Barry and the pretty young lady who had first awakened us, who turned out to be Tom's new wife. Tom worked part-time for Aaron's Limo Service, so the driver of the limo that night was a co-worker of his. While cruising Mulholland, Tom crawled out of the sunroof onto the roof, with us holding on to his ankles, so that he could stretch his arms down over the windshield, scaring the chauffeur half to death—in retrospect, not a bright move. His new wife did implore us to hold on tight.

Later, we pulled up by the curb in front of Tommy's, a popular burger joint in Los Angeles. The place was small, with windows lining the whole front. The reflection of the limo in those windows spanned the entire width of that little place. Patrons inside sat on seats facing across a counter to the outside where we were parked. Snowball powered down his window on the curbside of the limo. We could read the lips of the patrons, "Who's that?" The place had great fries served in large, brown paper sacks.

I was driving as we entered the parking lot of the Loveland ski area off of I-70 west of Denver. Pulling in, we were approached on foot by Marvin Spees, aka Starvin' Marvin, with whom we'd arranged rental skis. I set the brake. Then, instead of moving the gearshift lever to neutral, I grabbed the crank handle to open the door, and by habit let out the clutch. You'd have expected the coach to lurch and the engine to stall, but nothing much happened. A bit of a clunk was heard, but the engine continued to idle as if in neutral. A small shaft in a major component in the drive train had broken, disabling the coach.

We were so glad that this no-doubt defective shaft had snapped in the parking lot rather than out on the highway. Had we been geared down, descending the grade back into Denver depending on engine compression to hold our speed down, suddenly being, in effect, neutral, would have been very dangerous indeed, to say nothing of being stranded on the side of the highway after getting the coach stopped. But this is just the beginning of the story.

We had the coach towed back to Denver for repairs, which no doubt would take a few weeks because a replacement for the broken component, called a drop box, would have likely have to have been ordered from the factory. A church in Golden, CO, sent their church vans up to get us after a first day of skiing. We would use those vans for the next couple of days in getting to and from the slopes.

Of course we called the Wheels office for prayer and to plan for another coach to come out to Colorado to return our group to Goshen and Upland. Not yet knowing whether the slim possibility of Possum Four being repaired in time for our return to Indiana might indeed pan out, it was decided that I would call the office before 4:30 p.m. on the day before our return was scheduled to depart Colorado.

Miraculously, the repair garage managed to find the unusual part and had our coach ready to go just in time, PTL! I called the Wheels office with the good news about 4:20 p.m., 10 minutes prior to the deadline. Suella, Coach's Gal Friday at Wheels, told me that Geoff Schwartz had already left with Possum Three to come and get us.

Suella alerted the state police in Indiana, Iowa, and Illinois to please stop the bus if seen and ask the driver to call the Wheels office. Geoff was having to drive via Chicago, 249 miles farther to Denver than going I-70, because he needed Steve Manganello to help drive.

Steve and his wife, Kari, were in Chicago at the time for Wheels' staffer Kelly Koons's wedding to Wendy Soderquist, a former Taylor girl and friend. Geoff picked Steve up on the way by Chicago to help drive and they continued west, without any notice by state police, stopping at North Platte, Nebraska, for fuel and deciding to check in with the Wheels office.

Finding that we did not need Possum Three, Steve got a bit hot under his collar. He knew we would be at Casa Bonita, a popular Mexican Restaurant in Golden, CO, and so he called and had me paged. He was not happy to hear my explanation, though accurate, that their rescue mission had departed 10 minutes prior to the deadline.

We decided that he and Geoff ought to spend the night in North Platte, which we would reach early the following morning. Then we could convoy back to Indiana, which we ended up doing.

Late afternoon the following day we were entering the Des Moines area, eastbound on I-80, air temperature about 30 degrees, and it started to rain, with a high wind blowing from the south (our right). The rain on the highway turned rapidly to ice; traffic began dancing around like drunken sailors; Steve was at the wheel with Geoff in Possum Three, leading our little convoy, and had their two passenger-side wheels on the graveled, ice-covered shoulder. Wayne Dalland at the wheel of Possum Four (with me and our group of singles) was trailing by about 50 yards. Both buses were in first gear, moving just a few miles per hour.

The roadway at this point was steeply banked as it curved toward the north (our left). Possum Four, just passing over a bridge with the wind howling underneath, emerged from the bridge onto the bridge approach supported by solid earth, the wind now rushing up the earthen embankment hitting Possum Four full in the side. It then pushed us sideways across both eastbound lanes, down the steeply banked roadway to the left-side shoulder and into the guardrail (actual steel cables). We were leaning drastically toward the embankment on our driver side, by the median. Wayne got out of the coach to see how bad the lean looked from outside. Turned out the lean felt worse on board than it was in reality, and we were in no danger of rolling … yet.

Wayne stepped back into the bus, just onto the first step. He was telling us we had time to put on our shoes, jackets, and such before leaving the bus to walk down the embankment on our left into the median. We'd then walk under the bridge we had just crossed to a McDonald's located on the south side of I-80.

But then an out-of-control semi rammed us in the rear, shoving Possum Four farther into the cable rail, greatly increasing the lean we had been concerned about. The right rear wheels of the coach were a couple of feet off the ground. We were now tipped precariously to the driver's side, the low cable rail the only thing keeping us from rolling down that embankment.

Wayne, standing as he was on the lower step, thumped his head a good one into the doorpost and his forehead began to bleed like a stuck pig. It was time to evacuate the bus posthaste. Wayne and I stood just outside, beside the door, and had to catch every passenger by their arms as they stepped off the bus onto the ice, because their feet just flew out from under them.

Steve had seen in his driver-side mirror what had happened. As he and Geoff left Possum Three parked on the shoulder on the high side of the bank, Geoff had to grab Steve by the arm as the wind was just blowing Steve with his slick-soled shoes across the ice-coated pavement.

Quick-thinking law enforcement closed that section of I-80 immediately. The temperature did, however, begin to rise a bit by the wee hours and the ice disappeared, but the highway was blocked by thousands of what had been slow-moving cars, trucks, and buses that had spun out of control, colliding with each other and bouncing off guardrails like billiard balls on a pool table.

We all managed to get to that Mickey D's, spending the night in a roller rink next door. In the morning the group boarded our God-provided back-up coach with Steve and Geoff, heading to Upland via Goshen where Dennis and his group were dropped off.

We had just managed on the iced-over surface roads to get Wayne to an emergency room aboard Possum Three. Medics dressed his head wound and discovered that he did indeed have a concussion, which kept him from driving for 24 hours.

The collision had ruptured the heater core on Possum Four so our run to Blitz Bus Body in Chicago was done without heat, though we were thankful that Possum Four was still drivable. The left front tire had been punctured on a steel post supporting the cable railing, but we had a spare on board.

God's grace sure seemed to be favoring us. If the semi that had struck us had been traveling just a little faster, Possum Four, with all hands aboard, would certainly have been rolled down that embankment, greatly threatening life and limb.

Having a spare coach to use in getting our passengers home seemed a God thing to me. The circumstances conspiring to get Possum Three with us just when we needed it were just too coincidental: Possum Four actually getting repaired in time for our return; Geoff leaving those few minutes early; Geoff and Steve had actually been at the scene of a car fire, even taking fire extinguishers from Possum Three to put out the flames, yet state police at that scene did not alert them to call their office; Possum Three not getting blown off the highway as had been the case with Possum Four and the semi that had rammed us. Even getting me paged at Casa Bonita was unusual—Steve had called the Wheels office at just the correct time to find out that Possum Three was not needed so he might be able to connect with me at Casa during the hour-or-so I might be there.

No deaths were suffered in Des Moines as I recall, but if memory serves, there were 8,000 cars off the highway on a 15-mile stretch of I-80. The following morning long lines of cars parked on both sides of the highway could be seen, each line with a tow truck still working at its head, recovering more vehicles, one at a time, from the ditches.

"I see His hand of mercy, I hear His voice of cheer, and just the time I need Him, He's always near." ("I Serve a Risen Savior," Alfred Henry Ackley, 1935)

NUCLEAR THREAT?

How many coincidences must occur prior to one realizing that there may be a connection, or not?

One early morning in 1980, on my fifth Wandering Wheels Coast-to-Coast bicycle trip, we were all up early getting ready for the day at a church in Idaho in which we'd sheltered for the night. A radio was on when a news report aired. It seems that the US had gotten within 15 minutes of having a nuclear missile exchange with the old USSR caused by some computer glitch. Though 18 years after the Cuban Missile Crisis, the Cold War was still in full boom, er, bloom.

At this writing today, 28 May 2025, checking with ChatGPT to see if my memory could be backed up, we were told that this subject was off-limits to ChatGPT—go figure. However, DuckDuckGo had a report concerning such on 3 June 1980, which coincides with the 1980 Coast-to-Coast conducted that summer.

Anyway, my riding group of six (affectionately called a "six pack"), tending to be a bit slower on the pedals than other six packs of that year's 72 riders, needed to hit the road at first light else we would run out of daylight prior to reaching the evening's destination.

That news report fresh in our minds made the first few miles of the day seem a bit eerie to say the least. It was still cool and we, riding single file, were making pretty good time on the two-lane blacktop. Then, up on the left, right next to the highway, we spotted an unusual sight—in fact, the first such sight I'd come across along any highway anywhere ever before or since. It was a missile silo, either a Minute Man or Titan II.

My elder brother had been a missile silo maintenance officer in the US Air Force. As a result, I'd once visited a Titan II missile silo in Kansas, far off of any through-road, and got to go inside and see the missile standing ready below the massive, horizontal blast door covering the top of the in-ground silo.

From the outside, all that may be seen of a missile silo is about an acre of cleared land with a barbed-wire-topped chain-link fence surrounding it. In the center is a large concrete slab, the massive blast door mentioned above, with what looks like a big phone booth nearby—a shelter for the steps leading down to the command module located beside the silo itself.

On the heels of the radio report about our almost having a nuclear missile exchange with the Soviets, sighting an actual missile silo was cause for pause, let me tell you. Talk about eerie!

But within just a mile or two of seeing the silo, a third, large-than-life reminder of the nuclear powder keg we and the world lived with in those days appeared in the sky, at tree-top level, louder than thunder. It was a sight that, unlike the missile silo, I'd seen before, frequently, growing up on Okinawa with its two air force bases. But I'd never seen it this close up, certainly not after the events we'd just witnessed.

It was what is called in the Air Force a BUFF—big, ugly, flying fripper, or words to that effect. A B-52! It was low and loud and flew right across our group. So low was it that you could've read "No Step" on the wing even though we saw only the underside of the beast. If memory serves, though uncertain of this, the landing gear was down, indicating that it had taken off very nearby because it was gaining altitude.

That eerie feeling ramped up to full alert as I began looking for culverts or defiles in which we could throw ourselves should we see evidence that the US was indeed taking fire.

Looking today, at this writing, at a map I see that Mountain Home AFB, a Strategic Air Command (SAC) base, is near the route on which we would have been riding, though conflicting articles talk about it having been converted to Tactical Air Command (TAC) in 1966.

Each of these three minor events, taken by themselves, was hardly more than remarkable, but together they reminded me of a familiar if often forgotten truth: that God is in charge, that He is our protector, that His mercies are new every morning. PTL!

A follow-up note: We, at least three decades after this experience, were in South Dakota with a LtR group and stopped to see Badlands National Park. Something new to us, an old, decommissioned Minute Man missile silo, had been opened up by the US Park Service near the eastern park entrance off I-90.

Visiting that silo sure brought back memories for me. One feature caught my attention. Deep underground there were two large concrete vertical blast doors, one on each side of an air-lock entrance to the silo's command center. Both were shaped just like a pizza delivery box. The outer one was even lettered in a similar font and style as a popular national pizza chain. The lettering read, "Delivered anywhere in the world in 15 minutes or the next one is free." It struck me as so funny that I took a picture and texted it to my grandson. But I digress . . .

A COUPLE OF COAST-TO-COAST HIGHLIGHTS

My riding group on this Coast-to-Coast—nicknamed, as I recall, the Diner's Club—was moving rapidly eastward on a county road through rich-looking, flat-as-a-fritter farmland in Illinois, a very strong tailwind pushing us much faster than our generally lethargic pace.

The combination of flat terrain with a gale-force tailwind are the stuff of daydreams to bicycle riders on a 3,000-mile trek, having just conquered the mountains of Colorado and the headwinds of Kansas. But the dark clouds of a thunderstorm massed behind us, looming closer and closer, spoke more of the need for shelter than speed.

Up ahead on the left was an old white church, the only building for miles. It was quite dilapidated, abandoned as it turned out, but we stopped there, seeking shelter just as large raindrops began pelting all around. The church door was sagging ajar. We dashed breathlessly inside, leaving our bikes scattered in the small gravel lot.

We sat down in the one pew that had been left behind and askew, relieved to have found this providentially provided haven from the storm—what are the chances that our little group of riders should happen on this perfect shelter at the perfect moment along this vast stretch of open, rural roadway?

The din of rain on the old tin roof was deafening as the deluge grew to full force. It had gotten very dark, darker than dusk, in the middle of this day.

An old upright piano sat in the middle of the empty sanctuary. One of our riders, a 15-year-old girl, Terry Murphy, went over and sat on the rickety piano bench. Along with a 15-year-old boy, Peter S., she had been "copping a 'tude" the entire way from the West Coast, demonstrating why Wandering Wheels rarely allowed immature kids that age to participate. As a single guy, about 30, those two had me glad to be single, without children.

Then, as lightning flashed, casting a bright if eerie glow over the dark room, Terry's 15-year-old self began to tickle those eighty-eights like a concert pianist, pealing out the dramatic tones of Johann Sebastian Bach's "Toccata and Fugue in D Minor," deafening thunder chiming in perfectly, as if arranged by a master conductor.

My Diners Club and I were transfixed, mesmerized by this dramatic one-girl concert, accompanied as she was by the very hand of God backing her up with lightning, thunder, and the din of rain on tin! I get goose bumps just recalling it, feeling totally inadequate to fully describe it.

Man, what a full-house blessing, such a world-class—rather extra world-class—rendering of one of the most recognized pieces in the organ repertoire, done on a piano no less. And all of this by a skinny little girl not old enough to drive a car—I was shocked that this "tude copping" teen with whom I'd shared about 2,000 miles of highway over close to four weeks even knew the name of Johann Sebastian Bach, much less was able to honor him with such a fine performance of his masterpiece. All done in a little abandoned church, not ridden rapidly by without notice, but blessed with at just the right moment, providing much more than shelter from the storm, it became a concert hall enabling the performance of an indescribable musical blessing, a blessing greater than fiction, greater than one could even imagine, a duet of God and one of His children. God is good.

The incident reminded me of a similar event witnessed while in college at the University of Maryland in my days BC (Before Christ). I had attended a concert of the piano duo Ferrante & Teicher with my good friend and roommate Bruce Bendt. It took place in an old field house on campus that had a skylight running the length of the building, thousands in attendance.

All of the house lights were out as the duo played their two giant Baldwin grand pianos, placed back-to-back on stage, with red footlights casting their roof-top-high shadows on the backdrop. The two were playing a fifth encore, reaching the crescendo conclusion to "Exodus," when God chimed in—lightning lit the room through that glass skylight, thunder boomed, and rain created a din on the glass in perfect accompaniment with the pianos—more goose bumps. But I digress.

Terry Murphy was planning to attend Taylor University and promised she'd play Bach for me on the wonderful pipe organ in Taylor's Milo Rediger Chapel—sadly, that never happened. Terry graduated from Taylor, did some mission work for a couple of years, and ended up working on campus at Gordon College in Wenham, Massachusetts. We occasionally showered in the gym at Gordon when en route to Nova Scotia with folks on LtR's mobile retreats.

On a different Wandering Wheels Coast-to-Coast-with-the-Holy-Ghost bike trip, my group of six riders, eastbound on US 50 in West Virginia, had made the climb to Cheat Mountain pass, elevation 2,746 feet. We were sweating big-time. This stretch of road sported 28 curves with a 9 percent grade over three miles—no wonder they call West Virginia the Mountain State. We'd climbed much higher passes on this trip, like the 11,312-foot Monarch Pass in Colorado, but the grade was not nearly as steep. On a map, a 2,746-foot pass looked like a piece of baklava—it was not!

So we'd stopped at the pass, quaffing warm water from our water bottles, licking our wounds, so to speak, sore buns, chaffing, cramped muscles, and the like, yet grateful to have made it this far on our 3,000-mile journey, glad to know that by night we would have made it, God willing, to Winchester, Virginia, and the end of the mountains on our route to Rehoboth Beach, Delaware.

Then a lone rider heading west arrived at the pass and stopped to chat. He, a veteran, had just one leg. What a nice guy. After chatting for a bit, silently reflecting that our two-legged selves really had it made, we learned that he, by himself, with no back-up team as we had, had ridden from Washington State to Washington, DC, and was on his way back—a very humbling turn of events, let me tell you.

We did have a one-legged guy, Brooks Pfeiffer, who sold golf carts in Indy and got around on crutches better than most of us on two feet, ride with us. Brooks rode on several trips with Wheels, always riding with the Animal Pack. On one such trip, he pulled a hamstring and needed to ride with a slower group for a few miles. He chose to ride with my group, the slow group, but insisted on leading our little pack, breaking wind for our weaker selves. But I digress.

Seriously yucky warm drinking water is, however, less hazardous to bicyclists than unrestrained canines on the prowl. An excellent foil for such is the bike flag pioneered by Wheels. With a mount on the handlebars, the flag may be taken in hand and swatted swiftly down in front of charging canines who burn paws stopping and then feign lack of interest as they wander off elsewhere. It should be noted that flags mounted on the rear axle are harder to deploy in such situations and returning them to their holder after action courts disaster—bike flag poles in the spokes at road speed, never a good outcome.

I corrected this ridiculous warm-water nonsense and a few other needless bicycling discomforts by my last two Coast-to-Coasts. With a 32-ounce insulated water bottle mounted on the down tube, sporting a length of plastic tubing with a squeeze bulb and an insulated 32-ounce mug full of ice devised to hang on the handlebars, I never rode another mile with warm water. And only once did I have to purchase ice, as most all stops along our paths happily offered free ice to my endomorphic self.

The largest wooden church in North America: Église Sainte-Marie, Church Point, Nova Scotia

FOURTEEN

A Word or Two or Three Thousand Five Hundred Twenty Five of Testimony

Being raised an Army brat, it seems like there was always a church near where we lived. The US Army is very good at making chapels available for their officers, men, and their dependents, along with chaplains to fill the pulpits. It's that In God We Trust thing engraved on all US coins.

The Sukiran Army Chapel in Fort Buckner, where I lived on Okinawa from 1958 to 1968, was equipped for Protestant, Catholic and Jewish services. Mom dragged us boys there, sometimes kicking and screaming, every Sunday for the Protestant service. Steve and I even ushered, assisting a couple of Army colonels in collecting the offering and such. Had I been asked at the time if I were a Christian, I would have said yes. After all, I was an American, an Eagle Scout, and attended church, albeit reluctantly. God's plan for me, my salvation and life with and for Christ was just beginning to unfold.

The concept of choosing to be a Christian didn't become apparent to me until a pretty girl next door, a Christian, took a shine to my twin brother, Steve. She invited him to a youth revival service being held at Camp Chenin, a CIA base a few miles south of us. An evangelist, Bill McKee, no doubt a part of the Jesus Revolution talked about in a 2023 movie of that same name, journeyed 7,000 miles across America and the Pacific Ocean to share the gospel on Okinawa. Steve heard that message, believed it, and committed his life to Christ that very night. His life began to change, visibly, as he learned more about being a Christian.

It was Easter break 1969, and my good friend from Okinawa days Bruce Bendt and I drove from the University of Maryland down to Pensacola, Florida, for a five-day, 250-mile bicycle jaunt to Tallahassee with Wandering Wheels.

Well into this retreat with Taylor University students, I found myself riding with a group of 18 in a column of twos on a narrow two-lane highway near Tyndall Air Force Base, on a curve with a double yellow line, doing about 18 mph with a nice tail wind. I was second from the front in the curbside column when, being the complete rookie rider that I was, I overlapped my front wheel with the rear wheel of Julie Ringenberg in front of me, throwing me off balance.

I went right down, falling on top of the girl riding next to me on my left, causing the remaining 14 riders to literally pile up on top of us in a scrum covering most of the highway. A second or two later, once the screaming died down and the flying bodies had come to rest, I uncovered my head and looked back. A log truck had been right on our group's tail, anticipating the double yellow changing to a dotted line, permitting him to pass. That semi was so close to our pile of bikes and bikers that I could see only the grill of that conventional tractor—the windshield wasn't even visible from my perspective on the pavement. Had the life of my heathen (at the time) self been spared by the hand of God?

By His grace, there were no severe injuries, just some hamburgered knees and elbows, a few cuts and scrapes. My brother Steve, following right behind me, had run into my rump with the chain rings of the bike he was riding, adding a bit of blood and grease to my situation, though that bike suffered much more having had three welds in the frame torn apart. A few months later, near Cleveland for a wedding, having breakfast at the bride's home, I was telling this story when the young lad across the table spoke up: "That was my bike!" He'd loaned it to his sister, Karen Hall, the bride, who had let my brother Steve use it. Karen was marrying Larry Lemke, who would years later serve on the LtR board.

Two of the bikes had become unrideable in the collision. Mike Sonnenberg, the group leader, and I ended up walking a few miles carrying the disabled bikes while the group continued the ride. Walking with a mature Christian man for that hour or two, reflecting on the life-threatening experience we'd just encountered, continued in earnest God's softening up of my still-in-darkness heart.

Two years later, in 1971, Steve and I, sharing as we do the same birthday, each got the proverbial letter from Uncle Sam as the Vietnam War continued to rage. Steve got injured (could have been killed but for the grace of God) in a diving accident on a Possum trip and so he remained a civilian, continuing to serve the Lord at Wandering Wheels in Upland, IN.

Still living in Maryland following graduation from U of M, I reported to Fort Holabird in Baltimore. Joining a group of draftees there, we were then flown to Fort Knox, KY. It was December 1971. After being sworn in, having our hair cut and being issued uniforms, we were given a choice of either pulling guard duty for two weeks or taking two weeks' leave for Christmas. Choosing the latter, duh, I hitchhiked to Upland, IN, to spend the holidays with my brother Steve.

While at U of M, my foolish, adolescent self had, following six weeks of field training and completing three out of the four semesters of Air Force ROTC, washed out of that program because of poor grades in my other studies. Following graduation, I approached the Air Force about my taking that last semester of ROTC training to complete the program and be commissioned as a second lieutenant. The Air Force was open to the idea but would require me to carry a full-time undergraduate load of studies. Because of the cost of out-of-state tuition and the fact that I had already graduated, I foolishly (probably had had a severe brain cramp) turned down this opportunity.

Now, being drafted into the Army, it seemed all of that training ought to account for something. The young 2nd lieutenant at the Reception Station, who I had asked about this, was clueless and indifferent (to be expected from a "brown bar"). Talking with Steve about it while in Upland, he suggested writing to Colonel Schrader, an Army officer who had been on our Eagle Scout board of review back in high school.

Colonel Schrader had instructed the group of us young scouts at the time that if we ever needed anything to please give him a call. How we came up with an address I don't recall, but write to him I did.

Following my two weeks' Christmas leave, I flew back to the Army. Flying out of Fort Wayne, I sat next to a young soldier who had just finished Basic Training. Conversation with him helped remove some of the trepidation I felt about Basic. Changing planes in Indy, I bumped into the only flight attendant I knew, a pretty redhead and Taylor grad, Lana Caudle—nothing quite like a pretty girl to cheer up a gloomy young guy.

On the connecting flight to Louisville, KY, I sat next to a woman from the hometown (Hollywood, FL) of a girl I had fallen for while in Upland, a Taylor student, Julie Shambo. My spirits were continuing to get a boost as God's plan for me—my salvation and life with and for Christ—surreptitiously progressed.

After midnight, entering Fort Knox aboard a bus from Louisville full of gloomy fellow draftees, it occurred to me that God was sending me to the Army to find this Jesus that Steve had come to know five years previously. That thought suddenly made me very happy. In fact, looking back, I suspect Christ entered my heart that night. So, to begin my search for Jesus, I promised God that night on that bus that I would start attending church again, something I had quit doing when going off to college in Maryland.

The next day was Sunday and, true to my word, I attended church at a little Army chapel in the training area. Reverend Lackey, pastor of the largest Baptist church in Louisville, KY—no doubt a part of the previously mentioned Jesus Revolution too—was preaching there that morning. He asked if any of us soldiers wanted to know Jesus.

Raising my hand seemed natural—after all, God had sent me to the Army to find Him. The pastor asked me to see him after the service. We met. He talked me down "the Roman Road" (see note at the end of Chapter 33), convinced me that I, like everyone else, was a sinner, had fallen short of the Glory of God, and led me to the Throne, there to invite Christ into my heart. I had found Jesus! Phoning Steve back in Indiana with the great news, I learned that he had had all of Taylor University praying for me.

I still had questions, so queried Steve while on the phone. "What about six-day creation, bad things happening to good people, a so-called loving God condemning people to hell and such?" Steve quietly quoted Saint Augustine to me: "Understanding is the reward of faith, therefore seek not to understand that you may believe, but believe that you may understand." That old guy had it right: the longer I have believed the more I have understood.

God's plan for me, having accomplished my salvation, continued to unfold for my life with and for Christ. About three weeks later, a drill sergeant picked me up at the rifle range, and drove me in a Jeep to the Personnel Office at the Fort Knox Headquarters. The Officer in Charge (OIC), a light colonel, asked me, "What was my question?" "Sir, what are you talking about?" I asked. He said, "We have a letter here from a Major General Schrader . . ." I'd forgotten all about my letter to Colonel Schrader.

So I inquired of this light colonel OIC about my Air Force ROTC training maybe having some value to the US Army. He lamented that regulations did not accommodate such things. But he insisted that, despite my understanding that I was here to do what the US Army expected and needed of me, we discuss what I would like to do while in the Army. Where would I like to be stationed? It was embarrassing. Because I had graduated college, my being a truck driver was out of the question. We settled on personnel specialist. Because Julie Shambo had graduated Taylor and was teaching school in Suitland, MD, I requested duty in Washington, DC. The light colonel said I was not to worry about a thing, and that he'd be in touch. I was returned to the rifle range.

A day or two later, I was called out of formation with several other soldiers and loaded onto a truck. We were driven across post to a theater. We talked among ourselves, wondering what we were doing here. We realized that we were all college graduates that had been drafted. Soon, three men in three-piece suits with briefcases joined us. They asked if we'd like to dress as they were dressed and have the US Army pay for it. How would we like to eat in restaurants instead of mess halls and have the US Army pick up the tab? "Sign Me Up!"

It was the White House Communications Agency. They needed soldiers of several different Military Occupational Specialties (MOSs). It would mean being stationed in DC and traveling with then-President Nixon to set up and maintain communications for him wherever in the world he traveled.

"Never volunteer" was one of the first adages I'd learned as an Army brat, but volunteer I did. There was, however, one little glitch: they could only accept volunteers with a three-year hitch—and I, being a draftee, only had a two-year obligation. What to do? I wanted to talk to Steve, but we were not allowed to call anyone, and once we left this theater the opportunity would be lost forever. I prayed. Committing to a third year was more than I could handle, so I passed on this opportunity too, pretty dumb as the Vietnam War was still being fought.

Weeks later, while going through AIT (Advanced Individual Training) where I was being groomed as a 71B20 (that's the MOS for clerk typist), another drill sergeant picked me up in another Jeep and took me back to see that light colonel at HQ. He was beaming with the news that I was receiving a special assignment to HQ USEUCOM. Learning that it was in Germany, not Washington, my crest fell. "Gee, Private Manganello, we thought you'd be pleased." Apologizing for my seeming lack of gratitude while again stating my understanding that it was the Army's prerogative to use me where they needed me, I explained about my friend Julie living in Maryland. Evidently, the specter of possibly displeasing a major general had its limits. Or, more likely, it was God's plan for my life with and for Christ. HQ USEUCOM, the United States European Command Headquarters for American forces in Europe, was indeed a cushy assignment by any standard.

When I had told Julie that I was going to Advanced Individual Training, she asked me if I was an advanced individual . . . But I digress.

Seven months of training passed. Steve drove me to Fort Dix for air transport to Germany. But Steve had an inspiration and asked to see a chaplain. He asked if I, a new Christian, might be given leave to attend EXPLO 72 at the Cotton Bowl in Dallas, which was to be the largest gathering of Christians in history. Administrative leave was granted and we drove back to Indiana to board the Possum headed south. What a great event added to the beginnings of my life with and for Christ.

A week later Julie drove me back from Indiana to Fort Dix, spending one night in Princeton, NJ, at the home of my godfather, Merle Frampton, an ordained Presbyterian pastor, prior to flying on to Germany.

After a miserable weekend at the Replacement Station in Frankfurt, Germany, I found myself at the bahnhof (train station) in Stuttgart with a hundred-pound barracks bag and no one to meet me as had been promised; this seemed to be a wrinkle in God's plan, but was, rather, an important part of it.

Seeing a phone number scrawled on the wall by the name Robinson Barracks, which sounded like Army to me, I managed to connect with a support unit. A car was sent for me. Being a Friday night, the Officer of the Day (OD), unfamiliar with the unit on my travel orders, had me spend the weekend there at Robinson Barracks.

A young soldier who happened to be in the dayroom at that late hour offered to put me up in his room because his roommate was out of town, skiing for the weekend. The young guy was a Christian who had fallen away from his faith and God no doubt had arranged for my on-fire new-Christian self to fellowship with him. It was a great weekend.

On Monday morning, the OD figured out where they wanted me and so sent me on my way. The young soldier gave me a cellophane-wrapped packet of pamphlets written by Bill Bright of Campus Crusade for Christ, titled *10 Steps to Christian Maturity*. Years later I would learn that Bill Bright had been Bob Davenport's spiritual father.

My new duty station, Patch Barracks, was just across town. My first day had me assigned—despite the fact that I was of insufficient rank and had no security clearance—with a Sergeant Bauman on a detail to burn classified documents. Sergeant Bauman, due to rotate back to the States the following day, was indeed a Christian who right away wanted to know if I knew Jesus. We had great fellowship, too, and ended our day with him introducing me to a Colonel Maggard who, with his wife, led a weekly Bible study in their quarters.

Arriving at Colonel Maggard's quarters the following evening, the colonel informed me that his group of married officers and their wives, which I as a single young soldier was still welcome to join, was starting a new Bible study series so he would order the materials for me. The name of the series: Bill Bright's *10 Steps to Christian Maturity*. God's plan for me and my life with and for Christ was continuing to unfold before me.

My time with the US Army in Germany was rich with Christian fellowship, making it a time of rapid growth in my new faith and in knowledge of God's Word. A life verse came to me, 1 Peter 3:15: "Quietly trust yourself to the Lord, but if anyone asks why you believe as you do, be prepared to tell them with gentleness and respect." That's my recollection of it from the Living Bible that my mom had sent me off to college with back in 1968.

Though God used me in the lives of a couple of fellow soldiers, it troubled me that my life seemed to be happening at home in my absence while I made coffee and toted the mail for the American high command overseas. My brother Steve got married, our mother got promoted to Heaven, and my girlfriend in Maryland, Julie, still writing to me, was—I found out at Mom's funeral in Fort Worth, TX—engaged to be married to some other guy. Even the first car I'd ever bought, my beloved 1955 Chevy Belair Sport Coupe named Goliath, was rusting and deteriorating badly.

The US Army certainly cares for its men overseas when family emergencies happen back at home. Within a couple of hours of being notified of my mom's passing, I was packed and en route via government transportation to Rheine-Main, the big (at the time: 1945–2005), US Air Force Base near Frankfurt, Germany, where I awaited space available (Space A) on the next flight back to CONUS (Army jargon for Continental United States). Familiar with Space A travel from summers flying back and forth from Okinawa to and from college, this trip seemed almost routine, except for my emergency-leave status. The US Army was getting me home in time for Mom's funeral come h-e-double-toothpicks or high water. They even bumped a general also traveling Space A to get me on my way.

Upon returning to duty and the mundane, peacetime chores robbing me of family life back home, things seemed so futile that I went to see the Sergeant Major, the Army's go-to guy for soldiers with personal problems. He had me sit down with him in his office. Opening my mouth to begin logically pointing out my read of my situation, I burst into tears, sobbing uncontrollably—something I'd never, ever done before or since. He handed me a box of tissue and waited out the totally unexpected and emotional response. He'd seen it all before.

We talked and he proposed a plan, called an Early Out, a program to allow soldiers with nonessential duties to go home up to three months early if it lined them up with a college semester. It was then March of 1973, slightly short of halfway through my second and last year of active-duty obligation, which was up in December. The fact that I already held a college degree was not considered relevant.

Hence I applied to two colleges: my alma mater, University College at the U of M; and Taylor University in Upland, IN, where my brother Steve worked with Wandering Wheels. Acceptance came soon from both colleges. Going back to Maryland would enable me to pick back up with my job at United Parcel Service, which I had left upon being called up by the Army. UPS wanted me back too. My college roommate, Tom Provost, who had started work at UPS the same day as I had, still worked there.

In the continued unfolding of God's plan for my life with and for Christ, I selected Taylor, which would enable me to give back to the ministry of Wandering Wheels, which God had used in getting me prepped for salvation. It would also give me a place to stay. The GI Bill would cover my tuition but room and board was up to me. After three months, I could return to Maryland and the career potential at UPS. But that wasn't in His plan.

God knew what He wanted of me and lay ministry was it. Upland's been my home since being honorably discharged from the Army in September of 1973. Looking back, it sure seems like a lot of "Divine Appointments," unrelated decisions, good and bad, each one essential for me to have stayed on His course.

My favorite pastimes are eating, talking, and driving; being paid to do such has enabled the sharing of His Word, love, and grace with thousands of folks over millions of miles, to say nothing of my getting fat for free . . . God is good!

FIFTEEN

Observing Tradition Remembers Forgotten Truth

Most anyone in America with a motor coach will tell you that one of our most popular traditions is taking eighth-graders to Washington, DC, in the springtime. As such, Lake View Christian School in Marion, IN, a loyal Lightrider group, sojourned to DC every spring for several years. On many of those retreats, Stan Tyner, Lakeview's American History teacher, was front and center.

Typically, we'd board the Lakeview students Friday evening for the overnight drive to our nation's capital. Saturday would find us visiting the White House and US Capital Building, and spending time at the various buildings of the Smithsonian. After dark we'd tour the national monuments *shanks mare* and aboard the LtR, finishing the day at Cherry Hill Park in College Park, MD.

Sunday morning, following showers and breakfast at Cherry Hill, we'd drive to the US Naval Academy in Annapolis, MD, for worship at the US Naval Academy Chapel. Tradition is the name of the game in the US Navy. Admiral Nimitz once remarked that in US Navy tradition navy ships are referred to as ladies because they require so much paint and powder... Traditions,

The altar area of the US Naval Academy Chapel decorated for Christmas. Note that the flags have been posted. High above the altar, words from the Navy Hymn "Eternal Father Strong to Save" are engraved.

of course, are a tried-and-true way of helping future generations remember important people, places, self-evident truths, and events. The Academy Chapel, itself a beautiful cathedral, a treasure trove of such tradition, became a favorite feature of LtR's Washington, DC, experience.

One Sunday we arrived early on the front steps to the Chapel with, on this occasion, 30 high-schoolers, guys and gals, nicely turned out for church. A formation of midshipmen in uniform happened to be marching past, their Petty Officer counting cadence. "Give me an M," he bawled. The formation responded, "M!" "Give me another M," said he, the formation again, in unison, proclaiming "M!" "What's that spell?" A beaming formation responded with a happy hum, "Mmmm, Mmmm." The countenance of the gals in our group glowed bright red as if a switch had been thrown. But I digress.

Traditions, be they the magnificent pipe organ played by Monte Maxwell, an organist so skilled that when asked to play the piece that he had practiced in preparation for his job audition countered by asking, "What would you like to hear?" The stained-glass window here named for Admiral David Glasgow Farragut, the hero of the battle of Mobile Bay, honoring this deeply Christian man who was embarrassed that he was known for a curse, his statement, "Damn the torpedoes full speed ahead." After guest preaching, Max Lucado was honored with the presentation to him of a beautiful brass compass in a mahogany box, recognizing him for his lifelong efforts at guiding folks on their spiritual journey.

My favorite was the processional that always started the service. A large brass cross, held high on a pole, led the procession. A massive Bible, also held high, followed the cross. Then an honor guard of uniformed midshipmen marched solemnly forward with the American flag in a line abreast to the right of the Christian flag. Once on the platform, the honor guard would wheel left, keeping the American flag on its own right, as demanded by protocol. Then the American flag would be dipped to the Christian flag, representing the only power on earth to which the American flag is dipped: the God in whom we trust. The Christian flag would then be posted, followed by the American flag.

The first time we took American History teacher Stan Tyner and his Lakeview eighth-graders to the Academy Chapel he was stunned by this tradition, not realizing that there was any power on earth to which the American flag dipped.

Some while later, the flags were removed from the processional. When asked, the chaplain on duty suggested that we write to the Naval Academy Superintendent, which I did. That letter follows, though we never received an answer.

23 October 2007
  Superintendent US Naval Academy 121 Blake Road Annapolis, MD 21402

Dear Admiral Fowler,
  We at Lightrider Ministries have visited your Protestant worship service in the Academy Chapel on numerous occasions over the last 20 years. On each visit we have been accompanying groups of teenagers or adults from various churches or schools around the Midwest as part of our mobile retreat ministry. Worship at your chapel continues to be a highlight for my wife and me personally and for most of those who travel with us. Thank you for maintaining this welcoming, majestic, Christian fellowship.

  A couple of years ago we came to Annapolis with students from a school for troubled youth, White's Institute of

Wabash, IN. Then Academy Chaplain Luther Alexander presented the Gospel in such a way that one young man asked to be led to Christ—which Chaplain Alexander promptly did. On another visit I had taken our group of older adults down to the 3d row. After the service I asked one of them, a guy named Kyle Schoeff, if he enjoyed the service. He said it was ok except he couldn't see. "You were in the 3d row!" I said. Kyle replied, "I kept tearing up . . ."

Perhaps it's the traditions that are alive at the Academy Chapel that remind us of the doctrine that is the foundation of our belief that inspires us. Maybe it's the wonderful organ so superbly played by your amazing Monte Maxwell; the stained glass windows with their tales of Admiral Farragut and his Christian faith and humility; the words from the Navy Hymn inscribed above the alter, "Eternal Father Strong to Save;" or simply the warm and gracious welcome of your present chaplain, LCMDR Kimberly Sawatsky. Likely it's all of these.

However, on our visit two Sundays ago I was chagrined to see that the American and Christian Flags were simply present in the corners beside the altar instead of being marched into the service along with the Bible by an honor guard. I explained to a history teacher with the Lakeview Christian School Class of 2012 that we had brought there that in the past I'd seen the American flag dipped to the Christian flag. He did not know that the American flag dipped to any power on Earth.

As a Navy man, you certainly understand the importance of tradition in keeping ourselves and our Republic on course. The flags in procession are an important reminder of America's chain of command. We are One Nation under God. Indeed a former Commander in Chief of yours, President Reagan, said, "[We] are a nation under God, and if we forget that, we'll be just a nation gone under."

Acknowledgement of this truth at the US Naval Academy Chapel had been one of the few places I've seen such acknowledgement in many years. It is an acknowledgement desperately needed at this time in America's history, and one I strongly urge you to reinstate. Please, Admiral, bring back the flags to that magnificent processional that reminds all of us of our duty to God and Country.

Proclaiming the Truth with dignity and class at the Academy Chapel has been an important Navy tradition that I have gratefully witnessed over the past 35 years—a tradition that continues to bless and instruct your midshipmen as well as a few of us veterans and, I trust, gives pleasure to our Savior, Jesus Christ.

Stay the Fight and Keep the Faith,

Michael G Manganello, Co-Founder, Director Lightrider Ministries

This photo was taken years after entering service—note the custom features inspired by use: brush guard protecting upstairs windshields, which have been downsized to ease occasional replacement, and the faux grille guard, an actual ladder for getting the bugs off the upstairs windshield.

SIXTEEN

Lightrider's Miracle Bus

All three of the double-deckers operated by Lightrider during our 33 years of mobile retreats came to us through miraculous circumstances, but it was the second one that we actually called our Miracle Bus.

In the fall of 1999 Debbie and I had a houseguest, our friend Don Smith. Don was in Upland bringing his daughter Jenni to Taylor University for yet another year of study. As he said goodnight and headed for the guest room, he paused and said that one day he would like to give Lightrider a new bus.

In 1997 Don had purchased 1,200 shares of Yahoo stock for about $18,000. He decided to give that stock to Lightrider at the end of December 1999, then valued at about half a million dollars. Peter Rohn of Merrill Lynch in New York City made the transaction and held the paper. His office was the 44th floor of the building connected across West Side Drive with a two-storied, enclosed walkway to the North Tower of the World Trade Center. A year and a half later, on the six-month anniversary of 9/11, we would visit Peter and look down on the wreckage where the recovery operation was still ongoing. The walkway was still suspended across West Side Drive, but the North Tower was no more. But I digress.

We held that Yahoo stock for six days, during which time it went up in value by another $65,000 (that's how we were able to afford English wool upholstery). On the first Tuesday in 2000 my brother Steve and another LtR Board member, Dick Becker, got to talking about LtR's need to convert that stock into something more stable. I pointed out that it had gone up in value quite a bit in the six days we had held it. We had a LtR Board meeting coming up in three days, so why not let the board decide?

But even so, God led us to sell it that very day. About an hour later, the stock market took a steep plunge. So bad was the drop that the day became known as Black Tuesday. What had been our Yahoo stock dropped to less than half the value at which it had started that day. Had we not sold that stock at almost the exact moment on that exact day in history we would not have had the money to order the new Neoplan Skyliner for which the stock had been gifted to us. God multiplied that original investment, protected it, and put it into His service.

We did order that AN122 Neoplan Skyliner, which was to be built in Brownsville, Texas, at an old factory then recently purchased by Neoplan USA. China Clippers, B-25 bombers, and Silver Eagle Motor Coaches had been previously manufactured on that site. However, when 9/11 hit, in addition to the carnage and destruction in NYC, DC, and Pennsylvania, it took out, among many other industries, the American motor coach market, and so Neoplan USA had to close that factory in Brownsville.

In fact, on 9/11 I was aboard an American Airlines flight en route to Brownsville to check up on the progress of our new Skyliner. My flight landed at Dallas as scheduled but my connecting flight was grounded. Renting a car to drive the eight hours on to Brownsville the next morning, I found myself stranded in Texas for five more days. To this day. I wear a little American flag pin daily that had been a common sight in the days following 9/11, as a reminder that "In God We Trust" is the American way of life. We also fly the American flag, under lights, 24/7, at Lightrider and at home.

The hulking start of our Skyliner had to be towed to Neoplan's factory in Lamar, Colorado, where it was eventually completed, about 14 months late. We took delivery in October 2002.

Because of the delay in the completion of our once-again divinely paid-for new Neoplan, LtR was caught on the horns of a dilemma. We had scheduled a double double-decker bus run for a youth retreat to Colorado with the Church at the Crossing, a Church of God in Indy, planning to use our existing Lightrider and the yet-to-be-finished Miracle Bus. Fortunately, Neoplan heard of our dilemma and gifted us a well-used but quite serviceable 1990 Neoplan Skyliner, which we were able to outfit with bunk beds in time for the planned retreat.

Heading west with 60 kids on two double-deckers was really a historic event for LtR. The kids were great, and within the first few miles they had nicknamed each of the double-deckers. The 1990 was painted all white. The kids recognized this as a notable feature so named her "Vannah," after Vannah White, pretty co-hostess on the TV show *Wheel of Fortune*. Our soon-to-be-replaced LtR in its red, white, and blue livery was dubbed "Old Glory."

Once we arrived in Colorado at a Church of God youth conference in Denver, we found our two double-deckers parked right next to a third double-decker. The kids nicknamed the trio "The Three Amigos" after a popular movie of that time. But I digress.

Finally, upon taking delivery of our brand-spanking-new "Miracle Bus" in October of 2002, the intriguing yet time-consuming task of outfitting her for LtR's unusual duty, for a motor coach, began.

As in the past, God had been working before and behind the scenes to move this process along. On a weekend LtR retreat to the Smokies with Center Chapel UMC in September 2002 we'd had a particularly special time of fellowship. During our final devotional, one of the men, Dan Spencer, shared that boarding the LtR on the Friday evening that this retreat began was the last thing in the world he wanted to do. But he had promised his wife, Cheryl, that he would go on this somewhat strange-sounding (to him, anyway) adventure.

Now, on this Sunday evening en route home from the Smokies, gathered upstairs with his fellow parishioners, Dan said that in the future if he could just be told when the LtR was leaving, he'd be there. We would not even have to tell him where it was going or what it would cost, so special had been this retreat and he for sure wanted to be aboard next time.

Back at the church, as the group disembarked the LtR early Monday morning, another of the passengers, Kyle Schoeff, told me that if we ever needed help with any welding we should let him know. I'm embarrassed to say that I had not yet learned his name, so I handed him a scrap of paper and asked him to write down his phone number, which he did, and his name, too, as I had hoped he would.

So in October, when the designing and building of our new Lightrider's interior began, the person of God's choosing had already been introduced to me. Kyle was the man who designed our new idea for couches that could be raised, allowing one person to sleep on the couch with another under the couch, making for the efficient dual use of the same space for sitting during the day and sleeping overnight. He stiffened the frame such that no middle support was needed, which was essential if one could sleep under the unit.

Kyle even built in pneumatic struts to assist in the raising of said couches so that my sweet wife, whose duty it was to set up the bunks at night, could actually lift these heavy units.

Much of the weight of these bunks was the very heavy, dense foam used in the mattress. During the design phase, we had set up a prototype in the BusBarn shop. One of Debbie's small group girls, Annie Essenberg, happened through the shop. We asked her to please sit on this prototype bunk and tell us what she thought. Her response, "Is this supposed to be comfortable?" Admittedly, this was rather stiff foam, but it sure held up well. But I digress.

We had made a special request of Neoplan when manufacturing this unit. We did not want cargo bays so asked them to build the space usually occupied by cargo bays on the AN122 to be built as part of the downstairs passenger area. Cargo may be carried in a passenger compartment, but passengers could not be carried in a cargo compartment. Bay doors had become windows. For liability reasons, no staircase had been built.

Kyle, with his clever self, designed and welded together a wonderful stair: deep steps without risers. This allowed the driver in the driver's seat to observe the entire length of the downstairs via an inside rearview mirror, enabling him to well chaperone both the entire downstairs and with a camera covering the entire upstairs too. God knew what He was doing when he introduced us to Kyle Schoeff!

Another important custom feature requested of Neoplan was the creation of a trailer hitch receiver capable of supporting a 10,000-pound load, built right into the coach structure. Kyle Schoeff designed and built three important accessories that would utilize this receiver: a spare tire carrier, kind of a continental kit;

Note the swivel rocking chair in the foreground mounted with a '55 Chevy front coil spring to a bus rim and tire. One Saturday while working in the BusBarn I heard a very loud report so rushed outside. The swivel rocker was lying on the ground 10 feet out into the parking lot. We learned that day to put about five pounds of pressure in the tires supporting our bus tire benches rather than the customary 110.

Here the cook box is in use, with Steve Kuhn and his bride-to-be, Carrie, serving.

Kids help with bug removal prior to Kyle's innovative "roo bar" entering service.

a cargo ramp, 60" x 30", with running lights (some cargo, propane gas canisters, chainsaws, and the like cannot be carried in the passenger compartment); and a forklift to be used to lift and carry the cargo ramp when we had an electric cart aboard like the one used by Arlena Wood or an aluminum cook box with six gas burners built by Dave Russell, an HVAC guy from Zionsville. Dave and his wife, Lynn, staffed a few LtR retreats as well.

After several years down the road with our Miracle Bus, Kyle designed and built an aluminum bug masher (grille guard) like the steel ones you see particularly on Australian semis for protection from kangaroos on the highways in the Outback. Kyle's "roo bar," however, had a different purpose. Being aluminum, it could easily be lifted off two vertical steel bars bolted to the tow eyes under the front bumper, turned 90 degrees, and fitted into brackets deployed under the upstairs windshields, enabling its use as a ladder to provide access for removing mashed bugs from said windshield.

This ladder disguised as a "roo bar" proved to be a handy and practical replacement for the folding attic ladder, popular with fireman, carried on the first LtR. Fortunately, its lightweight self was never called upon to offer protection from a kangaroo in the road . . .

In April 2016, with just 643,000 miles under the bumper, we were shocked to discover that our Miracle Bus had to be sidelined due to serious corrosion underneath. It seems that a new ice-removal product being used on Midwestern highways had been creating serious structural damage to coaches, some that had been in service for just six years. This second Lightrider had served us for 14 years, traveling better than half a million miles over 1,713 days on the road, with 9,992 folks from 388 groups.

God turned our sadness at having to suddenly scrap our trusty, if rusty, steed to joy by bringing us such a timely replacement that we had only to postpone one Lightrider retreat.

God's people sent money. A small cloud of skilled volunteers created in just a few days a Lightrider from a 2009 45-foot Van Hool TD925. This former Mega Bus, being five feet longer than its predecessors at LtR, with its glass roof and dual stairwells, had enabled the creation of the best Lightrider yet. The electronic marquees over the downstairs windshield and beside the front door proclaiming our Republic's motto, "In God We Trust," have inspired more thumbs-ups from passersby than had our American flag motif alone in the 22 years it's served as Lightrider's livery.

Funding for this, our third Lightrider, seemed to involve a direct answer to prayer. Having been unable to raise the funds or to get a mortgage on this magnificent Van Hool, one Friday morning Rich Coolman called our staff to prayer on the front porch of our GrayBarn. Just as we were finishing up, we all heard the garbage truck enter our driveway on its regular scheduled Friday stop to service the LtR dumpster. A couple of us chuckled at the timing because we all knew that our garbage-truck driver, Arnold Floyd, looked just like Jesus. Then the phone in my office started to ring. It was the VIA Credit Union calling to say that they had reconsidered and would loan us the $300,000 needed to purchase the Miracle Bus's replacement. God is good.

Total mobile retreat stats at the time of putting this third LtR into service: 749 retreats; 20,992 passengers; 3,805 days on the road; and 1,493,000 miles traveled—all blessed with God's provision and protection. Thank you, Lord! LtR had then been in service for 28 years, 10 and half of which had actually been on the road—great honking beak, not a bad service record.

> "In God We Trust" became the United States national motto on 30 July 1956 by a joint resolution of the 84th Congress, having passed both the House and Senate unanimously, without debate, replacing *E Pluribus Unum*," which had been our de facto official motto. President Dwight D Eisenhower signed the bill into law.

The author with co-pilot Sweet Thing who, along with Steve Kuhn, were used by God in this story.

SEVENTEEN

A Girl's Life Saved by the Hand of God

My favorite example of seeing His hand in Lightrider's affairs happened a couple of decades ago in Florida with the youth group of our church traveling aboard the Lightrider. It was during a 15-year period when Lightrider had had the privilege of transporting our youth group on Easter break, usually to Indian Pass Campground in Port Saint Joe, Florida. Allen Mercer was our youth pastor; we were then the Upland Evangelical Mennonite Church (UEMC), some years later to be renamed the Upland Community Church (UCC).

We had met up with the Gaylord Evangelical Free Church's youth group from Gaylord, Michigan, led by UEMC's former youth pastor Newell Cerak, staying at the Port Saint Joe National Park, several miles from our spring-break digs at Indian Pass Campground. A large campfire was going, and we were having a grand time playing Chubby Bunnies and such with the 60-or-so kids in the combined group when the ice ran out. Remembering that there was a small store outside the entrance to the national park, I took the Lightrider out to get some.

LtR's double-decker always attracts attention, and this evening's stop at this small convenience store was no different. A gaggle of older guys were gathered inside shooting the bull. When asked about the double-decker, I was always happy to fill folks in, taking care to mention our mission of sharing Christ. We had an amiable chat prior to my purchasing a large bag of ice and heading for the door. One of the guys called after me, asking if I knew how to find a doctor in Port Saint Joe if we needed one. He went on to say that he knew of a good doctor there. He then tore off a scrap of paper and wrote down the doctor's name and address, but did not know the phone number.

Thanking him, always alert to not pass up a blessing, I put the paper on the dashboard and returned to the gathering. Once there I sought out Coleen, Newell's wife, an old friend from my days at Wandering Wheels, and showed her the scrap of paper so that she could copy down the doctor's information. Who knew, perhaps this info was intended for her and her group.

The next morning, back at Indian Pass Campground, while most of us were sleeping, my wife, Debbie, along with one of Lightrider's staff, Steve Kuhn, found one of the kids, Gabriel, a German exchange student, having difficulty breathing. She seemed to be in quite some distress. Seeing the scrap of paper on the dash with the doctor's name, Debbie and Steve decided to take Gabriel to the doctor. If they'd awakened me, we would have gone to the Port Saint Joe Hospital emergency room, a place well known to us from previous trips. The three got into the church van, which had accompanied us on this Easter break, taking off with only the scrap of paper to guide them.

Finding the doctor's office with a packed waiting room, they were told that there was no way that the doctor could see anyone not already scheduled. But then the nurse saw how blue Gabriel was, and realized immediately that her condition was indeed life threatening. She said the doctor would see her right then! The doctor took one look and asked Gabriel if she was on any medication. Speaking little English, she pulled a bottle of pills out of her pocket. It was labeled entirely in German. He said that without knowing what the pills were he could not prescribe treatment. The nurse spoke up, saying that the contractor that had recently remodeled their office was German. They called him and he easily translated the label, enabling the doctor to prescribe the treatment that indeed saved Gabriel's life.

The doctor told Debbie and Steve that if they had taken her to the emergency room rather than his office, they would not have known what the pills were either so would have had to put Gabriel in an ambulance to Panama City. So constricted were her bronchial tubes that she would not have survived the ride. No one knew that she was chronically allergic to campfire smoke.

Had the old dude from the night before, who had just happened to be at that store at the very time our attention-grabbing double-decker happened by, known the doctor's phone number, Debbie undoubtedly would have called before searching out a street address in a strange town. Being on the phone rather than in person, the nurse would not have seen Gabriel, would not have realized how deadly the situation was, would have told Debbie that the doctor was covered up, and that they should rather head straight to the emergency room. In fact, if either Debbie or Steve had awakened me, my move would have been for the ER too. In the years of Easter breaks taken at Port Saint Joe, we had never been out to the national park, had never even seen that little convenience store. Running out for ice would not have happened either had not I noticed and remembered that store being so nearby.

That alert nurse's memory that it was a German contractor who had worked on that doctor's office, that his phone number was found, that he was available to take the call, not out contracting somewhere else in this pre–cell phone age, adds to the intrigue.

When one considers the number of circumstances that coincided to get Gabriel the help she so desperately needed just at the time it was needed multiplies the probability that coincidence alone could not account for the happy outcome. Was not our encounter with that old dude at that little store a divine appointment? Sure seems that way to me. Seems like that plan of His for my life with and for Him was indeed continuing to be played out.

Those 15 years that LtR served on Easter breaks with our church were some of the richest in our ministry. They were years that Debbie volunteered with our youth group year-round.

Once, chatting about Christ late into the night, Debbie and I, while sitting around a waning campfire with a young English-speaking exchange student, Laura, from Hamburg, Germany, experienced God opening the eyes of and shining His Light into a young soul—Laura was saved!

Her host family in America was none less than Clyde and Sharon Eubank. Clyde would later serve as UEMC's youth pastor. It was great knowing that this young life in Christ would have a solid Christian family to nurture her new faith, at least for a season.

For four years during this period, we maintained a tradition of playing volleyball with some of the girls who played for Eastbrook High School, the school most of UEMC's youth group attended.

These girls were real athletes, and were serious about keeping up their skills while away from their school volleyball court on Easter break. Of course, these practice games were played on an improvised sand court on the beach.

Who had we found to offer these six really skilled girls a modicum of consistent competition? We managed to assemble a team of three guys whose aging, endomorphic selves, minus any volleyball training, with half the number of players, yet possessed of masculine advantage, might possibly overcome such deficiencies to at least offer a weak foil.

Mark Cosgrove, Bob Walker, and I made up this valiant trio, this missionary team willing to risk injury to our middle-aged, time-ravaged selves in support of these athletic young women seeking to maintain (nay, polish) their already impressive skills. Not wanting to appear in the least bit threatening, we humbly dubbed our threesome the Flounders.

What was innocently intended as a tool to give these ladies a workout, a team-developing drill, became a fierce competition—a competition that became fiercer, year to year, Easter break to Easter break.

We Flounders developed our skills as well, becoming a formidable foil rather than just a wimpy triad experiencing midlife crises. In fact, if memory serves, the Flounders were undefeated!

If truth be told, there was another factor in play outside of the obvious masculine advantage, an advantage being talked about at this writing because of biological males competing in women's sports. These skilled women, these serious players, had been trained and nurtured in the volleyball equivalent of Marquess of Queensberry Rules. We three Kings of Volleyball had learned under a less ridged set of rules, kind of a tacit understanding of play, sometimes referred to as Jungle Ball. This, coupled with no referees and the net set at women's height, kept us guys in the game.

I having long since succumbed to the fat-for-free syndrome rampant among bus drivers stationed at the net, kinda like a mobile—barely mobile in sand—court obstacle. Mark and Bob, spread out to my rear, fielded any balls that managed to get by me, which were legion. Of course a tall, large endomorph, lethargic though he may be, towering over the net might have been a bit of an intimidation factor . . .

In the face of such universal defeat, the ladies displayed excellent sportsmanship, though such occasionally was concealed just a bit by sad countenance and a less-than-cheery demeanor. Mark, Bob, and I always wondered whether the

Left to right: Mark, Mike, and Bob.

ladies were unhappier with the game's outcome, or with the fact that they had lost to a team of Flounders. All speculation aside, the initial goal of providing these skilled volleyball players with serious drill kept them competitive while in Florida, away from their required daily practice. God is good.

One of these ladies, Beth, was the daughter of a friend and client, Bob Gortner, a Taylor business professor who used Lightrider to take his senior business majors for three or four days visiting businesses in Chicago, like Service Master, Cook County Hospital, Western Cullen Hayes, and the like.

Getting a double-decker downtown in Chicago can be a bit of a chore. When a loop of elevated train track, the "L," was constructed in the downtown area, which took on the nickname the Loop, completed in 1897, it was built with a clearance above local roadways just less than 13 feet six inches. According to Gortner, this was done to keep highway trucks out of downtown, which meant such trucks would have to be unloaded and reloaded into smaller trucks, providing more union jobs. In recent years, three highways passing under the "L" have been lowered to allow taller vehicles entrance to the Loop area.

On one of these Taylor business junkets we were northbound on Michigan Avenue at lunchtime when I took a left on a side street and stopped immediately. Up ahead I saw the "L" and knew that this side street would not have sufficient clearance for our double-decker. Noon traffic was swirling and honking around us. A cop on foot looked up at our double-decker and approached my window, which I opened. He looked sternly at me saying, "Looks like you've got a problem!" He continued: "If you could get up enough speed perhaps you could just scrape under." He was joking, of course.

He offered to step out onto Michigan Avenue and stop the traffic so that we could back out. Talk about an angel in uniform—that cop was a Godsend.

Later, still heading north on Michigan, I had occasioned to drop our group off at a point a bit south of Water Tower Place, a very nice indoor mall, for a little free time. Continuing a block or two, I turned left on West Chicago Avenue to look for a place to park our beast. Sure enough, within a couple of blocks or so, right beside Moody Bible Institute, I spied a space on the right-side curb that looked like it might be long enough to accommodate our 40-foot coach—curbside parking three blocks from Michigan Avenue, PTL.

I lined us up and reversed into the space, managing to parallel park in that space, right

on the curb, without the need to maneuver or even pull forward—like butter. A car was parked about three feet behind us and one about the same in front of us. I performed this miraculous feat but there was no one there to see—a bit of a bummer, let me tell you. Perhaps God feels this way when one of His actual miracles goes unnoticed . . .

Always, on the last night of these Chicago junkets with the Taylor business majors, Bob Gortner would have us stop at the Pacific Garden Rescue Mission, located then on State Street.

We'd get a tour of the mission. One time, in the kitchen, one of the students poked fun at the very large chef. He patted his ample tummy and said something rather profound, "Everyone ought to have one of these." Being around hungry folks all the time no doubt gave this chef a different perspective.

We'd view their film *Miracle on State Street* about a young sailor who stops by the mission and is reunited with his estranged father whose down-and-out self is working there—it's a true story and a tearjerker. Then we'd join in worship with the homeless crowd there for the evening service.

Many of the students would tell us while en route home to Taylor that the stop at the Pacific Garden Mission was the highlight of their trip. In fact, at least two of the majors later left their chosen line of work to take up mission work.

Sorry to have digressed big-time, but I don't want to skip a little memory of a blessing to me that may be a blessing to y'all reading this book.

A typical fuel/rest stop, this one with a youth group, co-founder Bob (in the foreground) with one of the kids; the young lady on the far right is Cami Piekarski, one of our very best "lovely assistants".
(Notice sign advertising Green Stamps.)

EIGHTEEN

Left Behind

"I Wish We'd All Been Ready" is a song about folks being left behind when the Good Lord raptures His church. This chapter is not about that, but rather is about something quite akin to herding cats, to wit escorting groups of kids, adults, or families when traveling together aboard one of the Possums or the Lightrider.

Whether at Wheels or Lightrider, our track record in this regard has really been excellent, being able to count on one hand the occasions when we had driven off, leaving a cat, or, er, ah, passenger behind, though at least one of them had not been ready.

One prime example, frequently mentioned afterwards, mentioned in detail during group orientations with new groups traveling aboard the LtR, happened when returning from Alaska aboard Possum Six. We had stopped early morning to fuel the coach somewhere in Washington State.

Occupied with the fueling and, in this case, washing the bus, filthy from the 1,390 miles of gravel road that is the Alaska Highway, I was relying on our age-old system of accounting for passengers when stopped at times in which most were "comfortably ensconced in their respective accommodations of repose." All aboard had been instructed to leave their pillow on the driver's seat should they need to leave the coach at any time.

One passenger, Darlene Donaghey, a frequent flyer with Wheels then, happened to be awake, sitting in the front passenger seat. Her friend Gretna Hightower, another 70-something frequent flyer, having gotten up to answer nature's call, had asked her friend Darlene to hold the bus should we attempt to depart prior to her getting back on the bus. Darlene forgot.

Once finished fueling, we departed the truck stop and hit the highway. Three hours later, getting the whole group up for their matinal ablutions and breakfast, Gretna was missed. Having a fuel receipt from the truck stop where a now-more-alert Darlene recalled Gretna's departing the coach, I found a phone and called.

A nice lady answered. I inquired if they had a little old lady in a red flannel nighty with no purse, no shoes, and no money, hanging about? "The one that's crying," she replied. I said, "Please ask her to hang on ... It will take us three hours to get back to her." "Don't come back," the nice lady said. "Tell me where you are and we'll get her on an 18-wheeler and send her to you."

So Gretna Hightower, her 70-something old self, in her red flannel nighty with no purse, no shoes, and no money, climbed up into an 18-wheeler heading south on I-5. I do regret being asleep when she finally reboarded Possum Six to be reunited with her forgetful friend. Gretna left that retreat with a not-so-fond memory, but we acquired an excellent tale to hopeful convince future riders to be ready if found in similar circumstance.

We had another frequent flyer who didn't want to bother leaving his pillow on the driver's seat. Tom Shane. We stopped at about 3 a.m. at the Flying J on the south side of Indy en route home from Branson with a load of adults. We didn't need fuel so I just stood out front of the LtR while a handful of folks ran inside to drain their tanks.

Tom stood with me chatting for a bit. I even asked if he'd left his pillow on the driver's seat as had been strongly suggested. He said no, that he wasn't going inside. But a little bit later, unbeknown to me, he changed his mind and decided to go to the loo. Good thing he had his shoes on.

Stepping into the LtR, seeing that no pillows were blocking my seat, I buckled up and headed for home. Just at that moment, Tom, coming out of the truck stop, saw the back end of the LtR and started running after it. A yellow light at the exit failed to stop me as we rumbled on through the intersection onto the frontage road, continuing on our way (I rarely stop for stale yellow lights as slamming on brakes may catch standing passengers off balance).

About 15 minutes later, as we approached the exit for I-69 northbound, a car pulled up beside us on the driver's side, horn sounding and passenger waving wildly. Tom had managed to snag an emergency lift from an employee getting off work, a guy happy to chase a bus in the very slack, early-morning traffic. No harm, no foul. Thank the Lord for helpful folks. Aren't we glad that God looks after old ladies and younger guys alike?

Perhaps that off-work guy was a redneck looking for a chance to blow the carbon off his valves, an excuse to show off what his ride was made of. Reminds me of my brother Steve on Okinawa, where the top speed limit was 30 mph, the evening my appendix ruptured and I had to be taken, posthaste, to hospital. He really pulled the performance outta Pop's '62 Cadillac that night, fortunate that the MPs that usually hung around that area in swarms were not in evidence. But I digress.

Each time we meet a group for a mobile retreat we have a brief time, after getting underway, of welcome and orientation, informing all about traveling routines and praying for God's protection and watch care. Each passenger is assigned a number, one of a numerical sequence, to be shouted out when asked, in numerical order and so used as a head count prior to departing from stops made during our time on the road.

The alternative procedure of leaving one's pillow on the driver's seat when exiting the coach at times when most passengers are asleep has been explained. Though my brother Steve, with his hygienic self, blanching at the thought of his pillow being placed on the recipient of constant grinding by multiple, frequently wide-bodied drivers, suggested an alternative location for said pillows—the steering wheel, though handled by countless, germ-encrusted phalanges, was preferable, just, to the former. The Gretna Hightower incident is always recounted with emphasis.

Henceforth, after every stop, once it seems everyone is back aboard, the driver will get on the PA, request all to be quiet and attentive for a moment, and then say loudly, "Count off!" Then that herding-cats thing usually rears its inconvenient head.

Counting off, essential though it is, has been the most frustrating aspect of our travel routine.

Getting a coach full of folks, regardless of age, to shut up, listen up, and shout out their assigned number, in sequence with the other passengers, has been an exercise in futility, a frustrating attempt to organize a class of independent entities. It is the one disadvantage of the double-decker, because having passengers in two separate compartments greatly exacerbates the already exasperating procedure.

There was once a situation where it became necessary to deliberately leave someone behind, though as it turned out, it was not LtR doing the leaving.

In 2003, we were out West with a group Debbie had put together—adult, veteran travelers of various LtR groups—aboard our second LtR, our Miracle Bus, en route to Seattle, WA, to catch a cruise to Alaska. This double-decker had all but a couple of its passenger seats upstairs.

Seats upstairs were laid out in two rows facing each other across an open area, encouraging fellowship. Seat backs were against the bus's side walls so that riders could take full advantage of the scenic vistas by looking out the windows on the opposite side of the bus. We had installed a hatch in the upstairs floor just aft of the driver's seat for emergency egress and enabling communication between the driver and folks riding upstairs.

We had just arrived in Yellowstone National Park, entering through the north gate at Tower Junction, having climbed to and descended from 10,947-foot Beartooth Pass coming down from Montana into Wyoming.

My wife, Debbie, our lovely assistant on this retreat, suddenly appeared in the hatch above and behind the driver's seat, ordering me quietly but urgently, desperation in her voice, "Find a hospital right now!"

Joan Stahl, a British lady and veteran Lightrider from Fort Wayne, IN, had collapsed on the floor upstairs, was unconscious, and had even evacuated her bowels. Debbie's sister Linda, a nurse, a passenger this retreat, recognizing the gravity of the situation, had instructed Debbie to get us to hospital posthaste.

As you may know, Yellowstone is out in the boonies, far from any city of significant size. But within moments of Debbie's desperate plea, before the front-seat passengers, searching for a hospital in the trucker's road atlas that we carried in these pre-GPS days, could even find Yellowstone, what should we see but one of those normally anonymous but now beautiful blue road signs with a wonderful big white H and a small white arrow pointing to our left!

Turning safely left—not on two wheels, as one might imagine—we proceeded down a narrow, winding, paved lane for maybe a couple hundred yards, coming upon a small building with a big sign proclaiming, "Frontier Medicine." It was a hospital, albeit a small one, but a hospital nonetheless. Knelt down in the small grassy area in front of the building was a massive bull Bison just chillaxing, chewing his cud—thankfully, he took little notice of our big bus, which seemed unlikely if fortuitous.

We managed to get Joan inside where a well-trained EMT—aware of but unconcerned with the bovine squatter sprawled on the front lawn—quickly stabilized and evaluated the now conscious Joan's condition. She claimed her not-yet-elderly self to be in good health and having never had a seizure or event such as that that had just happened aboard the LtR.

The Frontier Medical team kibitzed, deciding that the best practice would be to transport Joan by ambulance the hundred-or-so miles east to Cody, WY, a cute Western village founded in 1896 by Colonel William "Buffalo Bill" Cody, no doubt named for distant kin of the fortunately dormant dude hanging about outside our providentially provided hospital.

Hence, it was our passenger, Joan, who left LtR behind, not the other way around. We cheered her send-off, chagrined to be losing Joan to this unknown medical issue and the necessitated geographic separation.

None of us had a clue as to what had happened to Joan. Some speculated that the collapse may have been a result of something that pilots call flicker vertigo, which is caused by flickering light. We had been driving on this sunny, cloudless day along a highway intermittently shaded by trees, which does cause a flickering light situation.

We were grateful that Joan had not collapsed while we were navigating Beartooth Pass. Hustling to hospital on that road would not have been practical, or even possible, in a 40-foot double-decker, let me tell you. We all felt that God's hand had been in the location of the event, virtually next door to a hospital rather than miles and miles of mountain road untold distance from the help needed.

God knew what was going on. The medical folks in quaint Cody ran tests and such but could find neither explanation nor lingering issues. Joan was free to go. She thus caught a plane and flew to Seattle where we met her dockside as we boarded our cruise ship, the magnificent Royal Caribbean MV *Vision of the Seas*.

A week or two prior to this retreat's departure, we had experienced what may have been a divine appointment prior to our leaving Upland. The president of Gray Line Seattle, a massive motor coach operation, called LtR out of the blue, checking to see if we perchance were interested in selling our double-decker.

We had a nice chat on the phone, discovering that we were both committed Christians. He had wanted to buy a used double-decker from which he could have the roof removed, creating an innovative sightseeing deck, a popular move in locations where the best view is up.

I told him that, no, we had no desire to sell our double-decker, but that coincidentally, we were to be in Seattle just a week or so hence, catching a cruise to Alaska. He, rather spontaneously, offered to provide us a secure place to park the LtR, long term, during our cruise, no charge, a great saving and peace of mind too, because parked coaches can be targets for theft and vandalism.

So, on the day we boarded *Vision of the Seas*, he met us dockside in his personal car to lead me, driving the LtR, to the Gray Line maintenance facility not far from the cruise dock.

This new acquaintance, whose name escapes me, wondered if I could take a few minutes once parked to share my testimony with his friend and co-worker, the Gray Line maintenance supervisor.

Always happy to share my testimony, I had a delightful, if brief, time sitting upstairs in the LtR parked at the Gray Line lot, retelling the story of LtR's beginnings, along with my own beginnings with Jesus, to a really nice guy still in darkness. Later, his boss gave me a lift back to the dock.

"Quietly trust yourself to Christ your Lord and if anybody asks why you believe as you do, be ready to tell him, and do it in a gentle and respectful way." (1 Peter 3:15 TLB)

Earlier in this writing, it's been mentioned that this has been my life verse, my favorite from the Bible, remembered from a Living Bible given to me by my mom. In writing it down today, I verified it in Mom's Living Bible, given to my Uncle Glenn by my brother Rick on my Mom's promotion to Heaven, per inscription in Uncle Glenn's hand on the inside front cover.

Uncle Glenn's widow, Aunt Bea, gave it to me when I was in LA in 1987 purchasing LtR's first double-decker. But I digress.

These happy diners are from Indiana Wesleyan University on retreat to St. Louis.

NINETEEN

Recycling God's Love*

The gal in stripes on the right of the accompanying photograph is a blind girl who traveled with us on four retreats. On the final retreat, we had got to the pick-up a bit early so were fast idling the LtR to keep the AC going. Then along came Wendy with her white cane, the first to arrive. She remembered the sound of the LtR idling and came right to us.

Sometimes during a devotional early on mobile retreats, it was our custom to suggest passing the hat, collecting a bit of all that God had already given each of us, creating a fund to be used to help someone we chanced to meet along the way, someone discovered by any one of the passengers.

One such opportunity presented itself to Steve's Taylor roommate at Taylor, Dan Donigan, along with his youth group from Hope UMC of Flint, MI, en route home on an SBD (see Chapter 28) aboard Possum Two. They had stopped at a Burger King at the Richmond, KY, exit on I-75, just south of Lexington.

Following supper, the group was meeting aboard the parked Possum for an evening devotional being led by Steve. There came a knocking at the bus door. The manager of the Burger King had found a young lady passed out on the floor. He wondered if she was one of the group on the bus. Steve rushed back to the restaurant to find that it indeed was one of their girls, Fawn.

Loading Fawn aboard Possum Two, they raced to the nearby hospital. Steve went in with her while the group stayed aboard the bus, finishing their devotional time.

While Fawn was being treated, Steve found himself sitting next to a ragged, distraught-looking woman, scraggly hair and missing front teeth, with a squirming sick young lad in her arms wrapped in a tattered blanket. On Steve's other side was an older guy, a veteran, whose demeanor and overpowering odor were evidence of his fondness for, in this part of the world, moonshine.

After a while, one of the boys in the group on the bus came in with a Disney souvenir bag full of cash, the fund that had resulted from the hat being passed earlier in that retreat. He asked Steve, "Is there someone here who could use the money?" After explaining to the few folks in the waiting room about where the money had come from, Steve looked at the woman with

---

*We have here recycled the name of a ministry in Denver, CO, "Recycled Love," that has opened a coffee shop named Little Drip that offers, among other things, employment to homeless folks.

the squirming lad in her lap. Her expression, conveying without words the very urgent and desperate need that she indeed could use some cash, said it all.

Steve held out the Disney bag to her, which she very gratefully accepted. The drunken veteran immediately stood to attention and saluted Steve, saying, "Mister, that's the nicest thing I've ever seen anybody do!"

Was that incident orchestrated by God or happy happenstance? My money's on God.

Another such incident happened, this time with an Upland group en route to the Canadian Rockies aboard the LtR, when we stopped for fuel outside of Cody, WY. We had just concluded our evening devotional, which happened to be the one in which we passed the hat, creating that fund looking for a person with a need. Philip and Velma Kroeker, along with their married daughter, Beth, her husband, Terry, and their children, made up part of this group.

There was a youthful yet beleaguered single mom working the register at this small fuel stop. Her young daughter was with her. She was filling in as cashier for her son who was at his high-school football practice. Her right hand was wrapped in a gauze bandage because she had badly burned it while attempting to recharge the air-conditioning unit in her old car.

All of this was learned by members of our group who were just being friendly to her. I was outside fueling the LtR.

Different passenger members came out to tell me about this brave single mom and her situation, wondering if she indeed was the one to whom God may have been directing us. After some kibitzing, a small group of our passengers circled the woman with her daughter, held hands and prayed for her and her little family's need, then presented her with the little fund—about three hundred bucks, if memory serves. Tears flowed all around then—and now, too, as this account is remembered and recorded.

Seems like God again, anonymously, spreading around His grace all over the place, just like that little four-year-old spreading peanut butter. The fund was given, as always, in the name of Jesus.

Of course, God's love manifests itself in far more ways than just handing out some cash when the hat is passed. "Count your blessings, name them one by one, count your many blessings, see what God has done." Sharing those blessings, too, is another great way to recycle His love.

TWENTY

Lightrider's Ministry Report—
25 Years OTR

Lightrider staffer Dave Moore sharing a biblical insight with a young passenger.

We've included this brief chapter as part of a timeline intending to show the growth in LtR's vision. Check out the following dated 8 July 2013, some 25 years after we got on the road:

Lightrider Ministries in Brief—1987 to the Present and Beyond

Lightrider began as a mobile retreat ministry, a spin-off of the pioneer of mobile retreat ministries, the Wandering Wheels. Motor coaches equipped with bunk beds and staffed with Christian drivers provide mobility while destinations throughout North America became places to retreat. **We call it adventures in Christian fellowship.**

A dream of using a double-decker motor coach to conduct mobile retreats became a prayer, then a vision, and finally, in 1987, a reality. Acquiring a 14-year-old Neoplan Skyliner, converting it to a sleeper coach, Lightrider began using pavement to connect folks with Him, with each other and with His Creation. Quality time enjoyed while traveling together allows Christian fellowship to blossom into spiritual rest and growth for individuals while strengthening the body of Christ, the Church. Strong churches make a stronger republic. **We call it strengthening America, one church at a time.**

Some time ago we prayed the Prayer of Jabez, "Oh that you would bless me and enlarge my territory. . ." (1 Chronicles 4:10). As God enlarged our territory, Lightrider, Inc., started doing business as Lightrider Ministries. So began our **RedBarn**, a place for at-risk kids after school. Partnering with Youth for Christ, relying on student volunteers from Taylor University and Indiana Wesleyan University, we provide safe haven for hundreds of kids, kids being influenced for Christ: From the streets into the Faith and off to Church. **We call it connecting kids to Christ.**

God has given us a heart for senior Americans, the most underserved people group around. So began our **GrayBarn**, a place where seniors gather for Christian fellowship. **We call it a sanctuary for seniors.**

Searching out a vehicle suitable for mobile retreats with seniors revealed the need for Lightrider to design a new generation of motor coach to serve seniors. Our concept is a commercially viable, 45-foot, **universally accessible** (step-less) motor coach with a mechanized overhead luggage system. (See Chapter 31.) **We call it the Lightrider H1213.**

As we approached our 25th year, God used a synergy of 34 people, prayers, and events to reveal His vision for Lightrider's succession and sustained growth: Manufacture and sales of the H1213 will fund our daily operation, greatly reducing user fees; provide an H1213 for our senior outreach; make possible the planting of H1213s in churches; and generate income allowing the hiring of successors to conduct mobile retreats with teenagers and to keep Lightrider in the fight until His return or the time comes for us to hang up our travel'n shoes. **We call it our Succession Plan.**

TWENTY-ONE

The RedBarn—Connecting Kids to Christ

YFC has partnered with Lightrider to provide before- and after-school activities for our local Eastbrook students at the RedBarn Teen Center.

Lightrider's RedBarn is the most successful outreach of Lightrider Ministries yet the one outreach for which the LtR staff has little operational responsibility.

Back in 2004 there was a rock-throwing incident in Upland that brought to light an adolescent intrigue that had been occurring on the footbridge on Second Street crossing the railroad defile. Three 14-year-old boys would stand on that bridge demanding cash tribute from younger kids walking home from Eastbrook South. The mother of the boy hit by the rock—who had been air evacuated to Reilly Children's Hospital in Indy—called a meeting in the Upland Town Building. Debbie and I attended.

The mother, completely dissatisfied with efforts of the police or town council to punish the three 14-year-olds, acknowledged that she was thankful that her boy wasn't blinded. I raised my hand, suggesting, "Then we do just that." She said, "Do what?" "Thank God that your son wasn't blinded." So we prayed with the 80-or-so townsfolk attending that meeting.

We went on to reveal a plan that God had inspired Lightrider with: putting up a building right beside that bridge that could serve as a safe place for kids after school. We'd put a security camera pointing at the bridge to discourage further extortion and the like.

Our desire was to help all the kids involved, including the three 14-year-olds. As the meeting closed, a man, the then-Superintendent of Eastbrook Schools, Jerry Harshman, stood up and removed his glasses, which had the right lens blacked out, revealing a glass eye. He said that when he was a youngster his eye had been lost to a rock thrown by a kid. But Jerry wanted, even as a youthful victim, to save that rock-throwing youth, not to condemn him.

At this time, across the tracks, near the corner of Washington and Main Streets, stood an old print shop that a couple of high-schoolers, Joe Lee and his sister Ellie, through Troy Shockey, had managed to get use of for a Bible study for teens that morphed into a shelter for kids waiting out front for their school bus.

They would have hot chocolate and a few games available for those kids. In sharing shelter and such with them, they were sharing the love of Christ. The kids catching the school bus there began to ask if they could hang there after school too, many of them being "latch key kids," and bring their friends. A Ping-Pong table was set up. But, because the growing crowd of kids began to outgrow the small, aging print shop, the timing of the RedBarn going up played right into the plan God had for my life with and for Christ.

Lightrider hired Fairmont Builders to put up the RedBarn, but it was finished inside entirely with volunteer labor. Even one of the 14-year-old boys, alongside his father, helped out. Professionals Greg Ballinger and Bruce Howard handled the electrical, plumbing, and heating— AC came along much later. Allen Goff lent a hand designing and building the staircase. We installed overhead doors on three sides of the RedBarn to serve as ventilation and to allow kids walking by to see what fun was happening inside. Roll-down screens were installed on these three doors.

A great gazebo was built from scrap lumber by Troy and his father. It's been a wonderful scene for spontaneous fun and fellowship during RedBarn hours, and was even used once for a wedding of a couple of "keenagers" who met on a Lightrider retreat, Mick and Jane Roush.

The Lees were okay with the idea of moving their print-shop ministry over to LtR's brand-new and much larger building nearby. They were okay, too, with our naming it the RedBarn, which was a nod to Don Odle's red barn, still to be seen on the south side of Taylor Lake, where evangelistic meetings had been held back in the late sixties and early seventies. My brother Steve had been a part of those outreaches to "townies," and he suggested the new name, which fit like a glove.

Troy Shockey, freshly retired from UPS, had been a volunteer working with Joe and Ellie at the print shop. He, too, was okay with moving that little operation over to our side of the tracks. Troy even approached Eastbrook about having the school bus stop at the RedBarn, which it started doing morning and afternoon. After Covid, however, it quit stopping in the morning.

Youth for Christ (YFC) was approached about partnering with Lightrider to run the RedBarn, and the arrangement has worked out great. YFC is able to raise the money to pay Troy as the RedBarn director and cover the power bills too.

LtR continues to maintain the building. In 2010, just five years after occupying the RedBarn, we added a 2,000-square-foot addition, 80' x 20', which included a pottery studio, the brainchild of Jillian Nash and the hands-on work of Mike Koch.

Troy had requested that we enlarge the main hall of the RedBarn for the purpose of enabling the growing Thursday Bible study to continue meeting in a large circle, as was their custom, because this arrangement was most effective for opening up these kids.

This addition, including the building shell, was constructed by the Indianapolis ministry of Big John Hilfiker's Sticks & Stones, whose mission is to build buildings for ministry. Micah Langmaack, LtR's number one volunteer driver over the years, was one of many others, locals and outta-towners, who lent a hand as well. Debbie and my great niece, Lindsay, traveled from South Carolina to help. The late Joe Harding, a Sticks & Stones volunteer, lent at least one willing hand to this project as his other hand very often was occupied with a cookie . . . but I digress.

Troy's wife, Liz, a volunteer, continues to be an indispensable part of the RedBarn ministry team. Dozens of local moms have become and served as RedBarn moms over these past 20 years, putting out hot chow every school day for the hundreds of kids who have made the RedBarn part of their daily routine. For 15 years, Susie Heth organized, shopped for groceries, and headed up this ménage of moms. In 2022, Susie handed the reins of running RedBarn's gargantuan grub affair, an essential ingredient in attracting kids to the building en route to His Kingdom, over to Rose Shanebrook.

There's more than grub going out at the RedBarn. God's Word goes out at a once-a-week Bible Study and at two major outreach events annually. In November there is a three-night event, the RedBarn Rally; while February has a one-night event, the RedBarn Mid-Winter Bash. Both are intentionally evangelical presentations of the gospel, complete with altar calls and counseling.

Currently (and for many years) we have even had three RedBarn Dudes, er, ah, Dads: Leo Robinson, who lives 20 miles away in Muncie, along with local men Roger Phillips and Brandon Fox—guys who are always improving their serve. Just today, as I wrote on 15 August 2025, Sweet Thing was suggesting to these three great guys, two of whom are octogenarians, that they split two packs of Pop-Tarts to avoid waste from kids who only nibble at one tart and trash the rest. Liz thinks these guys are excellent examples to the kids who rarely see men serving in the kitchen. *The problem, Pilgrim, is simple. Kids today don't know the fear of hearing leather rapidly being removed through seven Wrangler belt loops . . .*

Many others in the community, like Debbie and Jim Riddle, donate money and home-baked cakes and such that makes the hot chow possible. Students from Taylor and Indiana Wesleyan universities volunteer, becoming Christian role models for the kids, another essential ingredient in the RedBarn ministry mix.

The last four years (2021–2024) Rick and Cindy Wright and the Upland Lion's Club, having had a fire in their clubhouse, ran their Back Pack program out of our GrayBarn. This was a means of getting food for the weekend available to the RedBarn kids as well as to other community kids in need.

What's started out as a partnership of LtR and YFC forming out of Joe Lee's print-shop ministry and a horrible act of hostility has become a truly entire community effort—a sterling model for small-town America of a safe, dynamic community youth center where the love of Christ is spread around with reckless abandon like that four-year-old spreading peanut butter.

Youth pastors from neighborhood churches, especially most recently Upland Community Church's Matt Owlett and wife, Julee, following on the heels of Tom Nash, have conducted revival meetings, concerts, and such, on evenings and weekends. Many area churches have the RedBarn in their missions' budget, giving regularly, and on their prayer list too. Just today, 15 August 2025, $1,542 came in from Oak Chapel in the next county. Dozens of kids have been saved, some even baptized, right at the RedBarn.

Bob Mortimer, a Christian evangelist and motivational speaker, himself a triple amputee, has challenged the RedBarn kids on a couple of occasions, most recently being brought down by Ron Korfmacher as part of a Taylor University outreach. Speaking from a wheelchair that he wears like a glove, Mortimer has led several kids to Christ and encouraged all, with the Lord's help, to persevere through life's hardships.

One spin-off of the RedBarn (at least, that we know of) is SwitchUp in Van Buren. Bill and Jane Hemmick, members of our Sunday school class at UCC, kept hearing about the RedBarn and decided to make it happen in their town. Bill's mom and dad, Bob and Helen Hemmick, had traveled with me many times aboard both the Possums and the Lightrider.

Most recently, SwitchUp has partnered with YFC's City Life, providing the youth of Van Buren a safe haven where the love of Christ is shared liberally by Sarah McLeester and her staff of volunteers, including Ted Kluck, a retired pilot friend from my church (UCC).

Community seems like it has been a big part of that plan of His for my life with and for Him.

TWENTY-TWO

We Interrupt Our Sojourn with Great News

A bit of revival at a sunrise service on the edge of the Grand Canyon.

This date, 21 April 2025, several weeks before this writing is likely to be completed, news of unparalleled greatness has come our way! The day before yesterday was Easter. Reports of record-breaking church attendance have been coming in, along with accounts of thousands and thousands of salvations and baptisms from across America—indeed across the entire world and across many denominations!

In her article titled "We Are Seeing the Fires of Revival: Churches Flooded on Easter in Widespread Sign of Awakening" on 22 April 2025, CBN's Talia Wise reports:

> . . . a move of God has erupted across the country. From powerful outreaches on college campuses to spontaneous baptisms at churches on Sunday mornings, there have been reports of hundreds of people running to the altars and giving everything to Jesus.
>
> Pastors across America and even in Europe are reporting that Resurrection

Sunday brought huge crowds and big salvation numbers that indicate more than just the usual Easter bump—they're calling it revival.

"We are seeing the fires of revival burning and are on the cusp of Spiritual Awakening. Young men in particular are experiencing a hunger for God . . . it is a Jesus movement in the making," said Pastor Jack Graham of Prestonwood Baptist Church, Plano, Texas.

Greg Laurie, one of the leaders of the Jesus Revolution of the early seventies, which led to my own salvation, founding pastor of Harvest Christian Fellowship, said: "What a joy-filled, Heaven-blessed Easter Sunday at Harvest. Thousands came to hear the greatest story ever told—and over 500 people made decisions to follow Christ at Riverside and Orange County!"

Said Pastor Kap Chatfield: "We've never seen attendances like what we saw this weekend, 52 baptisms on Good Friday. Thousands were in attendance all weekend. Dozens of decisions for Christ. Many of whom young men. It's amazing. We're on the cusp of revival."

These quotes are a fraction of those in Talia's article. You may wish to Google the article to see more.

Dr. Steve Turley, the Patriot Professor, in his podcast of Monday 21 April 2025, queried, "Are we seeing the GREATEST RELIGIOUS REVIVAL IN HISTORY?" He went on to say, "Reports from all over the world point to this being the single greatest religious renewal ever."

Thank you to my college roommate, Dave Coleridge, for sending me Turley's report.

Video footage of 700,000 at one Easter service in Israel (I believe that was reported by Turley), millions more at a similar service in Ethiopia, 10,000 at Auburn here in the US, thousands more at Texas A&M, 150,000 at Thessaloniki, all seen as "just the tip of the iceberg!"

One hundred players portray the Passion of Christ at Trafalgar Square in London while thousands watch (this has become a tradition in London). In France, the Catholic Church reported an astonishing 17,800 converts this Easter—10,400 adults and 7,400 kids aged 11 to 17.

Please consider Googling this report, too, as these mentioned few are a fraction of the video coverage.

At our Senior Men's Fellowship, we've been reporting over the past year the more than 100,000 kids meeting at 12 big revival services held on 12 secular university campuses in the US, with over 15,000 salvations and/or baptisms. These revivals were conducted largely with students at these universities having requested UniteUS to organize and conduct them. In each case, local churches and ministries have done the groundwork and are available to mentor kids who make commitments to Christ.

At Lightrider we've been praying that "should He tarry might He save America" through revival, that we be a Nineveh rather than a Sodom. After all, the God in whom we trust is Jehovah, the God of the Bible, of the Jew and of the Christian alike.

TWENTY-THREE

A Proverbial Poke, with Love—Calling on Disney to Repent

A group of Girl Scouts, not at Disney World but in Long Beach, CA, having spent the night aboard the *Queen Mary* as part of a California adventure with LtR, the night before going to Disneyland.

The most popular destination for mobile retreats at Wandering Wheels was beyond a doubt Walt Disney World. We were there so often that Wheels sprang for Annual Passports for most of us staffers to save money on admissions. I personally was there over 330 times, each time with an average of 30 kids. Don't ask me why I kept track of my number of visits, but that number does speak to the herds of kids that heard the Gospel on Wheels trips, the scores of churches strengthened through the fellowship of their youth.

On my visit number 305, co-worker Steve Kuhn reflected that I, succumbing to the fat-for-free syndrome, was weighing in at 305 pounds… but I digress.

Disney World in Florida and Disneyland in California were safe, family-friendly, patriotic, extremely popular destinations. Entertainment at the parks had a pretty good balance of being okay for the teens at which it was aimed and the cultural corruption erupting in the arts, entertainment, and secular media.

Our Smoky–Beach–Disney retreat—referred to in-house as an SBD—would be conducted in conjunction with weekends during the school year as it only required kids to miss a couple days of school. Kids could get two days pre-arranged absences for church activities with little or no hassle from their school.

Disneyland would have to be visited during the summer when kids were out of school. It was the centerpiece of our California retreat, an 11-day adventure already described in Chapter 5.

By the time Lightrider got on the road in 1988, with American cultural standards continuing to disintegrate, Disney World had long been losing the balance between church and culture, right and wrong, indeed good and evil. The following letter, written after much prayer, and as a duty, pretty well describes how much we enjoyed Disney parks and our chagrin in having to change our Florida and California itineraries to include the far less popular yet still family-friendly venues like Bush Gardens or Sea World:

18 March 1997
Michael Eisner, Chair and CEO, the Walt Disney Company, 500 S Buena Vista Burbank, CA 91521

Dear Michael,

It is a sad thing I do in writing this letter—my mood matches the cold, gray late winter day outside.

Having visited Disneyland dozens of times, and Walt Disney World over three hundred times, I feel like part of the family. On each visit I was accompanied by 30 or so teenagers. From about 1977 until last month I have maintained a Charter Annual Passport. Letting it expire was a difficult decision.

For the past 25 years I have conducted mobile retreats with teenagers, offering an experience in Christian fellowship aimed at strengthening individual faith and life in Christ. Disneyland and Disney World have each been popular stops on those retreats.

I used to know the cake decorator at Sara Lee's on Main Street USA in the Magic Kingdom at Disney World. He'd make birthday cakes that we would surprise groups with while waiting for Bev Bergeron and Kay Kellogg to delight us with the wit and charm of the Diamond Horseshoe Review.

Michael Iceberg, an entertainer at the Tomorrowland Terrace, became a friend and would break into "Back Home Again in Indiana" whenever he'd see us in the audience with a gang of kids. He liked to sneak a few of us underground to see the tunnels below the Magic Kingdom and to share a visit in his dressing room.

Because of the fast-paced schedule we'd keep on our usual four-day, five-night retreats to Florida, I would want to catch a nap in the Hall of Presidents. But most often I was too stirred by the patriotic message so eloquently proclaimed in that program to get any sleep.

Many an evening I would thrill to hear the grand music and see the sky filled with the fireworks of Fantasy in the Sky, which always concluded with "God Bless America." Kids would straggle back to the bus at 1 or 2 a.m., exhausted, but saturated with memories of a fun-packed day with their friends. As we headed the bus toward home, the stereo played songs that had been sung (not lip-synched) by the Kids of the Kingdom on stage in front of Cinderella's Castle—songs written in the days when the Disney Company was a respecter, yea a promoter, of things American and things of the family.

But times have changed, and the Disney Company has changed too. No longer does the Hall of President's proclaim Lincoln's insightful warning about Americans being the author of their own destruction. Disney World, with its active accommodation of sexual immorality and evolution apart from God, is now actively helping to fulfill that prophecy.

Michael, sexual immorality, gay or straight, destroys individuals and families, and with them communities and nations. As Lincoln use to say, in the Hall of Presidents, "If destruction be our lot, it won't come from abroad. All the armies of Europe, Asia and Africa combined, could not by force make a track on the Blue Ridge or take a drink from the Ohio. No, if destruction be our lot it must surely rise up among us."

This destruction began to rise up among us, in earnest, in the sixties when the pursuit of pleasure overtook duty to God, family, and country. This selfishness began to break up the American family. Without the protection and nurturing of the family, young Americans bought into the "free love" lifestyle, leading to unwanted pregnancy and disease. Abortion and condoms came into vogue. But the destruction continued.

Drugs became popular to continue the craving for pleasure and to escape the guilt brought on by poor choices of unrestrained self-centeredness. Robbery and murder became rampant because of the need for bucks to buy the drugs.

Now forty million Americans are dead from abortions, and millions more are dying from AIDS or languishing in prison.

Just when the character of individual Americans so needs to be brought back to the values of fidelity and commitment to God, family, and country, the Disney Company defaults on its world-famous pro-family reputation.

[In my opinion] making bucks and promoting politically correct, godless philosophy are the major themes in Disney parks, movies, and employment policies these days. $40 admission prices, and $7 Mickey Value Meals, eclipsing beautiful Cinderella and Snow White with sexy and alluring Esmeralda and Pocahontas, Gay and Lesbian Day at the Magic Kingdom—these are the themes of greed and open immorality that greet Disney patrons.

Michael, there is one bright spot in the maze of immorality at Disney World. I understand that you personally are responsible for it, and I must congratulate you. "The Making of Me," in the Wonders of Life pavilion at EPCOT, is inspired. Not only is it creative, warm, and humorous, it clearly acknowledges God and endorses marriage. Without malice and judgement, it beautifully portrays life in the womb. Sadly, today, this strongly pro-family show is the exception at Disney World, instead of being the hallmark it might have been a few years ago.

No longer can Lightrider endorse the anti-Christian sentiments of Disney World. Our Board of Directors has instructed me to inform churches that wish to travel with us about these sentiments, discouraging them from visiting Disney World.

Disney World is visited more than any other place in the US by foreign tourists. It is sad indeed to realize that all those visitors to our country see America cast in the greedy, anti-family, and anti-God specter that [in my opinion] is Disney World today. Michael, you are one of the top three CEOs in the world, why not be a top ambassador for American values too?

Heed the warning of Abraham Lincoln that once resounded in the Hall of Presidents. America is being destroyed from within—and Disney has become a willing helpmate in that destruction. Can't you see what you are doing? Michael, please, change the Disney Company from the promoter of values questioned by most Americans back to the friend of the American family that it once was.

His and Yours,
Michael Manganello, Executive Director

cc: Roy Disney, Vice Chairman, Walt Disney CO; Lawton Chiles, Governor of Florida; Frank Ryll, President, Florida State Chamber of Commerce; Gary Bauer, Family Research Council, Dick Becker, Chairman, Lightrider, Inc.; Mike Cline, Editor, *Chronicle Tribune*; Marvin Olasky, Editor, *World Magazine*

At the time this letter was written, I did feel like a member of the Disney family, had indeed earned that position by shear presence, hence this letter, this rebuke, taking the high road rather than the easy path of just not coming back to Disney.

A rebuke in Scripture (from the *American Dictionary of the English Language* by Noah Webster, 1828) reads: "[A]ffliction for the purpose of restraint and correction." As Ambassadors of Christ, we at LtR feel duty-bound to carry His message, not our own, presenting it with gentleness and respect along our way. As a patriotic American, a veteran, seeing the historic family values of our Republic—values for which I stood on the wall to defend—misrepresented required at the very least a response.

Yesterday, 29 April 2025, some 28 years since writing that letter, we caught wind of encouragement regarding the Disney Company. More information about the revival reported in Chapter 22 has come to our attention.

It seems Disney and ABC aired *American Idol* as a three-hour special Easter Sunday afternoon titled "Songs of Faith" celebrating Christian music.

"The Resurgence of Faith in America," an article in the *Patriot Post* on 24 April 2025 by Samantha Koch, states, "[The] original producer (of *American Idol*) Simon Lythgoe said, 'For ABC and Disney to take such a stand on this holy day and celebrate worship music is truly inspirational.'"

One of the songs presented was Carrie Underwood singing "How Great Thou art." So inspirational was this majestic performance that we played it for our Senior Men Tuesday after Easter.

I'm reminded of the world-class Christmas shows presented outdoors in the Town Square at the Magic Kingdom with major stars like

Gary Sinise, James Earl Jones, and Pat Sajak reciting the Christmas story from the Bible while a 1,500-member choir backed each of them up with sacred carols and such. Those were favorite events on our SBD calendar, let me tell you!

God willing, those folks at the Disney Company are seeing the Light; that this resurgence of the Christian faith in the USA will bring back family values to their company's entertainment standards. Today, 1 May 2025, the National Day of Prayer, I've been charged here in Upland to pray for the arts, entertainment, and media in America. A bit of thanksgiving will be included in that prayer for this glimmer of Light in at least one corner of this industry.

While we're on the subject of Disney, I gotta tell you about a onetime, spontaneous event that should have gotten us kicked out of the Magic Kingdom. We had a herd of junior-high kids who had actually stayed with us until the heat of the day set in with a vengeance.

We had managed to get our group, exclusively, aboard one of those large Davy Crockett Explorer Canoes that were sometimes available to ply the half-mile or so of water surrounding Tom Sawyer Island. These behemoth craft, 35 feet long, hold 20 U-paddlers, two per row, and two costumed guides, one at the bow and one at the stern, charged with navigating the thing, without track or predetermined path, dodging other vessels like the Mark Twain River Boat or the Sailing Ship Columbia, each of which rode tracks submerged in the Rivers of America.

Anyway, on this occasion, as we were getting close to the dock at the end of our cruise, I got the urge to try a seemingly harmless maneuver I'd picked up river rafting on the Colorado. All the kids were obediently paddling in time with each other. I moved my paddle forward, putting just the tip into the water, but did not pull back. The canoe's forward motion curled a small wave of water up from my stationary paddle and over the gunwale into the lap of the kid in front of me.

His response was instant, never even considering that the wake-up call in his lap might have been accidental. Within just a second or two, the canoe was engulfed in white water, each soaked but gleeful kid jumping into the melee with the reckless abandon of the adolescent children that they were.

I managed a whispered word to the guide that all in the canoe were part of one group, which seemed to calm his understandable alarm. Close to foundering from the deluge, we had become dead in the water. The two guides should have been commended for keeping their cool and their course amid the total breakdown of discipline among the U-paddlers. With the guides doing the only motivational paddling, we miraculously managed to nudge the dock where the guides made fast the bow and stern lines.

Soaked to the skin every one, we escaped the swamped canoe for dry ground amid a hot throng of laughing, if concerned, U-paddlers waiting in line, we having found giddy relief from the midday swelter. The guides, trussed up as it were in their now heavier though suddenly cooler faux-leather frontier costumes, struggled to pull our water-filled canoe out of the line-up— hopefully, the two didn't have to do the bailing, no doubt a monumental chore.

We fled the area, leaving a watery trail, lest a roving security patrol fail to see the humor in our unconstrained yet unintended adventure. Have always wondered if the hot throng of waiting U-paddlers followed our lead once aboard the dry replacement canoe?

Another time, a small group of us Wheels staffers, including Coach Davenport, were walking through Cinderella's Castle when we spied one of the larger-than-life costumed characters standing very still against one of the inside walls. It was Little John from Disney's *Robin Hood*. A few young children were standing near the still figure, poking and prodding with their little hands, trying for a response. None came. The youngsters lost interest and went their way.

We had lingered watching, expecting some reaction from Little John. So a couple of us, junior staffers at the time, me and Eric Shegley as I recall, walked over to see if this was indeed just a static display. I reached forward to poke Little John's stomach. The thing rose up its clown foot and slammed it down on the ground with a loud smack! We two staffers jumped about two feet into the air. The thing ran away but we could hear a young girl inside laughing herself silly. We'd been had.

Davenport, having stayed away while watching this scene play out, was laughing harder than I can remember ever seeing him laugh. It served us right. Many of the stunts we pulled with kids while at the Magic Kingdom would make fun at others' expense, albeit good-natured fun.

One such stunt was taking a few of our group into the gift shop at Cinderella's Castle. The "front man" would approach one of the young ladies staffing the shop and ask her questions about the armor. What period of history is it from? Where is it made?

After a few more questions, he'd ask if it had been rustproofed, as we were planning to display a pair of the armor suits outdoors on either side of our garage door at home. The clerk was always interested in this question, often writing it down on a yellow legal pad to ask her supervisor when she had a chance.

A little later we repeated this scene, with another person asking the questions. Rust protection always came up.

Later still, a third guy or gal would find the girl really intrigued that there was so much interest in the armor's rust protection.

A fourth and final person, always one of us "adults," would approach the young clerk saying, "Hi, I'm with Ziebart. Does anyone have a contract for rustproofing your armor?"

Another favorite stunt was promoting Small World to our gaggle of groupies during our time together swarming the park attractions. We'd mention its great music and neat displays along the waterway in which you rode in a boat winding around in the cool dark—an inviting thought during sweltering Florida days. Bear in mind that those Disney employees who forgot their name tags were sentenced to ride Small World 20 times . . . or so the legend went.

Anyway, we'd get our anxious crowd of kids into the Small World line. But when the line passed through the turnstile we'd slip away, unnoticed, to run around the corner into the Pinocchio Village Haus, a fast-food outlet with massive windows overlooking the Small World entrance dock. We'd grab a table right at one of the large windows, waiting for our group boarding the boat to take them on the Small World journey, to notice us up above them sitting in the window. We'd put on a robotic act, mimicking the Small World Auto-Animatronic dolls that they would be seeing, though our actions were not greeting others—instead, we'd adopt movements that would not be seen on the Small World ride, like picking our nose and taking a look at our finger or some such.

Kids would point and laugh at our antics but would soon realize that they were stuck having to sit through that boring ride with its annoying, repetitious, soon-to-be-haunting melody assaulting their consciousness. Of course we'd meet them at the ride's exit, having lost all credibility but having had a good laugh together.

But I digress.

TWENTY-FOUR

The GrayBarn—A Sanctuary for Seniors

Debbie's family stayed at the GrayBarn while on a family retreat in Indiana that also included Amish country.

With Lightrider's fledgling senior ministry threatening to outgrow my brother Steve's upstairs office in our BusBarn, more space was needed as Lightrider, Inc., morphed into Lightrider Ministries, one of Steve's great ideas. Funding became available largely through help from John and Joan Horne, friends from the early days at Wheels running Possum trips with First Baptist Church of Geneva, IL, back when Jay Kesler was pastoring there.

Our LowRider (see Chapter 31) would need a home too, once it got off the drawing board and onto the highway. These factors inspired and informed the design and building of the GrayBarn—A Sanctuary for Seniors. The GrayBarn has matured over 20 years, through the work and wealth of a great cloud of His servants, into what participants have called a "warm," "inviting," "homey" place in which Christian fellowship may flourish.

Mike Mezo, next-door neighbor of Allen and Jan Goff, great friends and a big part of LtR over the years, drew an artist's concept of the GrayBarn with a 60-foot, low-floor, articulated Van Hool AG300 in Lightrider livery parked in what would be the east driveway of the 80-foot garage that forms the entire south side of the GrayBarn. (See Chapter 32.) Allen and his daughter Dawn did all of the finish work inside the GrayBarn to include the nicely crafted fireplace surround, funded by Dennis Smith's Jones-Smith Funeral Home.

We set the GrayBarn garage up with overhead doors on each end to permit drive-through operation with a 60-foot articulated bus, which is tricky to back up. An unplanned yet very welcome benefit is the terrific breeze that flows through the garage when both doors are up.

Fairmount Buildings, who put up the pole barn shell for the GrayBarn, installed four beautiful picture windows, with mullions, in the south wall of the garage—by mistake! But I am so glad

Artist concept of the GrayBarn.

we left them in place as they let in much light and make the garage useful for other activities besides just vehicle maintenance and storage.

The GrayBarn, begun in 2006, has continued to serve as a quality tool for ministry with and for groups, a static form of the venerable, mobile Lightrider, each unique enablers of Christian fellowship.

A variety of activities is scheduled, providing opportunities for sharing burdens and joys, one with another, in a Christ-centered, patriotic atmosphere in the GrayBarn Parlor. The painting hung on the Parlor's south wall, titled *If My People*, from 2 Chronicles 7:14, by American artist Jack E Dawson, mixes nicely our American Republic's "In God We Trust" way of life with the GrayBarn Parlor's atmosphere. Hidden symbolism in the painting depicts biblical values, which become evident if one spends a bit of time looking closely—even the identity of the person shown mending our flag is revealed.

Most of the unique artifacts, pictures, and such that adorn the walls or occupy shelves have come to us, largely unsolicited, from friends and family, many of whom are connected in some way with Upland and/or Grant County. (See Chapter 32.)

Our Veterans Corner came about through the vision, energy, and hands-on work of the late Chuck Moore, Korean War veteran, and his wife, Shirley. The artistic flourishes like the banner stating "Freedom isn't Free," the welcome sign painted on driftwood in the foyer, along with a painting titled *Time*, depicting the LtR traveling alongside a steam locomotive and covered wagon with a jet flying above, all being observed by an American Indian with headdress astride his horse, are the work of Jean Schaus, a dear friend and Lightrider frequent flyer. Her slate-on-wood rendering of the Twin Towers hangs in the parlor.

The late Ward Turner created the railed platform for live performances; Ron Wolf, former LtR board member, friend, and my dentist until he retired, handcrafted the speaker's podium and the corner cabinet that displays a collection of die-cast-metal (1/18th scale) model cars.

Jay Kesler, friend, world-class Christian, and member of the LtR board, handcrafted and installed the glass-front cabinet hanging on the south wall along with the two high-corner shelves of that wall. He also made the display stand for the spinner from the number-three engine of the *Niagara Special*, a B-24 of which Bob Vickers, cousin of the late Malcolm Evans, said, "I had to leave that plane in France." Its final flight depicted in the oil painting by my cousin Evan Mazellan, titled *Miracle Over Moauville*, hangs above the fireplace.

Bob Vickers' son Mark presented the spinner to us at Bob's gravesite at the Santa Fe National Cemetery in Santa Fe, New Mexico. Bob had used it as an ice bucket since it had been presented to him at the 50th Anniversary of the 16 January 1945 crash by the mayor of Moauville, France. An eight-year-old boy had dug down 30 feet at the time of the crash to salvage the spinner; Bob said he wanted LtR to have it after he passed.

Vickers had already given us his restored flight jacket (note that the second bomb in the group of bombs drawn on the jacket to commemorate each mission has a parachute), along with an engine ignition switch and portion of a bomb rack from the *Niagara Special* at a reception we held in his honor. He was in uniform then and said, "I believe that, if called upon, this current generation would acquit themselves as well as did ours." We're talking mega compliment given the service and sacrifice made for America by Vickers and his "Greatest Generation."

The photo of Malcolm Evans with wife Nadine and President George Bush the Elder

Cousins Bob Vickers (in uniform) with Malcolm Evans sporting Bob's World War II flight jacket in front of the mantle, with Bob's B-24 (nicknamed *Dugan*) displayed.

was taken on the occasion of a B-24 Liberator in the livery of Bob's second World War II aircraft, the *Dugan*, modeled on our fireplace mantle, being presented to the American Air Museum in Ducksford, England. The signed photo of Bob at that presentation was in the mail to LtR when I happened to be in Taos, NM, knocking on the door of Bob's quarters there.

Interesting to me is that Bob had been assigned to the same duty station as I at the same time back in 1972–73, though we did not know each other then: HQ United States European Command (USEUCOM), Patch Barracks, near Stuttgart, Germany.

A chunk of "Old Ironsides," rescued from a dumpster beside her quay in Charlestown Navy Yard, displayed on a stand created by Phillip Kroeker, and a cookie jar fashioned by Jillian Nash to look like our double-decker, are gifts from longtime LtR staff driver and good friend Rich Coolman.

We always visited "Old Ironsides" (the nickname for the USS *Constitution*), the oldest commissioned warship in the world, on Lightrider retreats that included Boston, being given tours of this, one of the original seven frigates built for the US Navy, keel laid in 1794, by US Navy sailors wearing uniforms of the period.

After one such visit, having dropped the group at Quincy Market, I was napping aboard the LtR, which I'd parked near the Charles River shore. Cannon fire awakened me, though I thought it was a cop banging on the front door having taken exception to where I had parked. It was the USS *Constitution* being towed on one of two annual turnaround cruises done to keep the ship evenly weathered. What a privilege to see and hear. But I digress.

The small piece of the flight deck of the USS *Yorktown*, CV-10, was given to us by friend and LtR board member Allen Goff. He'd received it as a thank-you for his work at Fellowship of Christian Modelers from Edward Sarisisian and his dad, a plank owner of the USS *Yorktown* (a plank owner is a member of the crew that sailed aboard a ship on its original cruise). Edward's dad is one of the two men in the photo on the weather deck beside the predominately white flag.

The wonderful, world-class photography—of old and new warbirds, a polar bear chillaxing, tigers checking you out, a panda nibbling, and cheetahs snuggling—was donated by an old friend from my days at Wandering Wheels, Dan R. Boyd, veteran of the US Coast Guard. The majority of his photos were taken from the ground here in Indiana at air shows in Marion and Fort Wayne. The two helicopter shots were taken on station in Florida while on active duty. Photos of the B-17 Memphis Belle, the Red Tail P-51, along with the Blue Angels and Thunderbirds, were taken at Wright Patterson AFB in Dayton, OH, a couple of hours' drive southeast of Upland.

In 2017 we actually saw one of the B-25s pictured in the GrayBarn Parlor, *Georgie's Gal*, which had been flown in for the 75th Anniversary of the Doolittle Raid held at Wright Pat. Colonel Dick Cole, Doolittle's co-pilot and last survivor of the raid, was there; his picture is on my office wall.

We'd taken a group of 50 down on the LtR, including an Upland son, Louis Benedict, a US Navy veteran of World War II. Louis was accompanied by a couple of Taylor gals, Rachel Pfeiffer and Hope Bolinger, students of TU Professor Donna Downs; Rachel and Hope had written *The Quiet and the Storm: A World War II Memoir—The Story of Louie "Bounce" Benedict*.

Our replica of the National Monument to the Forefathers, displayed on a turntable designed into a custom-built, wall-mounted platform beautifully crafted by a new friend and UCC parishioner, Greg Miller, was purchased from Kirk Cameron's ministry American Campfire Revival. Engraved on it are the names of all the 102 passengers who braved the Atlantic aboard the 90-foot *Mayflower*, departed from Plymouth, England, headed for Jamestown in Virginia. Blown more than 500 miles off course, they eventually landed on what would be known as Plymouth Rock at the place that would become Plymouth, Massachusetts.

The monument, envisioned in 1820—the 200th Anniversary of the Pilgrims landing at Plymouth Rock, Abraham Lincoln being the tenth investor in the project—and erected in 1889 in Plymouth, MA, stands 81 feet tall, making it the largest granite memorial in North America. The Civil War delayed its creation and reduced the funding, causing the monument to be half the size that had been intended. It was built to memorialize the unique form of government, biblically based, that would become the model for the American Republic.

A picture titled *Reflections*, depicting a middle-aged guy in civilian clothes leaning on the wall at the Vietnam Veterans Memorial, his upraised hand touching the upraised hand of one of a group of soldiers reflected from the wall, was donated to LtR by a retired Eastbrook High School teacher, Bobby Kroll.

The matted and framed copy of Public Law 97-280 declaring, among other things, the Bible to be the Word of God, establishing 1983 to be the Year of the Bible, was purchased directly from the National Archives in Washington, DC. Signed by three prominent Americans—Strom Thurmond, Tip O'Neil and Ronald Reagan—it evidences great nonpartisan possibilities.

The print, titled *Influence*, drawn by Arch Unruh from a 1967 photo taken at a Fellowship of Christian Athletes camp at Black Mountain, NC, portraying a little boy in a football jersey emblazoned with the number 18, a seemingly massive football held under one arm, observing a group of older guys huddled together in a field, was given to us by Stan and Cindy Tyner, along with the wicker settee in the foyer.

Hanging under the clock on the north wall is the decoupaged *Chronicle Tribune* article by Wende Wright, created and given as a thank-you to LaRita Boren on the occasion of Lightrider's 10th anniversary in 1997: ". . . for her confident investment that put Lightrider on the road for our first ten years of Christian Service."

Following Leland's recent promotion to Heaven, happening very shortly after LaRita too had passed, I asked Angie Darlington, longtime friend of the Borens and an Avis Industrial leader, if she could find this plaque among their possessions left behind, so that LtR might display it at the GrayBarn, continuing our grateful recognition of the Borens' contribution to His work at LtR.

It's a great article, too, well describing the efforts of LtR at "Strengthening America, One Church at a Time," reporting on two LtR retreats, one with Lakeview Christian School to Florida (pictured boarding the LtR); the other with Suzie Curfman Skager's youth choir journeying as far north and east as Peggy's Cove, near Halifax, Nova Scotia.

Named Right Direction, these sweet, talented kids presented the gospel in music at Saint John's Anglian Church, built in and serving continually since 1884. The elderly, saintly congregation had prepared and carried in a very nice potluck lunch for these young ambassadors for Christ and for America as well.

Next to the decoupage is a print of the 27 November 1943 cover of the *Saturday Evening Post* from the Norman Rockwell Museum in East Arlington, Vermont, a popular stop on LtR adventures. Depicting a young girl praying over her meal, one can observe from the picture's details her probable nationality, mean estate, and who had provided said meal.

It's fun to ask GrayBarn visitors, particularly kids, how many facts they can discern from the pictured clues while challenging them to be as grateful as the young girl for His blessings in our very likely safer and more prosperous estate.

Elsewhere in the GrayBarn are other Norman Rockwell prints, some with small signatures by individuals portrayed in those prints, signed by those individuals, who, now quite elderly, volunteer at said museum in Vermont. In their youth, they had posed for Rockwell as he created his wonderful remembrances of sweet, simple Americana, often with a remembered word or two from their personal experience, giving depth to one's understanding about that great American.

Hung high on the Parlor's south wall is a watercolor painting of a 1956 Cadillac on 57th Street in New York City at sunset done by good friend and nationally known watercolor artist, Tom Thiery. It was given as partial payment for LtR's conducting a mobile retreat to NYC with a group of kids from Tom's ministry, Overlanders.

Tom had for years sold paintings to fund evangelistic retreats aboard Overlanders' bus to Mexico or NYC. Of late, he's realized that the cost of using LtR's double-decker was less than just the insurance on Overlanders' bus.

Two portable, oak storyboards displayed together just outside my office are the work of friend, UEMC parishioner, and neighbor Dave Kastleline. He also had crafted four slide-out bunk beds for the first LtR, with really nice light-oak frames.

Most recent to this writing, a loft storage area in the GrayBarn garage has been converted into the "Learning Loft" by the efforts of many, including Daryl and Cathy Devers, my grandson Orrin Fromer, brother-in-law Joe Norris, along with legions of Taylor students participating in three separate Taylor Plunges. Portable air-conditioning units were provided by our Dayton friend and TU grad Tom Tobias.

Wood salvaged years ago from a tree that had been struck by lightning, having been milled and aged, was donated and delivered by Ward Turner a year before his passing. Working with this wood in converting said loft, my then 15-year-old grandson Orrin noticed a black line running through the grain of a scrap of that wood, guessing the black line might have been made by the lightning on its way through that old tree.

LeRoy Ling, one of our senior guys and a former farmer, confirmed that observation as being so. I was impressed, let me say, with Orrin's observation skills, given his youth.

The Learning Loft, once completed, will be used as the new headquarters of Task Force Upland as well as a micro campus for Upland community educational and fellowship activities.

LtR's Senior Men's Fellowship, begun in the late '90s by Paul E Turner, grew for eight years under the leadership of Jay Kesler into what one of our board members, Ken Strickland, calls a gathering of the Village Elders. SMF is open to guys 50 and older.

SMF meets at 4p.m. Tuesdays in the GrayBarn Parlor for a devotional time currently being led by Paul Bowen, a retired pastor from Australia and roommate (when at Moody back in the early 1960s) of already mentioned Tom Thiery. The devotional is followed by videos, a talk and/or discussion of historical matters and or current events relevant to Christian men, as well as to America's biblical heritage.

The red Fostoria glassware displayed in the Amish-built hutch with the 9-foot pull-out table was donated, along with the massive wood table, wicker credenza, and wicker-framed mirror, by Roger and Jan Jenkinson, he a former professor (over 50 years) of Geography at Taylor, both dear friends of Debbie and me.

The World War II uniforms displayed on the Jay Kesler-built shelf in the Parlor's southwest corner belonged to Geoff Schwartz's mom and dad, he a US Army corpsman and she a US Army nurse, their black-and-white pictures hung nearby on the west wall. The flag on the left was given to Geoff when his mom passed just a few years ago.

The flag on that display's right, with a US Army soldier's cap placed jauntily on it, was given to our family when my dad, Arthur Manganello, a Pearl Harbor survivor (see About That Bus Driver), passed in 2000. The cap was his. He had traveled, a 30-day journey, to Worcester, MA, from Hawaii for his brother's funeral about 1939 and had forgotten his cap. His niece, Joyce, sent the cap to me a few years back. The insignia on it was donated by a friend and SMF member, Neil Haglund.

The beautifully carved clock on the Kesler-built shelf on the southeast corner was made by Dick Darlington's father at a time when he had Parkinson's so badly that he could not sign his name. Yet he was able to guide his scroll saw through the thousands of turns necessary to create those hundreds of intricate carvings.

The parachute displayed on the west wall was used by God in saving the life of a young, 26-year-old US Air Force lieutenant, Tom Smoak, who was in a B-47 Stratojet (model built by Chuck Moore) that exploded above Little Rock, AK, at 6:08a.m. on Thursday, 31 March 1960. Three air crew and two civilians on the ground died in this tragedy (see newspaper article in the shadow box).

Smoak stood on that platform to speak to a gaggle of RedBarn kids on Veterans Day some years ago and had us adjust the attitude of the model to reflect the actual attitude his aircraft was in when it had exploded. He was to be the keynote speaker aboard the LtR, departing the next day, on a Military Heritage mobile retreat that included Camp Atterbury, Columbus, IN; the Patton Armor Museum at Fort Knox, KY; the USS *Alabama* at Battleship Park in Mobile, AL; Pensacola Naval Air Station in Florida (we happened to get there on the day of the Blue Angels homecoming for a great air show); the Mighty Eighth Air Force Museum in Savannah, GA, of which Bob Vickers was a board member; the US Marine Corp Museum in Quantico, VA; the Aerospace Museum of the Smithsonian Institution in Washington, DC, along with its branch in Chantilly, VA, home to the *Enola Gay* (the B-29 that dropped the Atomic Bomb on Hiroshima); and the US Air Force Museum at Wright-Patterson AFB, Dayton, OH.

Smoak had been blown out of the plane (his ejection seat was found in the wreckage), and his parachute (displayed) was burned open, the ripcord still on his harness. Some 25 percent of his chute had been burned away, the rest of it full of shock holes as it had deployed at such a high speed (estimated to be 500 mph), the perimeter strap keeping it in the shape necessary to do its job. Smoak, badly burned and missing a boot, had been an experienced jumper so determined that he would do his parachute landing roll when he got to earth.

Meanwhile, at home that early Thursday morning, Mrs. Hollman, having heard the explosion, had rushed outside, saw the fireball and the parachute, and began praying at the top of her lungs that God would spare that man's life. Her husband warned that she would wake the neighbors, but she prayed all the louder. Smoak came directly to her house. When he passed her TV antenna, she realized how fast he was going (afterward estimated to be 100 mph) and knew he would be dead on her driveway in back of her home.

She, a nurse, ran around to the back of her house to be confronted by a miraculous sight: Smoak standing in her driveway. He had passed between two tall trees, on either side of her driveway, which had caught the chute, bending down with the strain, absorbing the speed and force of his landing. He had done his parachute roll and then, as the trees returned to their upright state, he was hauled upright, too, to a standing position. No broken bones.

Mrs. Hollman recalled that they had intended to cut the two trees down the previous year but had not managed to get round to it. God is good.

Four days later a very young little girl came to visit Smoak in the hospital. She was returning his wedding ring, which she had found in her daddy's wheelbarrow in her backyard.

We once took an LtR retreat that stopped at Little Rock AFB, where my cousin, Captain (at the time) Scott Lawson, USAF, took us to see the memorial to the crash at the air base and to see Mrs. Hollman's house.

My family journeyed to Little Rock on the 4th of July 1955 in our brand-new Chevrolet Bel Air. En route home to Fort Smith, AR, we had car trouble, stranding us beside the highway. We got to spend the night in a hospitable farmer's home. Aged seven at the time, my big memory is of the massive feather bed the three of us boys slept in. (A loose front wheel caused my dad to pull over. He chose not to work on the problem, not wanting to void the warranty. Turned out it was just loose lug nuts. But I digress.)

The P-38 Lightning in the Kesler cabinet and the F-105 Thunderchief, affectionately known to pilots as the "Thud," in the roll-around glass cabinet by the exit door, are remembrances of Colonel "Bo" Bottomly, a three-war veteran and author of the book *The Prodigal Father*, a wonderful story of God's hand in his life. His testimony, along with Smoak's, is available on a flash drive we have for GrayBarn visitors. Both are riveting! Both men have been met personally. My brother Steve got to meet and chat with Bottomly at his home in California. Recently, August 2025, Smoak's son Thomas, in town to bring his daughter Violet to Taylor, spoke to our Senior Men's Fellowship about his family's 30 years of missionary service in Brazil, as well as the day God used that parachute to save his dad's life.

The shadow box on the west wall behind the platform honors the well-decorated US Air Force three-war veteran Colonel Richard Chenot, father of Steve Manganello's college classmate, Ross Chenot.

The charcoal drawing of Christ above the antique organ cabinet was done by Mark Kinnaman, one of our senior guys; next to it is the white clay cross with the image of Christ donated by my cousin, the late Marine Vincequere of Shrewsbury, MA.

If you find yourself in Upland, coming to Ivanhoe's for their famous strawberry shortcake, or to Taylor to check out that wonderful Christian university, stop by the GrayBarn; we'd love to share what God has been doing at Lightrider Ministries and indeed, historically, for our beloved America.

TWENTY-FIVE

Task Force Upland—Preparing to Weather the Storm

What began in 2013 as a Response to Aggression plan for the RedBarn became, in 2015, Task Force Upland (TFUp), a volunteer service outreach aimed at complementing the crisis management and response capability of our community.

Colonel (Retired) Ken Strickland, then recently discharged from the US Army and now serving with his wife, Sherri, on the LtR board and teaching at Indiana Wesleyan University, had developed the concept and plan for Task Force Upland.

Monthly meetings built a cadre through recruitment and training to give Lightrider a capability in three areas: First, the School Team is prepared to complement the school's state-mandated crisis response plan, making individuals available to assist the principal as a crisis-response counseling team. Second, LtR has become one of four reunification locations for Eastbrook South (located a block south of us) should the school need to be evacuated. The Lightning Team consists of volunteers trained and willing to complement first responders executing the County Emergency Management Plan (CEMP). And third, the Crusader Team offers faith-based assistance,

facilitating best practices in security and safety for area churches, ministries, and businesses.

A member of the Lightning Team had an idea for emergency transport and/or shelter that he had while at training 19 February 2016 near Indy. During the table-top exercise at a Senior Official Workshop led by Ronnie Taylor of TEEX (Texas A&M Engineering Extension Service), it became apparent that self-contained emergency transportation and/or shelter may be essential during severe winter storms such as the storm that hit North Central Indiana in 2005—zero-degree weather; blizzard conditions with ice, snow, and high winds; 33 miles of power lines downed; and a near-epidemic medical condition greatly complicating the shelter situation. The perhaps divinely inspired idea, in writing, was sent to TEEX for consideration but no response has ever been received.

The idea, springing from our unique experience using vehicles made from school bus bodies and chassis, adds credence to the thought that God had indeed inspired it. Hence, not wanting to pass up a blessing, perhaps from God, we've dusted the idea off for inclusion in this writing—who knows who might take it and run with it, perhaps saving lives down the road:

> School buses, omnipresent in central Indiana, with a very small amount of preparation and investment, could well serve as *self-contained emergency transportation and shelter.*
>
> School buses handle better on snowy, icy roadways than do most other vehicles. The addition of automatic snow chains would greatly enhance the already exceptional slippery road capabilities of these high-slung, readily available, safe, and reliable vehicles. School buses exist in great numbers, are regulated and inspected more than most vehicles, and are spread out in multiple locations throughout this state. Being as such pre-positioned, they could become an available resource during widespread emergency events.
>
> Think self-propelled, 40-foot, heated room, stocked with pre-planned emergency supplies and equipment, including a portable toilet, capable of moving on its own to locations where power failure and near-impassable conditions have stranded people in homes without heat, putting them at hypothermic risk.
>
> Transporting these formerly stranded people to fixed shelters would be the first move. But if conditions caused further stranding, or if quarantining was essential, such vehicles could actually shelter, in admittedly Spartan conditions, 20 or 30 adults and children per vehicle. Just 10 emergency-equipped school buses could pick up and keep 300 people warm and safe for a day or two or longer if necessary.
>
> The budget that provides and maintains school buses is already funded. State oversight systems keep school buses safe and reliable, even shiny. Equipping a single, daily-used school bus with automatic chains, emergency supplies, and equipment could be accomplished for about $2,500 per vehicle. Once the useful life of such vehicles has been reached during routine use, the chains, supplies, and such could be, with very little effort or expense, transferred to that vehicle's replacement.
>
> Certainly more investment could enable more emergency features. A generator and extra fuel could be carried on an external rack fitted into a trailer hitch receiver making AC power available for medical devices and battery chargers. A simple snow blade could be installed to further enhance vehicle performance in heavy or drifting snow conditions.
>
> Using school buses as emergency vehicles and shelter maximizes an existing resource at a time when such resources may be essential to saving lives.

Just saying . . .

TWENTY-SIX

God & Country Forum—Dialoguing the Biblical Heritage of Our American Republic

Williamsburg is one of many excellent locations in Virginia to learn much about America's biblical heritage.

Lightrider's God & Country Forum (G&CF) is a once-a-week gathering where information about America's biblical heritage from a variety of sources is presented, followed by an open discussion with those present. All who love God and country are welcome to join these informal gatherings for instruction, discussion, and prayer from a historical and biblical perspective about America's past, present, and, should the Lord tarry, future.

The following was shared, by me, on Marion, Indiana, FM radio station WBAT's *Thinking Out Loud*, on 29 August 1996, at the request of Pat Johnson:

One evening at supper, my 17-year-old daughter, Danielle, remarked that one of her new classes at Eastbrook High School that fall was Government. On the spur of the moment, I asked her what form of government we have in the US. Without hesitation she responded, "We're a democracy."

That's what they taught me in school. And it's no doubt what they taught you, too, and it's what we hear on the news and read in magazines all of the time.

But the United States is and always has been a constitutional republic—not a democracy. Every school child in the country knows this token by heart: "I pledge allegiance to the flag of the United States of America and to the Republic for which it stands . . ."

A republic, where the law is established first, and people are elected who swear an oath to uphold that law. Our Constitution is that law, and its foundation is the Bible—"That book, sir, is the rock upon which our republic rests!" Those words from our seventh president, Andrew Jackson, clearly proclaim what kind of government we enjoy and the basis on which it was formed.

Our elected officials, our soldiers, sailors, airmen, and marines, all promise to "uphold and defend the Constitution of the United States of America, against all enemies, foreign and domestic." Sadly, in this day and age, many of our elected officials fail their oath. They conduct the affairs of this nation in a manner that pleases the majority, rather than upholds the principles and standards of our Constitution.

The following quote was attributed to Sir Alex Fraser [Tytler], a Scottish jurist and historian: "A democracy is always temporary in nature; it simply cannot exist as a permanent form of government. A democracy will continue to exist up until the time that voters discover that they can vote themselves generous gifts from the public treasury. From that moment on, the majority always votes for the candidates who promise the most benefits from the public treasury, with the result that every democracy will finally collapse due to loose fiscal policy, which is always followed by a dictatorship." [This paragraph and Tytler's name revised per Wikipedia online 12 June 2025.]

If our schools keep teaching that this is a democracy, and our people and our leaders keep buying this tripe, then our fate as a nation will be just what [Tytler] noted to be historically true of all democracies, economic collapse.

Upon completion of the heroic efforts that resulted in the establishment of our Constitution, one of its architects, Benjamin Franklin, was asked by a woman, "Well, Dr. Franklin, what have you given us?" He replied, "You have a republic, madam, if you can keep it."

As the American flag stands for our Republic, so must the American people stand for our Republic as well, or our American Republic itself will stand no longer.

We digress a moment here to 6 May 2025, about two weeks after the news of Dr. Bob Jackson's promotion had come to me. He was a great guy,

Christian and servant of God, father and husband, Vietnam veteran, surgeon, 30 years the team doctor at Taylor University, and 34 years a member of LtR's board of directors.

Bob graciously passed along a bouquet to me in the inscription he wrote in a book about his life, *Bob, You Can't Do That*, which he'd written and published in 2021 and given a copy to me. The bouquet:

> Mike,
> Thanks for involving me in your Lightrider ministry. It has been a blessing to have you as a Christian Brother all these years. Hope you enjoy the book. My hope is that it will inspire and be a testimony to our Great God.
>
> Bob

Bob himself, indeed his life, was a great inspiration to me. I am grateful for the many medical blessings that he performed on me, each of which added quality to my life.

Perhaps God has orchestrated the timing of this saint's promotion with the writing of this chapter. Just a few years ago, we at LtR came across the Founder's Bible, which is packed with well-documented stories about the Bible's historic impact on America, such biblical heritage being the very reason for the G&CF. We had given a Founder's Bible to Bob along with a letter introducing it to him, a letter that really expresses much about LtR's direction at that time. That letter, written almost exactly four years ago, follows:

> Hey Bob, 25 May 2021
> We've been really blessed to discover the Founder's Bible just as we're embarking on LtR's mission tweak made necessary by selling our faithful steed in August 2019. May you, too, be blessed by it as you learn more about God's hand and purpose in launching, keeping, and using this Republic.
>
> Our desire is to help set the record straight about America's Christian Heritage.
>
> "Even when I'm old and gray O God do not forsake me until I declare Your strength to this generation, Your power to all who are to come" (Psalm 71:18). Andy Rooney said, "I've learned that the best classroom in the world is at the feet of an elderly person."
>
> Moses was 80 when God got him moving. I'm still three trombones short of a Big Parade but feel God mobilizing us gray-hairs to get the Bible back out there into the public square where it was from this nation's very get-go—off the shelf and out of the historical dustbin to which the progressive left and dormant Church have allowed it to be relegated. Into the hands of GRANDDADS, and through them to their spouses, grandkids, kids, and back into America's schools—schools founded to teach all Americans to read so that the truth of Scripture could be read for themselves that they ". . . not be deceived by priestly deceivers." "Fear of the Lord is the beginning of wisdom," which is why Bibles were used as textbooks in American schools for over two centuries.
>
> Learning the truth about America's Christian Heritage informs all people, of whatever generation or persuasion, of the need for *personally knowing God*, His love, mercy, and faithfulness, *not just knowing about Him* and these essentials truths; truths brought to life through the lives, actions, and testimonies of America's Forefathers, Founding Fathers, early Americans, and their families; truths borne out time and time again demonstrating that indeed "America, America, God shed His grace on

thee, and crowned thy GOOD with brotherhood from sea to shining sea."

"The wicked have drawn the sword and bent their bow to cast down the afflicted and the needy, to slay those of upright conversation. Their sword will enter their own heart, their bow will be broken" (Psalm 37:14–5). May the Sword of God's Word penetrate the hearts of the wicked before they self-destruct, that they not die but be saved—that America, too, would be a Nineveh rather than a Sodom and so be spared His much-deserved judgment.

Partners in His service,
Mike

Since penning that letter, LtR has adjusted G&CF's focus from just America's Christian heritage to America's biblical heritage as it encompasses both the Christian and Judeo origins of our great American Republic. Christianity had sprung from Judaism. Indeed, as you know, Jesus himself was a Jew.

For years the seemingly prophetic words of "America Again" were presented at devotionals aboard the LtR and at the G&CF by playing Carman's 1993 DVD of that name, as a reminder that America's hope is in Jesus and we need God in our nation again.

The US Supreme Court in the 1892 case of the *Church of the Holy Trinity v. the United States* declared the USA to be a Christian nation, on a variety of levels. Thankfully, we are not a theocracy but our laws and institutions of government are based solidly upon Christian principles. "America has the soul of a church but its laws demand separation of church and state . . . yet . . . Christianity is so intricately and delicately woven into the fabric of American civilization that if it were uprooted its foundations would be destroyed," said CK Chesterton.

We are reaping the reward for allowing our public schools to drift away from their intended duty, stated in "The Old Deluder Satan Act," to teach our children to read so that they could read their Bibles and not be deceived by priestly deceivers.

School days, school days
Dear old Golden Rule days
Reading' and writing' and 'rithmetic
Taught to the tune of the hick'ry stick
You were my queen in calico
I was your bashful, barefoot beau
And you wrote on my slate, "I Love You, Joe"
When we were a couple o' kids
    ("School Days," Will D. Cobb and Gus Edwards, 1907)

On 27 May 2025, Wayne Miller at our SMF recited from memory this little jingle:

"School days, school days, these are Golden Rule Days; readin' and ritin' and 'rithmetic, taught to the tune of a hickory stick." Origin of the Golden Rule is Mathew 7:12. For the last few years I've on occasion asked waitresses, preachers, people at random, if they know the Golden Rule. Most answer that they've heard of it, that it may have something to do with loving your neighbor or some such, but few get it right. Wayne's singing that verse was in response to that question. Most of LtR's SMF guys knew the jingle and the Golden Rule.

In the years leading up to the founding of Our Republic, the Black Robe Regiment—700 strong—named by the British Parliament, rendered to Caesar and rendered to God. We have spiritual duties and civil duties. These 700 preachers used their pulpits to inform and inflame their congregations about the abuses of our God-given liberty by King George, earning for themselves a price on their heads.

This is the whole quote, inspiring the words, highlighted below, on the Challenge Coin given to me by Micah Beckwith, Lieutenant Governor of Indiana, at LtR's Senior Men's Fellowship on 29 July 2025. John Peter Gabriel Muhlenburg of the Black Robe Regiment, writing to his brother William Augustus Muhlenberg, preacher at the Protestant Episcopal Church, wrote:

> "You say, as a clergyman nothing can excuse my conduct. I am a clergyman, it is true, but I am a member of society as well as the poorest laymen, and my liberty is as dear to me as to any man. **Shall I then sit still**, and enjoy myself at home, when the best blood of the continent is spilling? **Heaven forbid** it!"[4]

Ought not God's personally ordained building blocks of nations, family, church, and government lean on and support each other, functioning as a system, just the way blocks and mortar work together to form walls?

Hebrews 11:22–34 tells us that every saint listed as heroes of the faith were also involved with civil government. Every profit in the Old Testament was used by God to speak to the king.

Yesterday, 13 May 2025, wisdom surfaced at our Senior Men's Fellowship in an article by John Stonestreet and Glenn Sunshine of Breakpoint dated 7 May 2025. Titled "The Papal Conclave," it spoke about the system to replace Pope Francis, who had then recently passed, and the importance to all Christians of who would be elected as that replacement: "The brilliant theologian JI Packer once observed that we are justified by faith, not by believing in justification by faith. And so, Christians across faith lines can embrace what Chuck Colson called 'an ecumenism of the trenches,' which takes the forms of defending life, promoting robust dialogue, and where possible working to protect essential cultural goods such as life, marriage, and religious liberty." The article concluded with this admonition: "We must never sacrifice the truth on the altar of unity, but we should pursue unity within the bounds of truth."

Just now, 14 May 2025, driving the three minutes home for lunch, a commentator on the radio spoke about leaders being one or the other: thermometers or thermostats—the former reports the temperature while the latter sets the temperature. The Church in America today, unified within the bounds of truth, must again, like those 700 churches led by the 700 pastors of the Black Robe Regiment, set biblical standards for our culture, not just report on the standards of Satan that seem to be prevailing.

It's been said that we are a part of all that we have met. Perhaps that's why God has instructed us in Proverbs 4:23: "Above all else guard your hearts . . ." For our hearts are daily deluged with evil disguised as good, with good made to look evil.

Whether the bigger and bigger flatscreen at home or the now omnipresent small screen on the phone in our pocket, our Republic's foundation, the Bible, will filter the deluge, allowing

---

[4] http://orderofcenturions.org/muhlenburg.html (accessed 5 August 2025).

| IWU kids tying on the feedbag near St. Louis on a Lightrider retreat visiting historic sites. The girl in horizontal stripes, Wendy, had lost her sight as a teenager. She had the most winsome, gracious spirit of anyone we've ever met. | Wendy, on the same day as the last photo, enjoying hearing others describe the St. Louis Arch. The occupant, not pictured, of the electric cart had mobility challenges but had her eyesight. She had much to learn from Wendy's beautiful spirit. |

what's good to come to us, like that blessing on the radio mentioned earlier—but, like all filters, it must be taken off the shelf and brought online. The great thing about the Bible, it never needs to be cleaned or changed—just used!

Johnny Cash had it right back in 1956: "I keep a close watch on this heart of mine, I keep my eyes wide open all the time . . ." He was aware that evil lurks all about, that we must be on our guard if we're to "walk the line," if we're to keep fidelity, in our case, with our Lord to stay the fight.

Once, at Valley Forge, Pennsylvania, alive with stunning fall colors, my wife, Debbie, walking with Wendy, feeling so sorry that Wendy was missing the glorious fall scene, was surprised to hear Wendy speak up, saying, "Hearing the sound of the leaves underfoot brings to mind the beautiful colors that must be filling your sight! Please describe what you're seeing." Wendy wasn't missing anything!

As I mentioned a while back, on the fourth of our annual retreats with the IWU kids, we had arrived a bit early on campus so had fast idled the LtR to keep the cabin cool. Wendy was the first one to come aboard. She had recognized the familiar sound of the LtR at fast idle, and with white cane in hand, came confidently tapping up to us, passing an idling construction vehicle, smile on her face, once again confidently present, though unbeknownst to her, to humble us with her wonderful grace. As I recall, Wendy wanted to go into ministry to folks who had recently lost their sight.

Katie, who I knew at college, worked in the office of a truck repair shop. She told about how one cold winter day a fire truck pulled into the garage for repairs. A Dalmatian leapt off of the truck and curled up by the heater in her office. All day long trucks started up and moved about but that Dalmatian never stirred. Until, toward the day's end, the fire truck was started, repaired, and ready to go. That Dalmatian jumped up and ran out to the garage and confidently boarded his ride. But I digress . . .

(Appendix 1 contains a ream of important factual information, acquired in person, edited from this chapter, in an effort to prevent derailing this narrative with academic and experiential overload.)

TWENTY-SEVEN

The Dan Plan—Lightrider's Transition to Today

LtR's BusBarn being constructed in 1997. It served as such until 2019 when we leased it to Eagle Wings, who had purchased our third and last LtR.

Spring 2017 found Lightrider Ministries in a bit of a bind. We had hired a younger guy to take over LtR's Mobile Retreat program and had borrowed $300,000 to purchase Lightrider #3 (previously mentioned). Sadly, the young guy wasn't a good fit and had to be let go, leaving LtR holding the $300,000 bag for a wonderful newer coach for which we now had insufficient staff to operate. Of course, God was on top of the situation.

Gordon Vandermeulen, living in Grand Rapids, MI, woke up at 3 p.m. having been inspired by God with a plan to help LtR get past this bind: "When I remember You on my bed, I meditate on You in the night watches . . ." (Psalm 63:6). He called my brother Steve and told him what LtR should do—an idea we later dubbed the Dan Plan, named for the founder and director of Eagle Wings, a Christian bus ministry, Dan Bryant.

The plan was simple: Raise as much money as we could to pay down the $300,000 loan so that Eagle Wings could afford to purchase the Lightrider, and allow Eagle Wings to move into LtR's BusBarn, rent-free for a year, with a low monthly payment and lease option to follow that first year. Gordon and his wife, Elaine, put up $40,000 as a matching grant. A single donor family, Bob and Charlotte Canida, matched the entire $40,000, netting LtR $80,000. Along with another $10,000 LtR managed to raise on the Paul E Turner Memorial Golf Retreat gave us 90 grand to pay down a big chunk of the $300,000—which was sufficient enhancement that Eagle Wings signed on to the Dan Plan. God is good.

So in August 2019 LtR passed our double-decker to Eagle Wings, a 20-year-old Upland ministry, then a two single-decker motor coach operation, whose mission is to provide transportation to the Church. It was also time for us aging endomorphs of the LtR staff to hang up our traveling shoes . . . Eagle Wings has continued to prosper, adding additional motor coaches, single-deckers, to their growing fleet, at this writing numbering five coaches.

Simultaneously with the execution of the Dan Plan, LtR passed ownership of LtR's buildings and land on to the Paul E Turner Foundation. Presently, LtR pays a buck a year to that foundation, which enables us to use all of LtR's former assets in pursuit of our ministry. Our thinking here was to allow a seamless transition of LtR's assets into continuing ministry should LtR leave His service if the old A.G.E. were to overtake me, LtR's co-founder and current director, in the event a successor doesn't come along.

Then Covid hit America, and the world, pretty hard. Lightrider was designated by the Indiana governor to be an essential operation. We never missed a day of work.

Our Senior Men's Fellowship did meet via Zoom for a couple of months, but restarted in-person meetings by August 2020. Our Taylor University LITE (Life Independent Through Exercise) exercise class, interrupted by Covid, never restarted. Our ladies' chair-exercise routine, the longest-running program in the GrayBarn, started back up in the fall of 2020.

The motor coach transportation industry was hit as hard as any by the government's draconian response to Covid, but Eagle Wings weathered the storm by the grace of God, something for which we at LtR prayed and for which we are very grateful.

TWENTY-EIGHT

Wandering Wheels and the Mobile Retreat

Possums Four, Five, and Six with Wheels staff, left to right, back row: Wayne Dalland, Scott Pugsley, Phil Summerville, Mike Manganello, and Curt Anderson; front row: Mel Callison, Ted Bowers, Dale Patten, Larry "Spare Parts" Kleindienst, and Jim Gore.

Wandering Wheels, the brainchild of Coach Bob Davenport, then football coach at Taylor University, pioneered, among other things, mobile retreats aboard buses equipped with bunk beds, enabling overnight travel. Wheels named and numbered their sleeper buses and or motor coaches Possum One, Possum Two, and so forth. Mike Sonnenberg, Biology major at Taylor, came up with the name. The possum, the only marsupial in North America, travels at night, carrying its young . . .

Starting out in a pickup truck with a camper back, seven students from Taylor were taken to New Jersey. They traveled overnight on a Friday, with three drivers each driving about three hours. They then surfed all day Saturday and Sunday. Then they returned with their sunburned selves as trophies to Upland, driving overnight and arriving Monday early morning in time for school. The concept was born! Overnight travel allowed journey to faraway places without burning daylight getting there. Motel bills were eliminated. Kids could adventure with the church without missing school.

In the late sixties, a one-ton Chevy truck with an Omaha Standard Feed Bed was converted into a camper with 16 bunk beds inside. No windows, stereo, lighting, or even cushions were used. The highlight of a night's journey was standing stooped over in the aisle for a few minutes.

Then a school bus body was ordered to be built at Superior Coach in Lima, OH, on a Chevrolet chassis. It had special ribs built into the body to support bunk beds. Possum One became a reality. A Lilley Endowment footed the bill.

Down the road, moms, dads, and grandparents too were clamoring to be included. Steel leaf springs and 455 AC (four windows open at 55 mph) weren't going to work well with the wide bodies of advancing years. A well-used motor

We had to maintain these buses. "This Holly four-barrel ought to fit my 55 Chevy . . ." – the author on a bad-hair day.

coach with AC and air-ride suspension was purchased from Illini Swallow Lines in Champaign, IL. This 1963 35-foot GM PD-4106 had a million miles on its clock—that's to the moon and back, twice! It became Possum Three and an entry into adult mobile retreat outreach.

So popular were these mobile retreats that several Christian ministries spun off of Wandering Wheels: God's Night Crawler out of southern Indiana; Men in Motion out of Mansfield, Ohio; Circuit Rider out of Lebanon, Ohio; Retreat in Motion out of Fort Wayne, Indiana; Overlander's out of Adrian, MI; Fellowship of Christians in Action out of Titusville, Florida; Immanuel Baptist out of Richmond, Virginia; King's Coach out of Newton, New Jersey; Spirit of America out of Holland, Michigan; The Reaper out of Dayton, Ohio; Eagle Wings out of Upland, Indiana; Lightrider Ministries out of Upland, Indiana . . . to name a few.

Lightrider specified one additional adult amenity—more space—by going with a double-decked motor coach rather than a typical single-decked coach. Grown-ups really liked the extra room, and the double-decker provided a real "wow" factor for kids. It also enhanced our chance to share Christ with the legions of folks asking about what we were up to with these still, in America, eye-catching double-deckers.

Early on, Wandering Wheels had used the "wow" factor with kids by adding dual pipes with glass pack mufflers, using chrome by the yard, polishing the brass under the hood, playing a state-of-the-art stereo at full blast, air horns, and the like. Kids loved this stuff—even if the local constabulary did not.

One late evening, passing through College Corner, OH, my brother Steve was rattling windows in a neighborhood with Possum One's glass pack mufflers when he got pulled over by an unimpressed "yo' in a heap of trouble" small-town sheriff.

Steve got out of the driver's seat, left the vehicle, and walked down the curbside of the bus to face the music in the glare of the flashing blue lights. Meanwhile, the officer walked up the driver's side of the bus to the driver's window. One of the kids had jumped into the driver's seat just for fun. The cop at the window scared the heebie-jeebies outta that kid.

Steve finally connected with the cop who, becoming impressed with the effort being made in these kids' lives if not the glass pack mufflers, let Steve off with a warning and an admonition that "sounding like a low-flying aircraft" might "wow" kids, but was annoying to sleeping neighbors to say the least.

The Possums were used for mobile retreats but also to transport guys to America's West Coast who would be cycling to America's East Coast. Coach Davenport called these coast-to-coast bicycle trips for guys "putting hair on the chest of the church," an effort to associate more masculinity and toughness with the church. Coast-to-Coast with the Holy Ghost—bronzed bodies from the waist up were the order of the day.

In 1975, though, the first official Wandering Wheels co-ed coast-to-coast bike trip was run from Lincoln City, Oregon, to Rehoboth Beach, Delaware. That hair-on-the-chest-of-the-church thing was quietly dropped from the Wheels lexicon.

Center Chapel adults enjoying a campfire at Camp Mead in Vermont while on a Lightrider retreat.

TWENTY-NINE

The Lightrider Experience—Blueprint for Fellowship

At Lightrider we used the mobile retreat system learned at Wandering Wheels as a tool to get people closer together by getting them away together, with God. His Creation in all of North America became our camp—if there was pavement, we'd use it. We've also done a retreat or two where pavement went only so far, like Hawaii, and Israel.

From 5 July 1988 to 5 March 2020, LtR provided a mobile retreat program for groups of 30 teenagers or 26 adults located within a five-hour driving radius of Upland, IN. We'd plan the retreat, working closely with the group leaders, tailoring the experience to meet the needs and desires of the group. And then conduct the mobile retreat, including driving, cooking, conducting tours, devotions, and the like. Our desire was always to help initiate and/or renew the faith in Christ of individuals, congregations and families by:

Getting people away from pressures and problems of work and family and the lethargy of their comfort zone;

Surrounding them with a warm, friendly environment where most of the daily, distracting decisions regarding food, entertainment, where to go, and the like, had already been made;

Mixing them comfortably with new faces and fresh insights;

Worshiping God through song, prayer, sharing, and reflecting on His word together;

Joining people in an open forum on Faith;

Demonstrating life in general with Jesus Christ;

Devotional times became catalysts that helped stimulate one-on-one chats among the group during the many private moments afforded as we traveled, hiked, ate out, shopped, swam, and the like;

Social barriers fell and people found themselves on the same level as we: slept in the comfortable, albeit close quarters of a 40-foot, double-decker motor coach, changed clothes in the crowded but friendly confines of a McDonald's restroom, and woke up together in one's typical first-thing-in-the morning mess.

LtR followed exactly the staffing pattern pioneered at Wandering Wheels. With three drivers, we could cover several hundred miles at night while our passengers slept. Driving just three hours per shift allowed each driver to get over six hours of sleep each night, enabling them to participate with the group in the next day's activity. Generally our drivers, volunteers all, were guys. State and then federal licensing requirements created a pool of drivers that, for one reason or another, was predominately male—though we did, from time to time, have gals like Marsha Becker volunteer as drivers too.

Our non-driving staff—affectionately referred to as "lovely assistants," generally gals, and also volunteers—equipped our team to handle individual needs of both genders. Once we did actually hire a guy, Dave Moore, as a non-driving staffer. He was supporting a wife and kids at the time. Dave, though an excellent part of our ministry team each time that he participated, was, decidedly, not lovely, though the ladies seemed to find him at least okay.

Our most popular mobile retreat was what we called a Smoky–Beach–Disney, or SBD. Typically, we'd pick up a group after school on a Wednesday and drive overnight to the Great Smoky Mountains National Park, arriving Thursday morning. A park with a covered picnic area and heated bathrooms, Mynatt Park, in Gatlinburg, TN, made a wonderful place for us to get the kids up while we made breakfast. A portable cooking unit, called a chuck box, allowed us to prepare a hot meal within about 45 minutes.

Thursday would be a day of hiking in the park. Following breakfast and a visit to Sugarlands Visitor Information Center, we'd take the trail up to the Chimneys, though for many years we'd climb up what we called the "back way," no trail at all.

We'd make lunch for our group at the Chimneys picnic area, stream-side near the trailhead. Late afternoon we'd head into Gatlinburg for a couple hours of free time before loading up to head south, again driving overnight.

Friday morning the group would wake up for a sunrise at New Smyrna Beach, Florida. Again we'd make breakfast and lunch while spending the day bodysurfing, playing beach football, taking in the sun, and such. The evening would happen at the boardwalk in Daytona Beach or at a mall and movie east of Orlando at Altamont Springs, after which we'd all bed down aboard the Lightrider.

The duty driver would then head over to Colonial Drive and the Orlando Krispy Kreme bakery to purchase donuts for breakfast. We did discover that 10-dozen donuts reached the wholesale rate, which was actually less expensive than buying just seven dozen which we'd done for a year or two. Hot donuts at midnight contributed, certainly, to our fat-for-free lifestyle. Then off to a campground near Disney World where we'd all get some sleep.

Saturday, opening to closing, was spent at Disney World, usually at the Magic Kingdom. Kids were free to hang with us or take off on their own. We'd leave Bus Parking as a group, take either the ferry or the monorail over to the Magic Kingdom, then meet at the flagpole in Town Square for a short orientation.

The Town Hall would be pointed out where the kids could go if they'd lost their wallet or some such as the LtR staff would check in there periodically throughout the day. Each person would be given a Disney-provided stub with the parking spot number and told to be there after the park closed.

We'd then offer the group the chance to spend a few hours with the LtR staff, see the Diamond Horseshoe Review, beat a few lines, or to just take off on their own.

One memorable retreat back at Wheels, we had had a double busload of junior high kids.

When given their options, they all took off, leaving the eight of us staffers standing at the flagpole. What to do—we'd all been their dozens of times?

One of our drivers, Tom Haifley, had once worked at the Contemporary Hotel waterfront. We ended up getting eight one-man motorboats in which to frolic around Bay Lake for a couple of hours. Endomorphic me, suffering the fat-for-free syndrome early on, my heavy self diminishing the performance of my little boat, became sport for the others whose boats were not similarly affected. They took great fun speeding toward my slow-moving self, turning sharply at the last moment, creating a wave that soaked me good.

Following our, for me, watery adventure with a nice buffet lunch at the Polynesian hotel, we'd return to Bus Parking, crank up one of the two Possums, and nap in air-conditioned comfort for the afternoon.

Evening found us back in the Magic Kingdom, watching five live groups performing five short concerts each. Tabasco, Gabriel's Brass, Michael Iceberg, Kids of the Kingdom, and the like were excellent entertainment. We eight had had a great day, as did the kids. All 60 of them, having spent most of their time and all of their money in the arcade, arrived back at the appointed space in Bus Parking, tired and ready to hit the sack for the long ride home.

We learned a valuable lesson on one such late-night departure from Disney. It was 2 a.m. and rather than hitting the sack as we had requested, an entire junior high group talked me into letting them stay up until the first fuel stop 45 minutes out, Okahumpka Service Plaza on the Florida Turnpike. On arrival at the plaza, we discovered that the entire group had fallen asleep, piled together in a breathing yet dormant mass. Waking them up to hit the head prior to the sack proved a difficult task—sleeping teens are able to sleep through a whole lot of noise, prodding, and pulling. Heaven forbid, in a late-night bus wreck we'd have to be certain not to leave slumbering kids lie . . .

I recall only one time when our staff was paged in the park to come to the Town Hall. One of the kids, a Japanese-American guy, had been caught shoplifting. He was released into our care on the condition that we promised to inform his parents on our return home. Having lived in the Orient for 10 years myself, I was well aware of the importance in that culture of not losing face. The young fellow, repeatedly on the homeward journey, begged me not to tell his parents.

This group was high-schoolers from Second Presbyterian Church in Indy. Arriving early morning, we met the lad's parents, both doctors, in the church parking lot. Keeping my promise was indeed a tough chore. But I digress.

Each day of the mobile retreat, we'd have a devotional time with the group, a time of sharing and looking at a Bible verse or two. Devotions were largely catalysts to stimulate sharing one with another. Such sharing opportunities occurred while driving, often late into the night, two or three kids in rapt attention, thirsty to learn about all kinds of stuff kids of that age are curious about.

Devotionals Wednesday–Saturday were great if not too direct. Sundays, we had morning time we called "Church," then an early evening time in which we presented the gospel, usually giving the kids an opportunity to commit their lives to Christ.

The rest of Sundays were spent driving back to wherever we had picked up the group, arriving before school Monday morning. Often, after sleeping in until lunch at a Mickey D's or some such, followed by "Church" running down the road, we'd have hours and hours to horse around, play games, or find opportunities to chat with one or two kids at a time about life concerns of theirs.

One such chat happened upstairs with a group of high-schoolers from Second Pres in Kokomo—Lloyd and Laura Swartzendruber's group—en route home on an SBD. One of the athletic kids, a football player, had courageously asked me a sensitive question about teenage boy-girl relationships. Very soon a crowd of other kids had gathered round, each interested in the chat—all ears, as it were—but, being timid, not wanting to engage in it themselves.

This particular chat went on for several hours, interrupted by one fast-food fuel stop, but continuing on after the stop right where we'd left off, all the onlookers again present. That athlete kept asking lots of excellent questions—the 1 Peter 3:15 and the 1 Timothy 4:12 things had opened the door and kept it open to this memorable exchange of biblical information.

After four days of making their meals, tucking them in, horsing around on the trail, the beach, and at Disney, we'd earned their trust and had earned the right to share. Having developed a bit of a relationship with them really added weight to the invitation.

Having missed just a couple days of school, these kids arrived back at school, often sunburned and pretty tired out but fired up about their faith—a great time to share with their friends who had been stuck in school and having had a ho-hum weekend in the often-frigid north. Youth pastors who had been with the kids on the Possum or Lightrider often bragged about how effective this dynamic was.

Other mobile retreats took us out West where a variety of beautiful parts of God's Creation were experienced through hiking, whitewater rafting, or viewed along the way. One of my favorite devotionals about His Creation included asking the question, "What about His Creation causes you the most awe?" Responses varied by age, stage of life, and/or profession.

Tammy Brown, then the receptionist at Upland Tire, said that she was most impressed that God could hear and respond to so many prayers all coming in at the same time, not unlike the multiple phone lines she managed at work.

Another passenger, Merle, a music teacher, was impressed with reproduction and music. No monotone birds—always the same pitch, kind to kind. That was news to me, having always been accused of being a monotone.

Wilbur Williams, Bible prof at IWU, said, "Everything serves its assigned purpose, save for man." A rather profound thought, don't you think?

Redwood trees have always been the most awe-inspiring part of God's Creation to me. My grandfather used to take us boys to see a particular stand of these near Santa Cruz, California, which he simply called the Big Trees, within Henry Crowell Redwood State Park.

Mike and Debbie Manganello with frequent LtR flyer Arlena Wood at the redwood cross-section on display at Henry Cowell Redwoods State Park in Felton, CA.

After starting LtR, we had occasion to take a venerable group of travelers, the Grabill Gobblers, to see these trees. One of the trees, the General John C. Fremont—named for an explorer and military officer in California's history, had been struck by lightning in a far-ago millennium, starting a fire inside that tree's trunk, creating a massive hollow in the base. In 1846 General Freemont and his party had reportedly sheltered in that hollow, hence the tree's name. It took 17 of us, side to side and hand to hand, arms outstretched, to encircle the 96-foot circumference of that behemoth.

The redwood's circumference is measured six feet up from the ground on the uphill side, such height chosen to be above the characteristic flaring of the trunk at ground level. This flaring, called a butt swell (not referring to fat-for-free drivers), is a feature designed into redwoods. It provides a wider stance for stability, like an old Pontiac GTO, while deflecting falling vegetation away from the base of the tree, decreasing chances of injury to the tree by fire when that debris eventually burns.

I had the bright idea of seeing how many of the Gobblers we could get inside the hollow of what was then a 285-foot tree (it had been 360 feet tall before the top 75 feet had blown off in a storm thousands of years ago). My mistake was going in first, along with Dick McNiece. Soon we had all 30 of our group standing inside that redwood, the little bit of light coming in through the teepee-shaped entrance having long since vanished.

My back was pressed against the inside of that tree, and I could barely move. Fearing someone might get fresh and start tickling or some such, I managed to suggest that it was time to leave the tree, which fortunately was accomplished without incident.

Dick McNiece had been a B-25 pilot in World War II so was used to being in a cramped place. Regardless, he agreed with me that going in first was decidedly not bright. Later, leaving the park, we saw a newspaper clipping on a bulletin board; it seems that 55 UC Santa Cruz kids had managed to cram themselves into the General Freemont...

A cross-section of an old-growth redwood had been cut and displayed on edge under a small shelter, like a giant, solid-wood wheel. Little flags had been inserted into several of the growth rings, marking events that had happened in the particular year those rings had formed (such rings are formed annually).

A flag marking the end of World War II was located almost out to the bark while one marking the nativity of Christ was just about at the center. Between the two was a flag marking the Norman Conquest in 1066 AD. This cross-section, about eight feet in diameter, spoke of about 2,000 years, so one can only imagine how old the General Grant must be, measuring in at 36 feet in diameter.

As kids we boys, with Granddad, learned that redwoods grew to be over 4,000 years old, the age determined by counting growth rings, while the Earth was said to be two million years old. Now, so-called science, still recognizing the veracity of counting growth rings, using more "modern" methods, has determined redwoods to be only 2,000 years old and the Earth to be six and a half billion years old. My money's on a young Earth with 4,000-year-old redwoods, but I digress.

Joseph B. Strauss, the engineer who built the Golden Gate Bridge, wrote an inspiring poem about these trees, titled simply "The Redwoods." That a man capable of building such a magnificent bridge could see God's hand in creating these majestic trees has always impressed me—he must have been a humble man indeed. He was a Jew who no doubt had a great respect for our God.

"THE REDWOODS" – JOSEPH B. STRAUSS

Here, sown by the Creator's hand.
In serried ranks, the Redwoods stand:
No other clime is honored so,
No other lands their glory know.

The greatest of Earth's living forms,
Tall conquerors that laugh at storms;
Their challenge still unanswered rings,
Through fifty centuries of kings.

The nations that with them were young,
Rich empires, with their forts far-flung,
Lie buried now—their splendor gone;
But these proud monarchs still live on.

So shall they live, when ends our day,
When our crude citadels decay;
For brief the years allotted man,
But infinite perennials' span.

This is their temple, vaulted high,
And here, we pause with reverent eye,
With silent tongue and awestruck soul;
For here we sense life's proper goal;

To be like these, straight, true and fine,
to make our world like theirs, a shrine;
Sink down, Oh, traveler, on your knees,
God stands before you in these trees.

AMEN![5]

Interesting that Strauss, a world-class engineer, with his verse ". . . fifty centuries of kings," written 16 years before my birth, recognized the more-than-4,000-year age of redwoods.

Growing up, we'd always find Strauss's poem reproduced on pieces of redwood or on postcards at the park's gift shop. Yet the last time I visited this park in California, in 2012, on the occasion of my Aunt Thelma's promotion to Heaven at age 99, no such was available. Asking three of the park rangers, not one of them had even heard of the poem.

One must wonder whether this omission of such an inspiring acknowledgment of our Creator was a deliberate move by those in open rebellion against Him these days—perhaps the change in the determined age of redwoods was foisted on us by the same folks?

---

[5] Joseph B. Strauss, "The Redwoods," ca. 1932, public domain.

THIRTY

O Canada—Nice Neighbor to the North

Wide bodies Mike Manganello (left) and Merle McDaniel enjoying their fat-for-free selves on the rocks at Peggy's Cove near Halifax, Nova Scotia.

We at Lightrider have always considered mobile retreats to be a "dog and pony" show necessary to get folks together so He can work His wonders in human hearts and relationships, show off His Creation handiwork, and prompt the testimony of His saints one with another so essential to defeating the evil one—all while protecting with His hand of mercy, guiding with His grace and love.

North America has been the prime venue for such shows, with Canada providing a wonderful if slightly foreign aspect. With the exception of one French Canadian border guard at a Maine-to-Quebec crossing who took exception to our calling ourselves American, our encounters with the Canadian people have been really great.

From the Maritime providences in the east to the Canadian Rockies and points west, we've enjoyed wonderful fellowship aboard the Lightrider while experiencing much of the excellence that is Canada.

My one encounter with the Royal Canadian Mounted Police (RCMP) happened while climbing the two-lane northbound grade into Jasper, BC, a long line of traffic held up behind our slow-moving selves. Suddenly, a rear-end collision happened on the southbound side right beside us. A motor home's brakes had failed to hold, allowing it to rear-end a passenger car. With no shoulder on which to pull over, traffic already backed up, I chose to keep going, planning to stop at the very first opportunity—painfully aware that, as a witness, the RCMP would at least wish to hear my observations of the accident and at most take exception to my having left the scene.

One of the cars following us was driven by Tubby, a relative of Jan Goff, who along with Jan's husband, Allen, were staffing this retreat. Once we managed to find a pull-over, Tubby said that he'd quickly go back to the scene of the accident, offer assistance if necessary, and let the RCMP know why I'd failed to stop at the scene.

We got word from the RCMP, through Tubby when he caught up with us, that they understood my reason for not stopping, a great relief to me, and requesting that I stop at the police station in Jasper to make a report, which I was happy to do. Canadians are okay people.

On the opposite side of the country, arriving in Yarmouth, Nova Scotia, by ferry, our first activity was always going through the border-crossing process. We'd be directed to a holding area, along with other motor coaches and oversized vehicles.

On one such occasion, driving Possum Four, we were greeted by a pretty young lady in uniform. She asked me to step outside and open one of the cargo bay doors for inspection. Opening the door revealed, among other things, our chuck box, which we used to prepare meals along the way.

She inquired, "What's in this big box?" Being a single young guy at the time, unable to resist a bit of levity with the comely lass, my reply was: "The remains of my departed brother." Her inquiring expression morphed suddenly into one of incredulity on the way to indignation. She actually took a step back. Knowing better than to joke with immigration officials, I quickly identified said box as to what it actually was, winning a brief smile without repercussions or even further inspection. Canadians are alright.

The Anne of Green Gables home in Cavendish, Prince Edward Island, home to the author of the book of that name while growing up, was a favorite destination for many of our LtR groups.

Sitting once on the porch of a B&B in Cavendish, I was immediately engaged in conversation with a Canadian pastor who happened to be staying there, taking a bit of R&R from

Steve Manganello sharing the faith with an inquisitive fellow in Banff, a garden spot in the Canadian Rockies.

Kathleen and Gary Johnson, great friends and frequent LtR flyers, at Lake Louise up the road from Banff.

his home and work in Halifax. We had been chatting about the RMS *Titanic*'s foundering, following striking an iceberg some 700 miles east of Halifax in April 1912.

Visiting the graves of many of the *Titanic*'s victims at Fairview Lawn Cemetery in Halifax was a favorite stop on many of our visits to that picturesque city, a miniature San Francisco if you will, perched as it is on a hill overlooking a bay. To this day, White Star Steamship Company, owner of the *Titanic*, maintains those graves (see Chapter 32).

This pastor told me about a practice by one of the churches in Halifax during that time when survivors and bodies alike from the *Titanic* were being brought there. Two large signs were posted outside of that church, labeled "Saved" and "Unsaved."

Once, when visiting the Fortress Louisburg, on Cape Breton Island, part of Nova Scotia, we learned a couple of facts, holdovers from colonial days. Tourists who wear red clothing will be harassed by the docents at this formerly French historic site, attired in period costume. Red was worn by the despised British Regulars.

Also, we found that men's calves were particularly attractive to ladies of the day. Just ask Geoff Schwartz, who, attired in shorts, found to his delight, his calves to be pleasing to the young ladies of Fortress Louisburg, even in this century.

Taking Right Direction, Suzie Skager's youthful choir originally from Marion, IN, to sing at a 19th-century church, still very much in operation, at Peggy's Cove, was a highlight. The mostly elderly parishioners in that congregation carried in a fine lunch for our youngsters.

Whale watching off Brier Island, Nova Scotia, was always an adventure. We had to put the LtR on each of two small ferries going and coming from Brier Island. We would travel by small boat out into the Bay of Fundy, a body of water that experiences a high tide of up to 52 feet, with a group of researchers.

Northumberland Ferries keep the traffic flowing in the Canadian Maritimes. Departing aboard the *Scotia Prince*, an overnight ferry, from Portland, ME, or taking the MV *Bluenose* from Bar Harbor, ME, saved us about 750 miles of driving getting to Nova Scotia.

From Cape Breton Island, Nova Scotia, to Newfoundland, required another overnight ferry, the MV *Ambrose Shea*, retired in 1989, crossing from North Sydney to Argentia.

Getting to Labrador required two days and nights at sea, traveling from Lewisporte, NFLD to Happy Valley—Goose Bay, Labrador. The "Happy" in Happy Valley is no doubt a reference to the restaurant with the wonderful ribs!

The menu instructed patrons to not even ask about the secret ingredient in the rib sauce, though having been to the Canadian pavilion at EPCOT, I had an inkling. So I asked whether they used Grade A or Grade B maple syrup in the sauce. "Grade A," came the response—and the revelation that maple syrup was indeed the secret ingredient. Once back home, I synthesized a few flavors and came up with a fairly close duplicate to that sauce, verified by a few fellow travelers from that retreat, that I use to this day.

The one time we took this route, summer 1999, our RO-RO (roll-on, roll-off vehicle deck) passenger ship, the MV *Sir Robert Bond*, had to make an unscheduled stop at Cartwright, Labrador, to deliver food to this landlocked community. With no roads into or out of this town, people there depend on supply by sea, which is not available during the winter months due to ice.

We were given leave for 20 minutes to stretch our legs ashore. We ran into a group of teenagers. They were proud of their internet connection to the world. When told that we were from Indiana, they inquired if we knew Larry Bird. Allen and Jan Goff were with us that trip, and Jan exchanged email addresses with a couple of the teens and maintained contact for several years, wanting to get these kids connected with Christ.

Debbie and I roomed with Jan and Allen on this small ferry. We had to get dressed for bed, with one person at a time in the cabin while the other three waited in the companion way—we're talking close quarters! Jan told me recently that she got no sleep as the ship's fog horn sounding in the night made her fearful of icebergs.

The *Sir Robert Bond* had a very small dining area but excellent hot food—memorable were the French fries smothered with gravy, a Canadian delicacy.

We have a picture of Oris Reece's wife, Donna, reclining in a deck chair on a weather deck, reading a book titled *Hero of the Titanic*, as our vessel slipped slowly past a massive, glacier-blue iceberg.

Then, from Happy Valley to Goose Bay required driving 600 miles of gravel west and south to reach Baie-Comeau in Quebec. After driving for a couple of hours, we encountered our first obstacle: heavy equipment grading the roadway. While we waited, a massive ore-hauling truck performed a three- or four-point turn. The truck pulled right up to the front of our double-decker before reversing, the truck driver eye to eye with our passengers looking out of our *upstairs* windshield. A road grader then adjusted the grade such that we could pass.

Had we been a few minutes later, this crew would have already gone home for the day, and the road surface being worked on had been graded such that our long-wheel-based coach would not have been able to pass. Cars or pickups could pass, but not us.

Given the terrain and narrow roadway, turning around would not have been an option. We'd have been stranded, not knowing that this unmarked spot had even been worked on. Traffic, oncoming or following, was non-existent. God sure looks after the details.

As it happened, about halfway to Baie-Comeau we had to park overnight at a lonely, closed-for-the-night fuel stop at Churchill Falls—the only fuel stop likely to be had before reaching pavement.

We had managed, along this primitive roadway, to break the engine governor while over-revving our engine on a steep downgrade, which prevented the engine from idling. Once we reached pavement, we decided to head straight for Indiana, using limited-access highways, skipping our last remaining stop in Canada, the Old City of Quebec, because keeping the engine going at stoplights and such was very impractical as well as unsafe.

Barb Davenport was with us on this retreat. She really wanted to see the Old City but was understanding. Sadly, this was her second retreat with LtR to Canada and the second time our scheduled visit to the Old City had to be forgone.

Previously, Barb had been on a family retreat to Canada with the Walkers, the family of LtR co-founder Bob. We had three generations of Walkers and a dog on board. Bob's mother, Charlene, had a bad thing happen aboard the LtR on that retreat. She was leaving the restroom while we were underway. Holding the doorframe on the hinge side for support with her right hand, the door swung as if closing, cutting much of her right thumb completely off.

I was driving and got word that we needed to find a hospital. As God would have it, we saw that wonderful little white H on a blue field straight away. Finding that particular hospital was indeed a divine appointment. A renowned plastic surgeon was on call, and he was able to reattach Charlene's thumb and get us back on the road in fairly short order.

During the ordeal, one of the family observed that Charlene was more concerned that she was holding things up than with getting her thumb back to work.

We decided to forgo stopping at the Old City, heading straight home instead. So sorry, Barb.

My impression of rural Canada was that it seemed to be quite like rural America in the 1950s. Small communities, each with a church or two, two-lane highways connecting them, with occasional sections having a third lane for passing; people always friendly and welcoming of strangers.

Much of my Canadian experience happened while driving the Alaska Highway three times while with Wandering Wheels: 1,387 miles of gravel from Dawson Creek, British Columbia, to Delta Junction, Alaska, via the Yukon Territory, with sights of the Alaska pipeline, Northern Lights, brown bears, and eagles—high adventure indeed for motor coach travelers.

Each of these three retreats went to Alaska via the gravel highway but returned by water—what had been three days and nights of high adventure going north would have been pretty boring had we taken the reverse route south going home. While planning these adventures, it seemed the only way back by water was aboard the MV *Columbia*, an auto ferry of the Alaska Marine Highway. Calling at midnight on New Year's Eve to get staterooms aboard the *Columbia* for the four-day-and-night return proved fruitless, meaning our entire coach load of passengers would have to sleep on the deck.

So I checked with one of our scheduled passengers, Virginia Corll, Marsha Becker's mom, to see how she might feel about sleeping four nights on a steel deck. She said that she'd be

okay with that arrangement, but suggested—she always had a suggestion—that I call her niece, Terri Stanfield, a travel agent in California.

That proved to be a providential call, and one I was admittedly reluctant to make thinking it, too, would be fruitless; how could a cruise ship with our passengers to Seattle and the 1,600-mile trek getting the Possum to Seattle to meet them possibly fit into our already-tight budget?

God had it figured out. Terri got us passage aboard a very new, first-class cruise ship with a car deck, the MV *Stardancer* of Sundance Cruises—full cruise amenities, outside state rooms, gourmet dining, live entertainment, even a midnight buffet, all for just 50 bucks more per passenger than the alternative: sleeping on deck and choking down peanut-butter sandwiches aboard the Alaska Marine Highway!

As we cruised home through Alaska's Inside Passage on each of these three adventures we'd be tied up in each of two ports of call: Haines and Ketchikan. Leaning on the stern rail of the *Stardancer*, I'd see the *Columbia*, decks cluttered with brightly colored tents, tied up astern of us and whisper a prayer of thanksgiving that our passengers had been spared the Spartan conditions aboard the *Columbia*—conditions that would have been real hardship for their aging selves. Any future suggestions of Virginia were always cheerfully followed up, that's for sure.

The Canadian Rockies were a popular destination. Banff and Lake Louise, just north of our pristine Glacier National Park, are about the most beautiful places in North America. Jasper, too, is especially beautiful, as is the nearby Columbia Ice Field with its Athabasca Glacier.

Rides out onto the glacier in massive, all-terrain, all-wheel-drive vehicles with wheels taller than a short man, costing $3000 apiece, were a must on our visits to the ice field. Called snow coaches or Ice Explorers, these rigs could easily navigate slopes up to and including 45 degrees with 56 passengers onboard!

On one such excursion it started raining once we had reached the top of the glacier. The driver said that we couldn't get off the snow coach—seemed like our past practice of wandering around on the ice, drinking 2,000-year-old H_2O, wasn't going to happen. Suddenly, the rain cleared up and the driver relented. On leaving the coach, we saw a beautiful rainbow arching across the sky, ending in the distance upon another Ice Explorer.

Sure seemed like a wink and a nod from our good Lord, kinda like His hand in getting us aboard the *Stardancer*: "I know the plans I have for you, plans to prosper you . . ." (Jeremiah 29:11).

His mercy is easier to see in life-saving situations like with Gabriel in Chapter 17, but His grace is also evident in little niceties like the luxurious cruise ship rather than the austere ferry; disembarking rather than remaining aboard the Ice Explorer—such a pleasant turn of events and signed with a rainbow no less. One's perspective leads to crediting our Creator with such happy happenings rather than commending coincidence. Again, the choice is up to you, the reader.

"Count your blessings, name them one by one . . . count your many blessings see what God has done." This song, written in 1867 by Johnson Oatman Jr., just four years after Abraham Lincoln officially established Thanksgiving Day at the height of the Civil War, was a favorite played on his baritone by my friend at Wheels, Paul Eakley, following his sister Judy's promotion to Heaven in a car crash. Judy had been praying for Paul to turn to the Lord, which he did.

"When upon life's billows you are tempest tossed, when you are discouraged, thinking all is lost, Count your many blessings, name them one by one, And it will surprise you what the Lord hath done. [Refrain]

"Are you ever burdened with a load of care? Does the cross seem heavy you are called to bear? Count your many blessings, ev'ry doubt will fly and you will be singing as the days go by. [Refrain]

"So, amid the conflict, whether great or small, do not be discouraged, God is over all; Count your many blessings, angels will attend, Help and comfort give you to your journey's end. [Refrain]"

THIRTY-ONE

Manufacturing a Redefined Motor Coach a New Way—in the USA

At this writing, LtR's dream of a specialty vehicle to use in senior ministry, along with the project needed to produce, fund, and proliferate it into a nationwide tool to encourage and evangelize America's aging adults, has yet to gain the traction necessary to become reality. Yet this decade-long portion of the Lightrider story, too, gives the very strong impression to me of having been authored by God Himself.

While this book is being written in an effort to thank and glorify God, He may direct others to read about our dream for such a specialty vehicle, its manufacture and sales, be inspired by it, and so take action to make it happen for the furtherance of His Kingdom. This possibility is the purpose for which this chapter and Appendix 2 have been written and included in this book.

As this chapter was getting a little technical, we've decided to create—as was done in Chapter 26, as a means of side tracking, in this case, technical overload—Appendix 2.

Early in this century, in about 2005, we learned about vehicles with low floors—in other words, floors mounted below the center of the wheels transporting that vehicle. Most low-floors were 60-feet long, which required them to articulate (bend in the middle) as a semi (tractor-trailer) does. Such vehicles, without steps, might be better for use with senior adults whom we were serving with increasing numbers. We called such vehicles LowRiders.

The following article, published in the August 2007 issue of *National Bus Trader*, will inform readers about the LowRider as we envisioned it up to that date and time:

Engineering Future Motor Coaches by Applying Today's Transit Technology to Yesterday's Motor Coach Design by Mike Manganello

Though transit buses and motor coaches operate generally in different venues and for different purposes, both vehicles must accomplish the same task—the safe and efficient transportation of passengers. Transit buses and motor coaches have certainly become safer over the years. However, unlike transit buses, motor coach efficiency has failed to keep pace with the changing demographics of our trade.

The design of virtually all motor coaches in America requires passengers to enter the coach via a single door, then climb up 5 or 6 steps through a narrow stepwell in order to reach the passenger deck located above cargo bays—a design unchanged since the first half of the last century. Yet today's coaches must carry older passengers, and more of them, than did coaches of yesteryear. ". . . An estimated 60% of motor coach passengers are elderly . . ." and or ". . . disabled," according to Ned Einstein in the March 07 issue of this magazine. Advocating improved stepwells, he continued, ". . . the steady trickle of boarding and alighting accidents . . . will only worsen as our ridership ages and becomes even more frail."

A tour director from southern Indiana, timing the unloading and loading of a motor coach full of senior adults, found that it takes 18 minutes to empty a coach and another 12 minutes to reload. Now that's world-class inefficiency! In an emergency that could be a world-class tragedy.

If we add a bit of modern transit bus technology to the motor coach design equation—namely low-floor engineering—which eliminates the need for a step well, we've begun to get motor coach design in step with the demographic needs of this new century. Put in another door or two with flip-out ramps and a kneeling feature. Now you've got a vehicle that will warm the hearts and save the joints of today's aging passengers—a vehicle that will make over-the-road travel palatable and available to a far larger segment of today's market.

Of course, with a 40-foot low-floor transit bus there are no cargo bays. What do you do with the luggage? Also, the intrusion into the low-floor passenger area by fender wells, the engine, the extra doorways, and such, cut down on the number of passenger seats.

The tough answer is to design a two-door 45-foot low-floor coach with a mechanized luggage handling system installed above the passenger deck. This would not only provide the passenger convenience and safety of the low floor, it would further lower the vehicle's center of gravity, which is already lower than that of a standard motor coach. People weigh more than their luggage, so putting the luggage over the people makes better sense than putting it under them.

Until a motor coach friendly to elderly or disabled passengers is developed, a 60-foot, articulated, low-floor transit bus could be set up for over-the-road use—beef up the horsepower, add taller gears, a larger radiator, and heavier tires. The luggage of senior adults is typically wheeled these days and could be rolled up a flip out ramp, parked in the rear of the vehicle and restrained with a cargo net. Little lifting would be involved so luggage handling would actually be easier than the current under-the-floor system that requires our also-aging

> A motor coach, or over-the-road-bus (OTRB), is defined as a vehicle designed for long-distance transportation of passengers, characterized by integral construction with an elevated passenger deck located over a baggage compartment. It is at least 35 feet in length with a capacity of more than 30 passengers. A low-floor vehicle is defined as having a passenger deck located below the center of the wheels transporting the vehicle.

drivers to do so much bending. Using the forward 38 feet of the vehicle for most of the passenger seating would place most of the weight in the forward section, or "tractor," of the 60-foot bus, aiding stability. The aft 22-foot section, or "trailer," with a lavatory and accounting for above-floor intrusions of two fender wells and the fuel tank, would afford 1,252 cubic feet of space for luggage and or more passenger seating.

With the kneeling feature, multiple doors, and flip-out ramps, passengers may enter and exit this vehicle without encountering even one step. The familiar gaggle of senior adults huddled in the rain or wind outside the single front door and step well of today's motor coaches will have been transformed into happily seated, ready to roll, smiling patrons. It was just such a gaggle waiting to board their tour bus that was seen from the low floor of Lightrider's Skyliner out front of a theater in Branson, MO, that inspired this idea.

Lightrider has built a scale model of an artic (Van Hool AG300) with perimeter seating for 26 passengers plus our staff of four within the "tractor." Luggage space for 30 bags of a specified size (30" x 15" x 15"), a lavatory, additional "spread out seating" for 15 passengers, and a driver's bunk are fitted into the "trailer." Most of the seating converts into bunks so that all 30 aboard may sleep. Space is available for airline-style overhead compartments to handle carry-on bags. The floor area under the perimeter seating will be used by Lightrider passengers for their sleeping bags and pillows.

A low-floor artic could be designed to carry more seated passengers than Lightrider's arrangement if group dynamics and the ability to convert for sleeping were not needed. AG300s are set up to carry 100 passengers plus the driver; that's 43 seated and the rest standing. So the vehicle can handle the weight of, say, 43 seated passengers and their luggage. To make people and luggage fit would require engineering some kind of mechanized, overhead luggage system.

Several articulated motor coaches have been used at highway speeds around the world. The high-decked Prevost H5-60 and the double-decker Neoplan N 138 Jumbo Cruiser are two examples. Neoplan's AN460/LF, an articulated low-floor transit bus, sold for transit or shuttle service, uses two hydraulic cylinders within the articulated joint, controlled electronically, to eliminate jackknifing. Similar systems are used by New Flyer in the D60LF and by NABI in their 60LFW for the same purpose. Hundreds of artics are used on intercity lines in Hungary. Neoplan artics ply the New Jersey Turnpike every day.

Steering geometry of rear steer and non-rear steer low-floor artics differs

> The Americans with Disabilities Act (ADA), as of 2012, requires universal accessibility on most motor coaches, necessitating onboard handicapped lifts. These lifts are heavy, time consuming to deploy, carry only one passenger at a time, yet occupy the space of four formerly revenue-generating passenger seats and half a luggage compartment. Though necessary and state of the art for the high passenger decks of today's motor coaches, these lifts are expensive, maintenance-prone nightmares for coach operators.

from each other and from non-articulated buses, making driver training essential in using these buses over the road. The lower driver position inherent in low-floor configurations has not been a hindrance in the 20 years of low-floor highway driving experience at Lightrider (over a million miles).

To be sure, the view is a bit nicer from a high-decked coach, but is the sight of trees and interstate pavement worth the physical challenge that hinders stiff-jointed elder citizens from entry and egress? Improved passenger amenities in coaches, like state-of-the-art entertainment systems, are great, but do the aging 60 percent of coach travelers care more about woofers and tweeters than they do about getting on and off the bus?

Face the facts: Since the 1940s major design improvements have transformed our two- and three-lane roads into multilane, limited-access super highways; oil-dripping, smoke-belching engines are cleaner, longer running, much more powerful, and economical; four-speed unsynchronized manual transmissions have become multi-geared, computer operated, cruise-controlled automatics—like butter; bias-ply, low-mileage tires with inner tubes on split rims have given way to tubeless radials mounted on one-piece rims with onboard pressure and temperature sensing systems; drum and Jake brakes are being left behind by all-wheel disc brakes assisted by transmission retarders; even the heavy, bulky suitcase has become a lightweight duffel with ball-bearing wheels. Unchanged, however, is the basic motor coach design, seemingly locked in a time warp with the likes of the venerable GM PD4151 Silver Side, a post-World War II coach.

Testing is the next step. Lightrider's radius of operation, North America, ideally suits us to experiment with the use of an articulated low floor in a wide variety of travel situations. Overnight ferries to Newfoundland; small ferries (the ones we use to get to Brier Island off of Digby Neck in Nova Scotia); and campgrounds, county roads, strip-mall parking lots, to name a few. We'd be in and out of fast-food places, through many national parks and major cities; we'd climb mountains and cross deserts. We'd take a low-floor artic where no low-floor artic has gone before . . . Beam me up, Scotty. Sure, this may sound like science fiction, and it will be fiction, like all innovative ideas, until it is tried.

The motor coach travel industry, 40,000 coaches strong in the US alone, must demand that coach manufacturers design and build motor coaches that meet the ambulatory need of the increasing majority of our passengers. Articulated, low-floor engineering is here today; let's get it into service where it belongs—on the highway.

> A seven-year-old motor coach carrying 44 assisted-living-facility residents and nursing staff caught fire from an overheated wheel bearing on I-45 near Wilmer, TX, during the Hurricane Rita evacuation in 2005; 23 passengers died on that coach, while 21 others were injured. Emergency egress from motor coaches, wheel-bearing maintenance, and fire resistance of motor coach materials were among the factors mentioned by the National Transportation Safety Board in their Accident Report of 2007.

As Ned Einstein has stated in these pages, rather eloquently, "Our future is aging Baby Boomers staying alive for longer and longer periods of time, and whose lives we can make richer and more meaningful by transporting them safely from their dreary parlors and nursing homes to the venues of their remaining hopes and dreams . . . these passengers are our living."

LtR's GrayBarn was built in 2006 to accommodate an articulated, 60-foot low-floor: the Van Hool AG300; through much research, we'd determined it to be the best platform on which to create our LowRider.

But, as Van Hool would not sell us an AG300, God continued our pursuit of a specialty vehicle for seniors, which culminated in a redefinition of the motor coach that we call the H1213.

We believe that God gave us a bigger idea than the H1213 alone, an idea we call the **H1213 Project**, which became the center of LtR's Strategic Plan.

Strategic Plan for Succession and Sustained Growth of Lightrider Ministries

**THE LIGHTRIDER H1213 PROJECT
Revised 24 April 2016**

Executive Summary

Concept To expand our 27-year-old mobile retreat ministry into the most underserved people group in the US, seniors, we have envisioned a commercially viable, stepless vehicle that anyone can board. Lightrider Ministries will obtain, operate, and test this vehicle, the H1213. Then we create Lightrider, LLC, to purchase the rights to manufacture, market, and sell it, generating revenue to sustain, grow, and hire successors for Lightrider Ministries. The H1213 will be safe and affordable to own, operate, and maintain. Competitively priced, with durability measured in decades, 20–30 mpg fuel economy, and other unique features, the H1213 will *redefine the American motor coach.*

Manufacturing A prototype H1213, engineered by Bruce Emmons of Autokinetics, using his patented lightweight stainless steel structure, informed by Lightrider Ministries' combined 100 plus years' experience operating coaches, will be purchased by Lightrider Ministries. Following 50,000 miles of operation a refined, final design version will be manufactured by Autokinetics as a demonstration coach for Lightrider, LLC. Profit from sales of H1213's to be used to open a micro factory in Upland, IN. Purposely engineered to minimize capital investment in its manufacture and using a revolutionary concept in manufacturing, the H1213 will *redefine America manufacturing.*

Marketing and Sales The demo coach is to be driven on a 10,000-mile marketing expedition, showing it off to coach passengers and coach operators all over America. Locations where seniors travel (Branson, MO) and live (The Villages in Florida) will be key destinations. Passengers and tour directors, recognizing the unique, passenger-friendly features of the H1213, will become "marketers" of the H1213 as they demand that it be made available to them by the travel industry. A targeted, glossy mailing to the 3,954 North American coach operators, a feature article published in *National Bus Trader*, along with a year of advertisements in *NBT* and an internet presence will direct buyers to Lightrider LLC. With The Golden Rule as our guiding principle rather than maximizing profit, the H1213 will *redefine the way America does business.*

Serviceability and Parts A driver-friendly website will assist diagnosing problems in the field and direct users to truck or coach garages near locations where emergency service is needed. Excellent serviceability will endear the H1213 and its service needs to America's massive, 2.5 million–vehicle truck system (the 40,000-vehicle motor coach system may be used, too, if preferred). Lightrider, LLC, will stock, sell, and ship any proprietary parts that are unique to the H1213. Component manufacturers, through their sales outlets, will stock parts used in their components. Because of our lightweight design, many parts on the H1213 will be those used on Ford pickup trucks, available in over 6,000 NAPA stores. An exhaustive Bill of Materials listing components used in the H1213, with contact information for vendors of parts for those components, will accompany H1213 sales contracts. With the truck mechanic–friendly design and ready availability of less-expensive parts, the H1213 will *redefine American motor coach service.*

OVERVIEW OF THE H1213 PROJECT

For over 40 years we at Lightrider Ministries have been using motor coaches to take thousands of passengers in dozens of groups hundreds of thousands of miles on mobile retreats around North America. We've found that a great barrier, and hazard, to America's aging citizens that travel are steps—steps that have been removed by the ADA from all the places we go yet still exist within the very coaches Americans use to get to those places.

For the past 10 years Lightrider Ministries has been working to remove the barrier of steps on coaches by developing a universally accessible motor coach primarily for use with senior adults. We envision a 45-foot low-floor motor coach with a mechanized overhead luggage system. We call it the H1213 for Hebrews 12:13, "Make level paths for your feet, so that the lame may not be disabled, but rather healed."

Prime safety features of the H1213 are having four front tires; a rear emergency exit; unique shock-absorbing bumpers; an all-vehicle video monitoring system; three-point seat belts w/shoulder strap; fire-resistant double-wall stainless construction, and NO steps.

Other passenger-friendly features include an *accessible lavatory*; two entry doors with flip-out ramps; and WIFI, video, and USB outlets.

Features agreeable to the coach owner/operator are 20–30 mpg; an extremely strong, durable, lightweight cast and corrugated stainless steel structure; a crew rest compartment; and over 600 cu ft. of cargo space with mechanized luggage handling.

The driver will appreciate the maneuverability and all-weather traction afforded by the all-wheel drive design. A very powerful, quiet, diesel electric drive train will enable this coach to effortlessly climb mountains and maintain highway speeds. A digital passenger-counting system will assure that no one gets left behind.

This motor coach will be made in the USA using a new system for making products that will lead the way to bringing manufacturing back to America's shores.

CONCEPT: A NEW DIMENSION IN SENIOR MINISTRY

The elderly, the most underserved people group in the US, are the largest traveling group in the US; they have the time and the money to travel. For 27 years Lightrider Ministries has been successfully using travel time as ministry time for kids and younger adults on what we call mobile retreats. Now we want to conduct mobile retreats with seniors.

Redefining the Motor Coach See *NBT* August 2007 article reprinted on pages 145–149.

In Support of Due Diligence The following are comments from Thomas Crumm, a major contributor in focusing Lightrider's vision [More on Thomas in Appendix 2]: "I am a believer in extreme due diligence myself. When risking the funding of others you have to trust the team you engage. You have to expect that everything that could go wrong will go wrong and choose engineers with the determination and patience to see it through. There were big names in automotive engineering with proven track records in the latter half of the 20th century—names that the Big Three trusted for decades. People I considered outstanding in their ability to navigate high-investment engineering risks. Their names launched technical advances that risked great wealth. Those trusted names often relied on Bruce [Bruce Emmons, the engineer whose design will be the H1213—more on Bruce in Appendix 2] and his team, and others like them, to do the math and conduct the experiments for their ideas. Many things moved out of Bruce's lab and into production. Many more never made it. As time went on there were marketing, material supply, and other strategic reasons that some ideas never reached the market. The experiments still on the shelf in Bruce's lab reflect the breadth of Bruce's ability to do due diligence. Many new ideas fade because of changes in the market, competitor moves, or changes to material supply strategies.

If what Bruce is working on were already on the market it wouldn't be new. If Bruce were a rookie I would not be part of this. People deciding to invest in Bruce's coach-development expertise will have to decide to invest in Bruce. They will also have to invest in you [LtR] and your belief in the value of an ease of entry coach with overhead storage. They will also have to believe that what Bruce designs can be manufactured at an acceptable price and its quality can be assured.

Do I believe Bruce can do his part—yes. Do I believe I can manufacture this coach design—yes. Do I believe you when you say the design will be superior to other coaches—yes.

Expect investors to want to do due diligence, but know that the competition will dish new ideas and/or begin their own parallel development. Verification of design and processing begins the race to market. —Thomas A Crumm, industrial engineer, advisor to two GM Chairman, third-generation auto worker, and author of *What Is Good For General Motors? Solving America's Industrial Conundrum.*

REDEFINING AMERICAN MANUFACTURING

Massive unemployment, uninspiring jobs, offshore and lights-out manufacturing, a dismal economy; 2015, a perfect time to redefine manufacturing in the USA.

There exists in America a steadily growing need to re-shore manufacturing—bring the jobs, and the wealth, home. Manufacturing creates wealth. Gold in the ground is just dirt until someone mines and refines it. Sales spread wealth. Wealth must first be created before it may be spread.

Two factors have come to our attention during Lightrider's 10-year odyssey to find a senior-friendly vehicle with which to expand our ministry into the senior realm. Both came on the same day, at the same place, one factor from each of two men, in August 2013: Bruce Emmons, CEO of Autokinetics, with his revolutionary lightweight, electric, low-floor coach design, engineered to minimize capital investment in micro factories for its manufacture; and Thomas A. Crumm, author of the book *What is Good for General Motors?*, with his revolutionary manufacturing system envisioned to replace the assembly line.

Dovetail Bruce's micro-factory idea and simple yet profound design with Thomas's system and Lightrider's vision to manufacture our senior-friendly vehicle in Grant County, IN, along with our need to generate revenue . . . seems like a divine appointment to say the least.

The presence of several universities and trade schools in our area adds yet another dimension to this convergence of factors. Applying Thomas's world-changing manufacturing technique along with his expertise on world trade make for the creation of a brand-new business course—a course in which students could intern at the very factory using said technique. High school students in our area could earn "credits in escrow" at any of these higher-education schools while interning in summer jobs at the micro-factory. They might even graduate high school with the job skills to begin working without the need for college or trade school.

The micro-factory concept allows manufacturing to be gradually begun in existing, small start-up buildings without massive venture capital investment. It locates these factories close to where the products manufactured are to be used, allowing for future maintenance to happen at those same factories. Autokinetics will franchise these factories.

A huge aspect of Bruce's coach design allows for vehicles of varying lengths to be made, accommodating needs of a greater range of customers. We envision Bruce Emmons's micro-factory concept using Thomas A. Crumm's manufacturing technique of mobile workrooms moving through successive areas of stationary tooling and equipment, which allows a variety of products to be built within the same factory simultaneously. His technique, totally divorced from the inefficient assembly-line system, calls for small teams of skilled laborers building each vehicle. No need to retool between products or at the end of a model year. Highway coaches, city buses, airport shuttles, nursing home activity vehicles, motor homes, and RVs . . . the potential product lines are legion. And all could be built efficiently within the same factory simultaneously! Tom's book *What is Good for General Motors?* is a must-read to best understand the whys, wherefores, and wisdom behind this technique.

Because the H1213 is built of stainless steel, no paint is needed, nor is the expensive paint booth required in manufacturing virtually all other vehicles. Typically a paint booth uses 40 percent of the energy used to manufacture a vehicle. Graphics, if desired, may be wrapped instead of painted.

The micro factory has the potential to bring jobs and wealth creation to different parts of the country with relatively small investments.

SUSTAINING AND GROWING LIGHTRIDER MINISTRIES

Lightrider Ministries, like many nonprofits, has become convinced that to survive in the coming years, much less grow, we must generate a revenue stream by producing something. The H1213 seems to be that likely something for five main reasons:

1. Because of our decades of motor coach operation and mobile retreat experience, coupled with our 10 years of searching, Lightrider Ministries is ideally suited to inform the design of the H1213.
2. The H1213 is the senior-friendly vehicle that we need to get our senior ministry on the road.
3. We've discovered a new method of manufacturing that will enable us to get started building H1213s with minimum investment. In fact, the H1213 has been engineered to be built without the need for the traditional, very expensive, heavy machinery used in today's factories.
4. Several universities and trade schools located in our area could teach this new method, interning their students at our factory.
5. The county and state where we live want to attract manufacturing, and, having a manufacturing history, has skilled labor readily available.

Income from manufacturing and selling H1213s would generate the revenue to sustain Lightrider Ministries. It would also support our "planting" H1213s as ministry tools for other senior conscience outreaches to use in their efforts at reaching and serving seniors for Christ.

The following is the most recent detailed summary of the H1213:

The Lightrider H1213—A New Breed of Motor Coach A Universally Accessible, 45-foot, 50-Passenger, Low-Floor Motor Coach The H1213 is all about safety, accessibility, dependability, economy, serviceability, durability, and it has curb appeal. This is a later version of the H1213. A final design, developed in the future, will no doubt be a combination of these two.

UNIQUE FEATURES

Corrugated and Cast Stainless Steel Structure, super lightweight yet strong, durability measured in decades with no need for paint—graphics may be wrapped; Lightweight structure with an aerodynamic, smooth bottom contributes to greatly increased fuel economy.

Diesel Electric All-Wheel Drive greatly reduces exhaust emissions while increasing fuel economy; provides power for mechanized luggage handling, lighting, individual passenger needs, and operation of the **all-electric HVAC** without idling a main engine in this increasingly no-idle world (seniors are most sensitive to harsh cabin temperatures that often result at destinations with three-minute idle regulations).

Four-Axle Oleo Strut Suspension provides a smooth ride with adjustable height while reducing compressed air need; more rubber on the road providing better traction for motivation, braking, and steering; two tandem axles up front with four-wheel steering and two tandem axles at the rear prevent a single blowout from stranding the coach with elderly passengers for whom stranding is a hardship.

Entrance Ramps with Dual Handrails at each door eliminates steps, a barrier for 60 percent of America's coach ridership—the elderly—increasing coach use by this growing, underserved demographic, reducing per passenger cost, and increasing profits for coach operators while complying with new ADA requirements. Eliminating steps eliminates the number one cause of lawsuits, falling on steps; steps have been removed everywhere coaches go, why take them with you? No need for a wheelchair lift—mobility-challenged passengers roll right in and tie themselves down using a self-securement system. Driver may see to the luggage rather than having to assist exiting passengers.

Two Passenger Doors: Improved pace of entry and egress enhances safety by easing tight scheduling (today's high-deck coaches take 30 minutes just to unload and reload their elderly passengers); parking brake cutout prevents coach from moving while either door is open.

Emergency Exit Door, step-less, located just 11" above ground level in the one area of a coach historically undamaged in fatal motor coach accidents, the rear. Tragedies like the recent, fiery semi-truck/motor coach collision in California, which took 10 lives, will be greatly mitigated by this quick, universal exit system.

Crew Rest Compartment: The best hedge against driver fatigue, an almost universal factor in fatal coach accidents, is a second, rested, onboard driver; alleviates much of the expense of getting relief drivers positioned down the road to take the wheel from drivers when their hours of operation expire; provides a rest haven for drivers to nap during passenger activities.

Mechanized Over head Luggage System, electronically operated and supervised, luggage containers are presented curbside within one minute; locating the greater weight of people and seating below the lesser weight of their luggage lowers the H1213's center of gravity; greatly increasing vehicle stability; eliminates eight ground-level luggage compartment doors and the traffic-side luggage removal of typical motor coaches; Mechanization will reduce worker's comp claims.

Lavatory, ADA-accessible, vacuum operated w/ fresh-water flush, positive ventilation, and a door that seals—what happens in the lavatory stays in the lavatory. The semi circular sliding lavatory door is easily removable from outside the lavatory in the event of an occupant emergency. It also closes off the toilet area when the lavatory floor space is being used as an entryway for the aft passenger door during coach loading and unloading, or when rear emergency exit is needed.

Windows with a tilt-in panel at the top, allow ventilation while parked (w/out compromising security) or running down the road, regardless of the weather. **Made in the USA**, the H1213, a revolutionary motor coach design built using a revolutionary manufacturing system . . .

MOBILITY IS INDEPENDENCE– INDEPENDENCE IS PRICELESS

We at Lightrider ministries believe that He presented us with the energy, experience, and will to develop the ideas expressed above, connecting us with the right people to make the H1213 Project happen. We will continue to be available as long as He gives us strength, to share all that He has taught us, all that we've learned, with any who pick up that gauntlet, who are called to invest in redefining the motor coach, redefining the way America manufactures, and/or advancing His Kingdom through mobile retreat ministry. Please email Mike Manganello at mike@lightrider.org, contact us through our web-site www.lightrider.org, or snail mail at 168 South Second Street, Upland, IN, 46989.

THIRTY-TWO

Snapshots and Short Stories

The first six pages of this chapter are a copy of LtR's *Good News Gazette* referenced in Chapter 7 about Debbie's "Year of Miracles" from December 2022 to November 2023.

Good News Gazette
December 2022 to November 2023

Senior Men's Fellowship guy **Wayne Miller,** also a member of the **9th Street Gang Car Club** of **Fairmount, IN**, presents a gift check to **LtR** from that club following our 6 December 2022 SMF meeting. Two others of our  SMF, **Mark Kinnamen** & **Jim Riddle** are also with the 9th Street Gang. It's always fun to see which set of vintage wheels these men arrive in Tuesdays at 4pm for SMF.

Wayne Miller has been a wonderful visiting prayer warrior & friend to Debbie & me throughout her fight to survive & come back from the ongoing **Year of Miracles** which began 14 December 2022 when **Debbie Manganello** (aka Sweet Thing) took ill with what was to be diagnosed as Legionnaires' disease. Lightrider's entire year has been colored both by this life threatening malady's insidious course & the constant **God Sightings** happening almost daily as He intervened on her behalf. Family & friends became God's voice in essential encouragement & His hands in providing much needed help and support. **Dan Boyd** & his therapy dog **Bailey** were frequent, welcome visitors at all three locations at Ball Memorial in Muncie where Debbie was treated. She was one month in the ICU, three weeks in the Long Term Acute Care (LTAC) & later, after spending three months in residential physical therapy at Colonial Oaks in Marion & two months at home, 29 more days' in-patient at Ball following ileostomy reversal surgery.

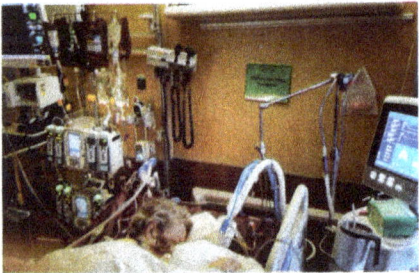

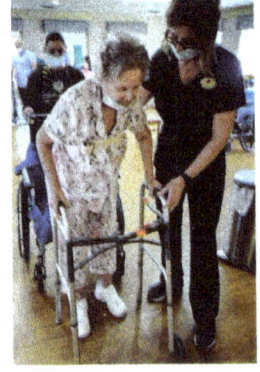

voice; a young nurse from Nigeria, upon hearing that Debbie had sung in church & on TV insisted that Debbie sing 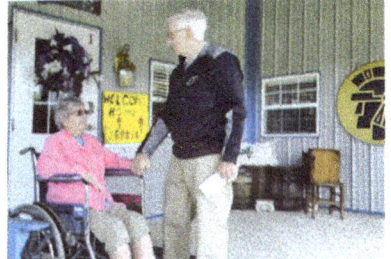 with her for Debbie's husband, choosing "Amazing Grace" for this extremely touching moment; the dozens of friends  and family who deluged us with visits, cards, prayers, even cash & gift cards to buy the gas for back & forth hospital runs, home care equipment, pay medical bills & such; the loving, expert care given by techs, nurses, physical therapists, ambulance drivers and transport staff; the  welcome back to Lightrider upon Debbie's first day being there to greet our senior guys, including the welcome banner made by a 10 year old neighbor of LtR's, **Miracle,** as well as one made by our 9 year old neighbor at home, **Myah**; our 15 year old grandson **Orrin**, while visiting from New Mexico with his mom, our daughter Danielle, volunteering to help out at LtR by building a half wall and railing for our Learning Loft (**Michael**, his dad, had well trained Orrin in carpentry let me tell you).

Taylor Universities' annual plunge once again proved invaluable to LtR's continuing work on our Learning Loft by varnishing Orrin's handiwork & adding furring strips to fill gaps in the rough cut lumber, salvaged from a lightning struck tree, donated by **Ward Turner** over a year ago.

Year of Miracles Highlights: God's mercies new every morning; eight family members from South Carolina journeying to Muncie, renting a house near Ball Memorial, &,  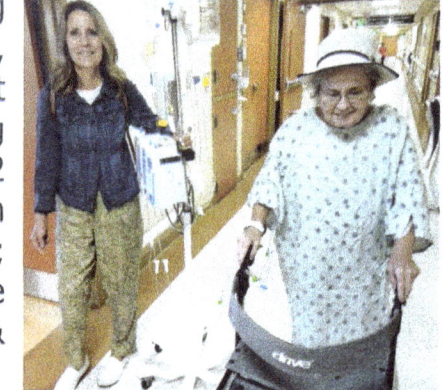 for the better part of a week, taking turns spending 12 hours a day with Debbie in the ICU; an alert nurse in the ICU spotting signs & symptoms prompting a 3am call to a surgeon, **Dr Brittany Kern,** who was able to perform a "best case scenario" removal of 3 feet of dying small intestines before it ruptured, while our daughter, **Danielle,** visiting from New Mexico, & I, waited in an empty waiting room; the 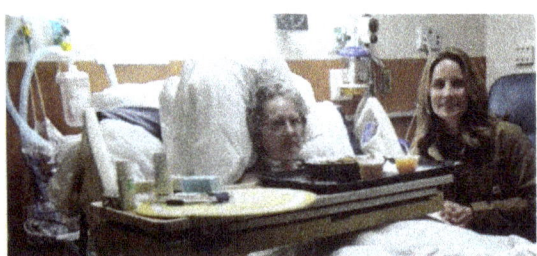 pulmonologist who diagnosed and supervised the treatment for the Legionnaires disease, **Dr**  **Natasha Dudiki** & **Dr Amit Shetty**, Debbie's LTAC doctor, begging Debbie to let them take her back to the ICU to show her "Miracle Self" off to the nurses & techs who God used to save Debbie's life (Debbie still remembers none of those ICU days 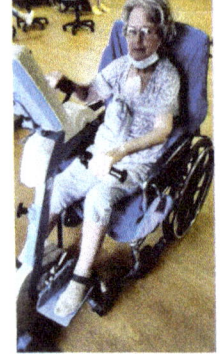 & nights, but was so touched by the outpouring of love from those ICU nurses and techs who were so delighted to see her smile & her pretty baby blues, to hear her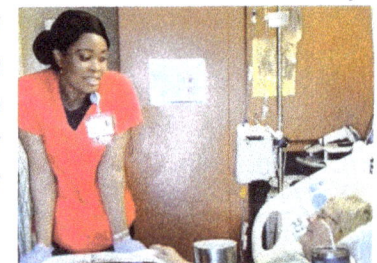

Keith Freer, another of our senior guys, a police officer & firefighter, spoke to SMF about our 2nd Amendment rights, which given these turbulent times gave all of us a lot to think about—after all, our families, and our Republic, are most certainly worth defending.

The **National Monument to the Forefathers**, Plymouth, MA, envisioned in 1820, 200 years after the **Pilgrims** arrived here, was erected in 1889. The replica pictured here, recent addition to the **GrayBarn's** "passive witness," is greatly enhancing Lightrider's active efforts to inform visitors about America's Biblical Heritage ("My people are destroyed for lack of knowledge" Hosea 4:6). Platform built by **Greg Miller**, a friend from **Upland Community Church (UCC)**. We've stocked & displayed tri-fold flyers that document the factual history of our Biblical Heritage memorialized by this largest granite monument in North America, this Biblical "stack of stones" if you will. **Kirk Cameron's** film, **"Monumental—In Search of America's National Treasure"** inspired us to obtain this replica, which had been commissioned by Kirk's outreach, **American Campfire Revival**. The "National Treasure" spoken about is " . . . the people, places, & principles that made America the freest, most prosperous & generous nation the world has ever known." These Biblical Principles, without which our Republic cannot long survive, must be revived!

Our **God & Country Forum**, suspended during much of our Year of Miracles, resumed 15 September, is now enjoying a video series **"Constitution Alive! A Citizen's Guide to the Constitution."** Billed as an "in-depth course on the original intent of the

Constitution recorded live at **Independence Hall**," this well documented presentation really captures the God fearing, Bible believing wisdom of those dedicated Americans who sought to preserve our God given freedom for themselves as well as for us, their posterity.

Tara Schwartz (Shellabarger), 1999 TU grad & basketball star, made a presentation at the GrayBarn introducing to Upland **Life Wise Academy**, an outreach that brings "Bible education for public school students during school hours." Life Wise Academy is a Gospel centered, character focused, local church driven, plug & play operation for the nation. Check 'em out at lifewiseacademy.org.

The **RedBarn Rally** really rocked the neighborhood for three evenings this

week! 6 kids had their names entered into the **Lamb's Book of Life** while 15 plus rededicated their hearts to Christ. A couple of the guys asked for Bibles, one even asked for a Bible for his mom. Seems 3 of the lads want to be baptized right soon, too. **Zeb Nelson**, senior at **IWU, Campus Life**

Director at **Marion High School**, & **Matt Owlett,** our own youth guy at UCC, were each tapped by **God** as key note speakers to sow seeds, harvest souls & inspire many still clinging to the growing cultural darkness shadowing our beloved America. Praise be to God & many thanks to Zeb & Matt as well as to **Troy & Liz Shockey** with the host of volunteers who supported His effort at reaching the lost at this year's RedBarn Rally.

Alayna Rolling, a sometime RedBarn volunteer & intern at UCC, won a grant from the **Ball Brothers Foundation** to purchase a pottery wheel for the RedBarn pottery studio. This wheel was a replacement & enhancement as unlike the wheel it replaced it is capable of operating in either a clockwise or counterclockwise direction. Thus left handed potters find parity with right handers when plying this art at the RedBarn. Thank you Alayna

As **2023** draws to a finish, with Debbie getting a bit better each day, we are mindful of & grateful to God for seeing us through this, the start of our **36th** year in His service & the end of our Year of Miracles. His hand has been much in evidence during this year's scary miles of miracles, miles in life rather than highway miles to be sure, though my Ford's put on a few of those, too, commuting to Debbie's various medically mandated whereabouts . . .

We are mindful, too, that His provision for our operation has come through the prayers & generous hands of many of y'all, **Thank you!** This 36th year, like each of the 35 before it, will continue to depend upon His provision. Please continue your partnership with Him in LtR's support through your prayers & gifts. Or, if newly acquainted with LtR, please consider beginning such partnership. And don't forget, **Pray for peace in Jerusalem!**

Stay the Fight; Keep the Faith,

Jesus is Real & Relevant

LtR co-founders getting roughed up in a rodeo at Lone Tree Bible Ranch, Capitan, NM. This is a great camp: horseback riding, archery, repelling, shooting, camping out under the stars, hiking, and such. Aboard the LtR en route home after a week at Lone Tree with kids from Toledo Christian School, many of them declared the highlight of their adventure was time together on the LtR.

Another group of Girl Scouts that had spent the night aboard the *Queen Mary* in Long Beach, CA. Note the conning tower of a Russian submarine and the two guys scouting for girls: Rich Coolman on the left and Micah Langmaack.

Kari Manganello (left) and Marsha Becker in Jerusalem on one of two LtR retreats to Israel.

Arlena Wood in her electric conveyance in the Jerusalem marketplace. We were always glad that we could get this courageous lady from Anderson, Indiana's North Side Church of God all over the place.

Debbie Manganello in Jerusalem—note the street name above: the Via Doloroso, the road Jesus walked to Calvary.

Debbie striking a pose at the north end of the Golden Gate Bridge, the north tower shrouded in fog: "The morning fog may chill the air, I don't care, My love waits there in San Francisco . . ." Once when visiting from Okinawa as teenagers, my twin brother, Steve, and I were walking the Golden Gate with our twin cousins, Don and Dave. The towers were both shrouded in fog. I remarked, "They're outta sight," getting seriously chided by our cousins—my Okinawa-dwelling self unfamiliar with stateside slang.

RedBarn kids with Troy and Liz on a LtR excursion to the Creation Museum, an outreach of Ken Ham's Answers in Genesis, in Petersburg, KY. A sister attraction, The Ark Encounter, located a bit farther away in Williamstown, shares the slogan "Prepare to Believe."

Many years ago, Taylor student Doug Laskowski, presently a missionary in Southeast Asia, organized two LtR loads of TU students to visit the Creation Museum, a strong advocate for Young Earth Creation. Doug had also invited me to a forum being held in a student lounge in Morris Hall to speak about America being a Republic, not a democracy (see Chapters 26 and 33, as well as Appendix 1).

Lightrider staff at the popular Tennessee attraction Dixie Stampede. Left to right: Vinnie Manganello, Mike Manganello, Kevin Webb, and Micah Langmaack; front: Debbie Manganello. Always grateful to God for legions of volunteers that staffed LtR retreats.

Lowe's in Marion, IN, sold us building materials and appliances at cost. Photo circa 2006. Allen Goff and daughter Dawn did the finish work in the GrayBarn Parlor.

Debbie Manganello, aka Sweet Thing, with a very happy homeless guy in Gettysburg, PA. Debbie usually packed scads of bag lunches to give to homeless folks we'd encounter while in New York City. This time she had been bummed to have left NYC with a single lunch still in hand.

When arriving at Bus Parking in Gettysburg National Park the next morning, I spotted this fella foraging in a dumpster, got on the PA, and gave Debbie a heads-up. She rushed downstairs and outside with her remaining lunch, which she blessed this fella with along with a big hug—and a brand-new garbage bag to replace the holey one he was using.

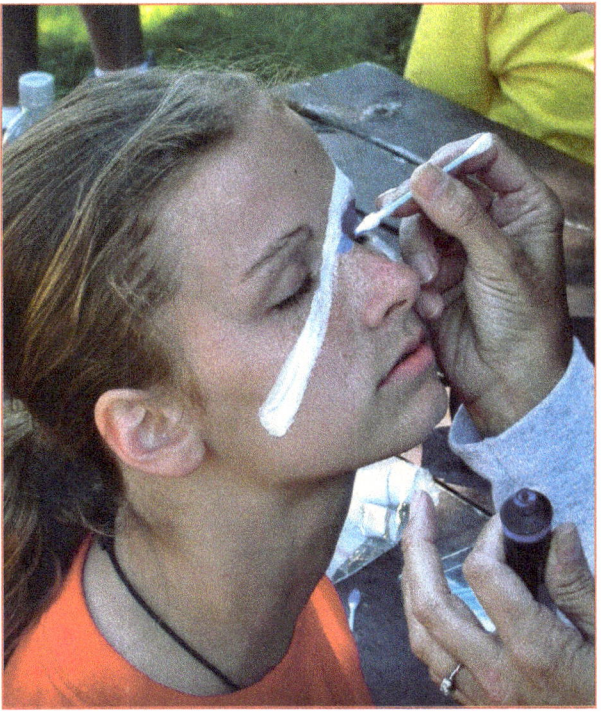

This young lady with North Side Baptist, Indy, getting made up for a wordless, evangelical play, *Freedom*, written by Colin Harbinson, to be performed in each of three Canadian cities, Halifax, Quebec, and Montreal. My wife, Debbie, led Peggy, a homeless lady in Halifax, to Christ after one performance, keeping in touch with her for several years after. Rusty Kennedy, the youth pastor, along with his wife, Michele, and Big John Hilficker were the energy behind the production.

Sometime later God spoke to Rusty, at about 3 a.m. one morning. Rusty was awakened with the thought that he was supposed to leave North Side Baptist Church. Shortly after, Michele woke up and said to Rusty, "God wants you to leave North Side." So the Kennedys left North Side. Then Rusty started a group of people who desire to help others through life. Named Leavener, this group has met at Pinheads, a bowling alley in Fishers, IN, since 2008. LtR has had the privilege of fellowshipping with Leavener on many a mobile retreat, doing hurricane relief, or building relationships with their youth.

The original Lightrider amid fall colors on the Taylor University campus following years and miles after the speed bump with the vertical clearance mentioned in Chapter 6 and the addition of our new livery in Chapter 12. Air spring noted in the following photo is just visible too.

A major engineering feature of the Neoplan AN122, not available on other coaches, is the full coach-width location of the air springs (air bags) on the drive axle that greatly enhance vehicle handling.

Thomas Smoak and family in the GrayBarn under the parachute God used to save his father's life.

The last surviving member of the Doolittle Raiders, Lieutenant Colonel Dick Cole, taken at the 75th Anniversary of the Doolittle Raid celebrated at Wright-Patterson Air Force Base in 2017. Cole had been Doolittle's co-pilot.

Lightrider had taken 50 interested people down for the celebration, including an Upland son and World War II vet, Louis "Bounce" Benedict, along with the two Taylor students, Rachel Pfeiffer and Hope Bolinger, who were writing his book *The Calm and the Storm*. Their professor, Donna Downs, came too.

We had met Bounce at LtR's long-running Saturday at the Barn Blue Grass & Gospel event hosted by fiddle-playing Gary Friesen, son-in-law of Chuck Holsinger, also a World War II vet and member of our Senior Men's Fellowship. Gary Felton at the town's barbershop had clued us in about Bounce's growing up in Upland. We learned of Bounce's incomplete memoirs so connected him with Donna and the girls.

Studmuffin Bob Walker aboard the MV *Viking Serenade* en route to Ensenada with a group from Kokomo. At the first lifeboat drill, we found our life jackets in a closet in our stateroom. The jackets had the name *Stardancer* stenciled on them. This ship had been the MV *Stardancer* in which we'd cruised back from Alaska during my days at Wheels (see Chapter 30).

Mike Crafts baptizes a Lenawee Christian School senior in the ocean off Clearwater, Florida, on one of dozens of senior-class retreats with that school.

Debbie Manganello, still eating, poses in front of the *Peking*, a four-masted windjammer moored at South Street Seaport in New York City.

Youth pastor Allen Mercer assists Jessica Boatwright framing a wall on a short-term mission retreat with Upland Evangelical Mennonite Church. Allen's father-in-law, Larry Winterholter, attends LtR's Senior Men's Fellowship.

Co-founders Mike and Bob at work slinging hash in a Rhode Island church kitchen on an early LtR mobile retreat with Christ Presbyterian Church of Nashville, TN. In Providence, RI, doing mission work with Habitat for Humanity, our project house was next door to a drug house doing active sales—we even witnessed a gunfight there.

Glacier National Park in Montana was a popular stop en route to Alaska via a cruise out of Seattle, WA, or Vancouver, BC, and/or to the Canadian Rockies. The Lightrider was too long a vehicle to take the Going to the Sun Road up to the Logan Pass, the Continental Divide and highest point on this scenic drive, so we had to hire the smaller, red 1936 White Motor Company Model 706 tour bus pictured here.

Phillip Kroeker waits with other LtR's to board the white tour bus with the rollback canvas top.

Pulling the grade up to Logan Pass, these wonderful vehicles carry 16 passengers and sport four doors on the passenger side, one on the driver side (originally had eight doors but was modified for safety).

Heraldry on the grill evidenced the $7 million restoration of the Glacier Park fleet of White Motor Company Model 706s in the early 2000s by the Ford Motor Company.

Tom and Cathy Jones's Pioneer Associates company retreat with LtR to Lake Fork, Texas; the guy claiming that handsome catch was actually asleep, line in the water, when that wide mouth bit. A co-worker saw the pole bend, grabbed it, parting the line; the fish (with float) headed away, right into the path of another of our group's boats; aboard that boat, a third co-worker grabbed the passing float and landed that big sucker—an assisted catch if ever there was!

White tour bus back-seaters: Micah Langmaack at the window with Tom and Cathy Jones with cap and visor.

Fueling the Lightrider at Hemmings Motor News in Bennington, VT, with volunteer driver Dave Russell at the hose. We had stayed at Camp Meade in Middlesex the night before, and Dave had shared seriously at devotions around the campfire. He had spent time checking out the very old cemetery on the camp grounds, and had been moved by a stone with the just-visible name Ben Dover, a doctor . . .

Camp Meade with a group from Oak Chapel—at least three generations of Pearsons and that Lightrider couple, the Clesters.

View from the Rocky Balboa steps at the Philadelphia Museum of Art, with Philly's City Hall in the distance; notice Micah, Mike, and Sweet Thing looking back toward the steps. In Philly we often met up with our good buddy Tony Proto who we would introduce to our group as Tony Rizzo, then-mayor of Philadelphia. Our subterfuge was once overheard by passing Jewish ladies who insisted on getting their pictures taken with the mayor—Tony happily obliged.

Tony was one of the Three Bears, a trio of fun Taylor students living in the Wheels trailer in Upland: Tony Proto, Dick Becker, and Scott "Froggy" Hughes. Scott went on to become a sheriff in Jackson, WY, where he scared the heebie-jeebies outta Phil Summerville by pulling over the Possum. Phil opened the bus door and Scott, in uniform, asked, "Are the Manganellos on board?"

Lightrider Staff in the LtR office suite on Washington Street, Upland, provided by Doc Oliver, retired flight surgeon, circa 1994. Left to right: Candace and Bob Walker, Debbie and Mike Manganello, and Steve Kuhn.

Notice the pigeonholes in the background, a system built by Don Clark, his wife, Yvonne (aka Yolanda), serving as our bookkeeper, with a pigeonhole for travel literature from each of the 50 US states, 10 provinces, and three territories of Canada—seems primitive in today's internet and AI age, as does the heavy, laminated trucker's atlas we used prior to GPS. LtR's eight-minute VHS cassette describing our ministry, created by Barry Pavesi, formerly of ABC *Monday Night Football*, along with a few TU students, shows me using an adding machine to calculate mileage being found by finger on such atlas, along with an IBM Selectric typewriter being used for correspondence—we have come a long way, Ba-Baby!

An aside: According to US Navy sailors aboard "Old Ironsides", a popular LtR stop when in Boston, the term "pigeonhole" originated from square holes in capstans aboard tall ships in the age of sail. Pigeons would nest in those square holes. When weighing anchor or raising sail, square-ended, capstan bars would be thrust into those holes, making a (literally) bloody mess out of the hapless pigeons. These holes were painted red as camouflage, mitigating the sight of such.

LtR's longest-running administrative assistant, Cheryl Ziegler, with daughter Katie in office daycare at our new office circa 2005.

Snapshots and Short Stories

Dear friend Tom Provost, college roommate and high-school chum from Kubasaki High School, Okinawa, with wife Linda and me, your author, the wide body on the right.

Kids from St. John Flatrock, Monroeville, IN, Class of 2006, horsing around with one big gun at the US Naval Museum, Washington, DC. These grounds and the building in the background served as the headquarters of NCIS in the popular television series.

LtR Staffer Rich Coolman doing his pig-pen imitation . . . When bus maintenance was needed OTR, Rich really got into his work.

John Wain, an actor from Legends in Concert, at the Chocolate Factory outside of Las Vegas, with co-founder Bob Walker. Portraying John Wayne, John went upstairs in the LtR to share his testimony with the "Odds & Ends"—our faithful travelers from Hessen Cassel, IN.

A favorite stop when traveling to Branson: Lambert's Café, Home of Throwed Rolls, in Ozark, MO.

Gloucester Fisherman's Memorial, Gloucester, Massachusetts.

"Odds & Ends" dining out near the Grand Canyon. Those are the folding picnic tables we used when preparing meals OTR. Maryland Sorg, leader of the "Odds & Ends," is on the right, with Bob Walker, mooching food as usual.

Cooking at New Smyrna Beach, chatting with a local guy; Mark Cosgrove, LtR board member, doing the dishes.

Serendipity at New Smyrna Beach, FL, with kids from North Suburban E Free, Deerfield, MI. The bagpiper was getting pumped for a funeral at which he was to play.

New Smyrna Beach is a safe, secure town with a wonderful beach, bathhouses, and such, ideal for LtR and Wheels. Notice the bucket of water by the front door. We learned this trick from our Taylor friend Tom Beers, former Marine: barefoot kids would rinse the sand from their feet by dunking them in the bucket, while kids with shoes would use a whisk broom, which really cut down on sand in the coach.

Lightrider's AK '94 group aboard the Royal Caribbean MV *Nordic Prince*: a mixed bag of Mike's extended family members, Ken and Barb Lawson, Dave and Linda Lawson, Mike's Aunt Thelma with husband Walt, Debbie's mom, Arlena Wood and friends, and local friends like Jessie and Carol Rush, and Paul and Betty Turner.

A LtR retreat post-1995 stopped at Glacier National Park in Wyoming—Cousins Ken and Barb Lawson with the famous little red White Model 706 roll-top tour buses.

Possum One pulling into Wandering Wheels' BikeBarn circa 1973.

The latest LtR pulling into LtR's BusBarn circa 2017, a 44-year upgrade in mobile retreat equipment.

LtR Campus seen from the air (drone shot compliments of Vinne Manganello).

LtR Campus circa 2017; notice LtR's Miracle bus on the far left being stripped of useful parts and equipment prior to being scrapped, as it had fallen victim to extremely corrosive ice-abatement chemicals being used on Indiana highways.

Notice double robins' nest over Vinnie's right shoulder.

Marquee showing our national motto on our latest LtR. Notice the circle of 13 stars around a cross; a part of LtR's livery signifying that Christian values were the center of our Republic at the very get-go when the USA was 13 states strong.

Banner that hung on the side of LtR's GrayBarn in 2017, part of our celebration of God's 30 years of faithfulness.

Another drone shot of our Van Hool TD925 Astromega Double Decker in LtR livery standing in the GrayBarn's east driveway; notice the full-length glass roof with two escape hatches; notice, too, the Upland water tower with the black panther, logo of East Brook High School.

THIRTY-THREE

Adventures in Christian Fellowship— Five Takeaways

You've read this far, spent a few hours sojourning with me, getting to know a bit about me, my heart and perspective, and I thank you for that.

In our experience at Wheels and LtR, we've considered such hours sojourning together, fellowshipping aboard a special coach, or reading about such, to be "earning the right to share."

Once again we interrupt our narrative with sad, shocking news: Charlie Kirk was assassinated just four days ago. Kirk's friend Gary Hamrick of Cornerstone Chapel, Leesburg, VA, sharing from his heart this 14th day of September 2025, heard by me online, was indeed profound. Gary mentioned Proverbs 17:24 and went on to say: "Kirk had biblical views which shaped his political views which challenged cultural views." Hamrick asked the question of his congregation, "Do you love people enough to tell them the truth?" He quoted Denzel Washington, now a pastor: "Some people will never like you because your spirit irritates their demons." Hamrick was clear to not make any man an idol but to use their example to lead you to a deeper walk with Christ.

It seemed to me, from the few clips I'd seen, that Charlie Kirk lived out my life verse, 1 Peter 3:15 (see Chapter 14). When asked what he believed, he was prepared to tell the seeker or scoffer just that, and he did so with gentleness and respect. God willing, Kirk's ministry, Turning Point USA, while maintaining the 1 Peter 3:15 formula, will continue the essential work for which it has become known.

As Paul asked his friends, recorded in Galatians 4:16 (ESV), and as I now ask you the reader: "Have I then become your enemy by telling you the truth?" I pray not!

Resuming the narrative, I now share five takeaways from our verbal sojourn:

First, the most important thing I have to share is that the same God that has protected, provided for, and led me millions of miles with thousands of people wishes to know you, the reader, on a personal level. My prayer is that if you have not yet entered into such a relationship with God, the God of the Bible, Jesus Christ, that you make it a priority to do so. (*See note at the end of this chapter.*)

Second: We as a nation *trust in the God of the Bible*.

Third: We have a *republican form of government*.

Fourth: *The family*, the first of three institutions ordained by God, is of paramount importance. The breakup of the American family, acknowledged by President Bill Clinton to me in person, as recorded in Appendix 1, the number one problem facing the American people, must be reversed. As the number one building block of the second and third institutions ordained by God, the Church, and government, restoration of the biblical family is imperative. Healing our Republic by healing existing families and creating new ones was Charlie Kirk's message to herds of young people.

Fifth: As observed in Chapter 26, the only real hope for America is REVIVAL—revival of, in the hearts of Americans, faith in our Lord and Savior Jesus Christ. This is not a call to theocracy! Rather it is a call to heal the Church in America as well as the biblically inspired republican government established by our founders to secure our God-given rights. This, too, was a part of Charlie Kirk's message.

Understanding the second and third may have escaped you, the reader, if educated in America's school system that has, along with the American family, been in steep decline since 1962. Being aware of all five is critical if one is to well carry his or her load as an American citizen and/or a Christian.

As previously mentioned, "In God We Trust" is much more than a motto or slogan; it was the creed of the seed of this great nation—it is the American way of life. A wonderful, if lengthy list of historical happenings supporting the fact of our Republic's dependence upon God and His Word has been recorded in Appendix 1.

We were warned back in 1793 by Alexander Hamilton: "Foreign influence is truly the Grecian horse to a republic. We cannot be too careful to exclude its influence." Yet in 2009 the US Supreme Court was using foreign law as precedent in determining US law while the Obama administration seemed to be forcing us to adopt a European style of socialism . . . Sounds to me like that Grecian horse had found a home in Washington.

Ron Paul, six years prior to running for president in 2008, said: "We have allowed our constitutional republic to deteriorate into a virtually unchecked direct democracy. Today's political process is nothing more than a street fight between various groups seeking to vote themselves other people's money. Individual voters tend to support the candidate that promises them the most federal loot in whatever form, rather than the candidate who will uphold the rule of law."

Teddy Roosevelt noted: "The Roman Republic fell, not because of the ambitions of Caesar or Augustus, but because it had already long ceased to be in any real sense a republic at all. When the sturdy Roman plebeian, who lived by his own labor, who voted without reward according to his own convictions, and who with his fellows formed in war the terrible Roman legion, had been changed into an idle creature who craved nothing in life save the gratification of a thirst for vapid excitement, who was fed by the state, and who directly or indirectly sold his vote to the highest bidder, then the end of the republic was at hand and nothing could save it. The laws were the same as they had been, but the people behind the laws had changed, and so the laws counted for nothing."

When the sturdy American patriot goes the way of the sturdy Roman plebeian, then the end of our Republic will be at hand.

Now think about America as you read this second scenario written in today's vernacular by William Federer: "Rome fell 4 September 476 AD. It was overrun with illegal immigrants. Visigoths, Franks, Anglos, Saxons, Ostrogoths, Burgundians, Lombards, Jutes, and Vandals, who at first assimilated and worked as servants, but then came so fast they did not learn the Latin language or the Roman form of government. Highly trained Roman Legions moving rapidly on their advanced road system were strained fighting conflicts wordwide. Rome had a trade deficit, having outsourced most of its grain production in North Africa, and when vandals captured that area, Rome did not have the resources to retaliate. Attila the Hun was committing terrorist attacks. The city of Rome was on welfare, with citizens being given free bread. One Roman commented: 'Those who live at the expense of the public funds are more numerous than those who provide them.' Tax collectors were 'more terrible than the enemy.' Gladiators provided violent entertainment in the Coliseum. There was injustice in courts, exposure of unwanted infants, infidelity, immorality, and perverted bathhouses. Fifth-century historian Salvian wrote: 'O Roman people be ashamed . . . Let nobody think otherwise, the vices of our bad lives have alone conquered us.'"

Might we, the American People, be similarly ashamed? We ought to be!

Let's conclude this chapter and this book with a word of encouragement and a thought or two from a great American who had a personal relationship with Christ, who recognized our need as a nation to trust in God and knew that America is indeed a Republic, Abraham Lincoln.

In his Inaugural Address on 4 March 1861, Lincoln encouraged the nation, saying in part: "Intelligence, patriotism, Christianity, and a firm reliance on Him who has never yet forsaken this favored land, are still competent to adjust in the best way all our present difficulties."[6] I submit that the same is true this day.

Lincoln's pastor, Dr. Phineas Gurley of the New York Avenue Presbyterian Church, Washington, DC, affirmed that "the death of Willie Lincoln in 1862 and the visit to Gettysburg battlefield in 1863 finally led Lincoln to personal faith in Christ."[7]

Speaker of the House of Representatives Schuyler Colfax, at a memorial service for Lincoln on 24 April 1865, stated ". . . that the last act of Congress ever signed by him was one requiring that the motto, in which he sincerely believed, 'In God We Trust,' should hereafter be inscribed upon all our national coin."[8]

---

[6] Federer, William J. *America's God & Country Encyclopedia of Quotations*, 1994, page 378. Used with Permission.
[7] Ibid, page 383.
[8] Ibid, page 392.

In a letter of condolence dated 21 November 1864 to Lydia Bixby of Boston, who had lost five sons in the Civil War, Lincoln said, "I cannot refrain from tendering to you the consolation that may be found in the thanks of the Republic they died to save."[9]

Gettysburg was a favorite destination on many of our mobile retreats at Wheels and Lightrider both. Gene Haney's American History class from Heritage High School in Monroeville, IN, went there many times. Perhaps more impacting for Lincoln than us, such visits were nonetheless profound, moving, and inspiring for our groups. We would stand on the very place from which Lincoln delivered his famous Gettysburg Address.

Steve and Carrie Kuhn, Mike and Brian Carter with a field piece at the Eternal Light Peace Memorial at Gettysburg National Military Park, with the Lightrider with field kitchen in the background.

Gettysburg Address

Four score and seven years ago our fathers brought forth on this continent, a new nation, conceived in Liberty, and dedicated to the proposition that all men are created equal.

Now we are engaged in a great civil war, testing whether that nation or any nation so conceived and so dedicated, can long endure. We are met on a great battle-field of that war. We have come to dedicate a portion of that field, as a final resting place for those who here gave their lives that that nation might live. It is altogether fitting and proper that we should do this.

But, in a larger sense, we cannot dedicate—we cannot consecrate—we cannot hallow—this ground. The brave men, living and dead, who struggled here, have consecrated it, far above our poor power to add or detract. The world will little note, nor long remember what we say here, but it can never forget what they did here. It is for us the living, rather, to be dedicated here to the unfinished work which they who fought here have thus far so nobly advanced. It is rather for us to be here dedicated to the great task remaining before us—that from these honored dead we take increased devotion to that cause for which they gave the last full measure of devotion—that we here highly resolve that these dead shall not have died in vain—that this nation, under God, shall have a new birth of freedom—and that government of the people, by the people, for the people, shall not perish from the earth.

---

[9] Ibid, page 389.

Always remember that in America we the people are Caesar, "In God We Trust" is our standard, and our Republic is His master plan to secure our God-given, unalienable rights.

God Bless America. And may He bless you too as your adventures in life continue, hopefully by His side: "The Lord bless you and keep you; The Lord make His face shine on you, and be gracious to you; The Lord lift up His countenance on you, and give you peace." (Numbers 6:24–26 NASB)

Stay the Fight. Keep the Faith.
Mike Manganello

Note: The beginning of my personal relationship with God happened in a small chapel in the training area of Fort Knox, KY: "He [Reverend Lackey] walked me down 'the Roman Road,' convinced me that I, my patriotic American, churchgoing, Eagle Scout self, like everyone else, was a sinner, had fallen short of the Glory of God, and led me to the Throne, there to invite Christ into my heart. I had found Jesus!" (See Chapter 14.) I had been born again.

> According to Noah Webster's 1828 *American Dictionary of the English Language*, "unalienable" is pronounced *una'lienable* and defined as "not alienable; that cannot be alienated; that may not be transferred; as unalienable rights."

> The Roman Road:
> - All have sinned and fall short of the glory of God (Romans 3:23);
> - The wages of sin is [eternal] death (Romans 6:23);
> - The free gift of God is eternal life in Christ Jesus our Lord (Romans 6:23b);
> - Confess with your mouth that Jesus is Lord and believe in your heart that God raised Him from the dead (Romans 10:9).

BORN AGAIN

You don't need to be with anyone, or you may choose to ask a friend or pastor to join you. In prayer, acknowledge that you have sinned, that you wish Him to forgive you, that you want Him to enter your life as Lord. You may or may not feel joy or a surge of happiness or relief, but as promised, Christ will have sent the Holy Spirit to dwell within you—you will have been born again (see John 3:3). As I shared in Chapter 14, those feelings came to me on the bus going into Fort Knox the evening prior to my praying with Pastor Lackey, the evening when I made my decision to earnestly seek Him.

Understanding that our one God exists in three persons—God the Father, God the Son, and God the Holy Spirit—may be confusing. Jay Kesler once likened this Trinity of God's character to water. Water exists in three different states: liquid, gas (steam), or solid (ice)—each of which is still H_2O.

If I may digress once again, yesterday (1 July 2025), Jay Kesler's sweet wife, Janie, began walking the "streets of gold." She will be greatly missed. Please be in prayer for her wonderful husband, Jay, as he continues his sojourn, solo, and her wonderful family, as well.

Making your conversion known to friends is an important part of creating accountability for your reborn self! Find a Bible-believing and -teaching Christ-centered church and get with it on the oars! Spend a little time each day in prayer and in His Word. Look for Him to bless you with a life verse while bringing you in touch with those who may mentor you in your new faith.

Get baptized. (Because of my work at Wandering Wheels, I was never in town when baptisms were held. Though it was seven years after my rebirth before I managed to get baptized, and it happened in the Jordan River in Israel, which was a special blessing.)

Christianity is not an individual lifestyle—it is a family thing, "not forsaking our own assembling together, as is the habit of some, but encouraging one another; and all the more as you see the day drawing near" (Hebrews 10:25 NASB).

Belonging to a church, the body of Christ, is an essential part of being a Christian. Jesus said, "I am the vine, you are the branches . . ." (John 15:5 NASB). If one cuts themselves off from the source of nourishment and growth, the vine, then they will wither and die. All Christians need the fellowship of believers.

Remember, as shared earlier in this narrative, that it takes two things to defeat the evil one: the blood of the Lamb (that is, Christ's death on the Cross, His atonement for the sins of all of mankind) and the testimony of the saints, believers, in whose ranks your reborn self is now a soldier.

You, like Paul, will need courage, when asked (see 1 Peter 3:15) to share your testimony, which will grow as you learn to apply your growing faith into every aspect of your life. "Ignorance is the seedbed of fear . . . truth is the cure for ignorance."[10] ". . . know the truth and the truth will make you free" (John 8:32 NASB).

One way that I chose to get my testimony out there was to write letters to the editor, taking the name of Christ into the public square. From time to time, such letters got pushback, but seemed like to me it was folks likely in darkness asking me about my faith, so more letters from me went out. One such, published on or about 16 February 1998 in the *Chronicle Tribune*, Marion, IN, under the headline "Can't have faith without works," follows:

In reference to Marian Thompson's letter about not liking letters with expressions of religious faith: Expecting people who are serious about their faith to express their views on other subjects without reference to their faith is like expecting a preacher to give a sermon without a Bible. For people of faith, their faith colors every aspect of their life, or their faith gets very little use.

Saying that God intended us to think, but that applying the Bible to our thinking may only happen in church, is leaving God out of most of life.

Can that be what He intended?

As morals are the purview of religion, leaving religion out of the public dialogue is to leave morals out of the public square.

Bryon Cannon's views are decidedly secular, and stated with the weight of his position as news editor. Is it not reasonable to allow people of a more biblical perspective to think about and respond to his ideas? After all, they pay just as much for the paper as everyone else.

If articles of a religious perspective are annoying to someone, there's a simple solution. Don't read them; just like Don Elliot doesn't read Bryon Cannon [Don was a good friend and member of CBMC].

---

[10] Beckman, Red. *Born Again Republic*, Freedom Church, page 96.

LtR board meeting in our new building circa 1998. From left to right: Jeff Evans, Dick Becker, Steve Manganello, Mark Cosgrove, Jerry Cline, Leonard Fisher, and Allen Goff.

Expecting the paper to carry only articles void of perspectives different from your own is to write the paper yourself.

A last thought: Christianity lived out in every aspect of one's life is not a religion—it's a relationship.

For more info contact following:
Dr David Jeremiah www.DavidJeremiah.org/Saved

Or

Lightrider Ministries www.lightrider.org

Lightrider's Board of Directors, past and present, men and women, each having answered the call of the LtR board to serve this essential duty, remembered from past to present: co-founders Mike Manganello (Taylor U Distinguished Friend 1990) and Bob Walker (Taylor U '80), Tom Gearhart (Taylor U '80), Oris Reece (Taylor U '60) (deceased), Bill Thompson (deceased), Ron Keller (employed by Taylor U on or about 1973–2008) (deceased), Chip Wehling (Taylor U '73), Jim Mathis (Taylor U '64), Wayne Dalland (Taylor U '78), Yvonne Clark, "Big Pete" Wilbur Carlson (Taylor U '67) (deceased), Jerry Cline (deceased), Kelly Koons (Taylor U '82), Jim Walker (deceased), Leonard Fisher (Taylor U '84), Mark Cosgrove (Taylor Prof 1990–2023), Bob Jackson (Taylor U '59) (deceased), Tom Lathers (Taylor U '80), Barry Pavesi, Jeff Evans (Taylor U '80), Allen Goff, Dick Becker (Taylor U '72), Darren Campbell, Larry Lemke (Taylor U '71), Steve Manganello (Taylor '70), Paul Turner (deceased), Ron Wolf, Karyl Wolf, Jay Kesler (Taylor U '58; President 1985–2000), Eric Turner (Taylor U '74), Bob Wright, Mattie Wright, Ken Strickland, Sherri Strickland, Jonathan Secrest, Steve Brinkerhoff (Taylor U '95).

Lightrider's Mission Statement: Lightrider proclaims the message of Jesus Christ, encourages individual faith in Christ, and strengthens Christian relationships through fellowship.

Lightrider's Doctrinal Statement: Lightrider is a non-denominational Christian fellowship ministry. The Bible is the Word of God. Jesus Christ is who He said He is, the Son of God. Christ died for the salvation of all people, young or old, and desires to know each of us on a personal level. If we accept Him in faith, He stands ready to care for us as mortals and to usher us into God's presence for eternity. As Ambassadors of Christ we are to share His love with the world. As Christians, it is essential that we maintain close bonds with the body of Christ, the Church, sharing the burdens and benefits of that body. We trust His Spirit to guide and direct all areas of our lives.

APPENDIX ONE

House Resolutions 397 and 443; NAE Insight Briefings '94 and '96; Scripture, Quotes, and General Facts With Regard to America's Biblical Heritage

A large portion of my adventures in Christian fellowship has brought me in contact with so many places, people, books, monuments, and memorials evidencing our Republic's biblical roots that failure to include such in this tale about those adventures would be to fail God Himself who arranged those contacts.

Realizing that the sheer volume of information about such heritage could likely induce slumber, boredom, or worse, offense in the minds and hearts of you, the reader, it seemed prudent to perform, if you will, a "lateral arabesque," not to diminish the importance of such, but to allow this narrative to reach conclusion without such an academic overload interrupting our admittedly already meandering style.

Sidetracking, as it were, this discussion of biblical heritage to this appendix will allow a bit of editorial license though an effort to throttle back my verbosity and whining will be attempted.

While God is the author of America's biblical heritage, the Church has been His primary instrument in establishing and encouraging such heritage. Public schools and universities had been His scribe, recording while teaching about this heritage up until 1963 when we allowed the Bible, "the Rock upon which our Republic rests,"[11] the very foundation of our heritage, to be removed from the former.

What follows is factual information gleaned primarily from my travels with Wheels and LtR

---

[11] President Andrew Jackson, a Democrat, in his Farewell Address, 1837.

around our magnificent Republic. I sincerely hope that you take the time to peruse it, perhaps with your kids and grands—it's a wonderful, bipartisan, American history lesson.

Republic! What a great-sounding word! "Republic . . . it means people can live free, talk free, go or come, buy or sell, be drunk or sober, however they choose." (John Wayne playing Davy Crockett in *The Alamo*, released in 1960)

On 4 April 2023, Lieutenant Colonel (Retired) Allen West stated on *Victory News*, "First and foremost, this is not a democracy, we have a constitutional republic, which means we are supposed to respect and regard individual rights, freedoms and liberties, and our rule of law."

In fact, our founders reviled democracy. Ben Franklin said, "Democracy is two wolves and a lamb voting on what's for lunch. Liberty is a well-armed lamb contesting that vote."

Thomas Pain said: "Democracy is the vilest form of government that there is." (Red Beckman, *Democracy Vs Republic*, as quoted on Facebook, 2 July 2025)

John Adams was more to the point: "[D]emocracy never lasts long. It soon wastes, exhausts, and murders itself. Democracy will soon degenerate into an anarchy, such an anarchy that every man will do what is right in his own eyes and no man's life or property or reputation or liberty will be secure . . ."

James Madison said, "Democracies have ever been spectacles of turbulence and contention; have ever been found incompatible with personal security, or the rights of property; and have, in general, been as short in their lives as they have been violent in their deaths."

The word *democracy* does not appear in the Declaration, the US Constitution, or in the constitutions of the 50 states.

The following is further support of the fact of America being a republic, downloaded directly from CONGRESS.GOV. Said Norman Thomas, who ran for president in 1928: "The difference between Democrats and Republicans is: Democrats have accepted some ideas of Socialism cheerfully, while Republicans have accepted them reluctantly. Yet the main negative factors in the national life today, according to spokesperson for this country's largest political party, are corporate greed, tax cuts for the rich, and poverty-stricken old folk crying out for life-saving medications. Plainly we need still more socialism. Don't worry, we'll get it." This statement was made in 1962 but sounds a whole lot like the talk coming out of the mouth of Democrat Zohran Mamdani, who was elected mayor of New York City in 2025.

Benjamin Franklin stated in a letter to the French Ministry in March of 1778: "Whoever shall introduce into public affairs the principles of primitive Christianity will change the face of the world." He also stated, "A Bible and a newspaper in every house, a good school in every district—all studied and appreciated as they merit—are the principle support of virtue,

> The term *lateral arabesque* is borrowed from The Peter Principle, suggesting the sidetracking without prejudice in this case, not of a loyal but ineffective employee, but of a large body of information not crucial to reaching our narrative's end. This principle is laid out in *The Peter Principle: Why Things Always Go Wrong*, by LJ Peter and R Hall, 1969, a favorite textbook of mine in college.

morality and civil liberty."[12] Perhaps most of the Fourth Estate and our public schools possessed a bit more integrity in Franklin's day than do they in 2025 . . .

A bit of levity from Federer: "As an ambassador of the United States, Benjamin Franklin was at a dinner of foreign dignitaries in Versailles. The minister of Great Britain proposed a toast to King George III, likening him to the sun. The French minister, in like kind, proposed a toast to King Louis XVI, comparing him with the moon. Benjamin Franklin stood up and toasted: 'George Washington, Commander of the American armies, who, like Joshua of old, commanded the sun and the moon to stand still, and they obeyed him.'"[13]

Visiting Independence Hall and the Liberty Bell in Philadelphia were favorite stops on Possum and Lightrider retreats. The following account about the spiritual state of affairs at the Constitutional Convention held at Independence Hall was also taken from Federer's book:[14]

On Thursday, June 28, 1787, Benjamin Franklin, delivered a powerful speech to the Constitutional Convention, which was embroiled in a bitter debate over how each state was to be represented in the new government. The hostile feelings, created by the smaller states being pitted against the larger states, was [sic] so bitter that some of the delegates actually left the Convention.

Benjamin Franklin, being the President (Governor) of Pennsylvania, hosted the rest of the 55 delegates attending the Convention. Being the senior member of the convention at 81 years of age, he commanded the respect of all present, and, as recorded by James Madison's detailed records, he rose to speak in this moment of crisis:

"Mr. President:

"The small progress we have made after four- or five-weeks close attendance and continual reasonings with each other—our different sentiments on almost every question, several of the last producing as many noes as ayes, is methinks a melancholy proof of the imperfection of the Human Understanding.

"We indeed seem to feel our own want of political wisdom, since we have been running about in search of it. We have gone back to ancient history for models of government, and examined the different forms of those Republics which, having been formed with their own seeds of dissolution, now no longer exist. And we have viewed Modern States all round Europe, but found none of their Constitutions suitable to our circumstances.

"In this situation of this Assembly, groping as it were in the dark to find political truth, and scarce able to distinguish it when presented to us, how has it happened, Sir, that we have not hitherto once thought of humbly applying to the Father of lights to illuminate our understanding?

"In the beginning of the Contest with G. Britain, when we were sensible of danger, we had daily prayer in this room for Divine protection—our prayers, Sir, were heard, and they were graciously answered. All of us who were engaged in the struggle must have observed frequent instances of superintending Providence in our favor.

---

[12] Federer (op cit), page 246. Used with Permission.
[13] Ibid, page 250.
[14] Ibid, pages 247–49.

"To that kind Providence, we owe this happy opportunity of consulting in peace on the means of establishing our future national felicity. And have we now forgotten that powerful Friend? Or do we imagine we no longer need His assistance?

"I have lived, sir, a long time, and the longer I live, the more convincing proofs I see of this truth—that God Governs in the affairs of men. And if a sparrow cannot fall to the ground without His notice, is it probable that an empire can rise without His aid?

"We have been assured, Sir, in the Sacred Writings, that 'except the Lord build the House, they labor in vain that build it.' I firmly believe this; and I also believe that without His concurring aid we shall succeed in this political building no better than the Builders of Babel: We shall be divided by our partial local interest; our projects will be confounded, and we ourselves shall become a reproach and bye word down to future ages.

"And what is worse, mankind may hereafter from this unfortunate instance, despair of establishing Governments by Human wisdom and leave it to chance, war and conquest.

"I therefore beg leave to move—that henceforth prayers imploring the assistance of Heaven, and its blessing on our deliberations, be held in this Assembly every morning before we proceed to business, and that one or more of the clergy of this city be requested to officiate in that service."

The response of the convention to this speech of Benjamin Franklin was reported by Jonathan Dayton, the delegate from New Jersey: "[The] Doctor sat down; and never did I behold a countenance at once so dignified and delighted as was that of Washington at the close of the address; nor were the members of the convention generally less affected. The words of the venerable Franklin fell upon our ears with a weight and authority, even greater than we may suppose an oracle to have had in a Roman senate!" [This eyewitness account of the visual impact of Franklin's call to prayer upon Washington and the others seems to me to be quite telling.]

Following Franklin's historical address, James Madison moved, seconded by Roger Sherman of Connecticut, that Dr. Franklin's appeal for prayer be enacted. Edmund Jennings Randolph of Virginia further moved: "that a sermon be preached at the request of the convention on the 4th of July, the anniversary of Independence, and thenceforward prayers be used in ye Convention every morning." [Of note is the fact that prayers have opened both houses of Congress ever since.]

The clergy of the city responded to this request and effected a profound change in the convention when they reconvened on July 2, 1787, as noted in Jonathan Dayton's records: "We assembled again; and . . . every unfriendly feeling had been expelled and a spirit of conciliation had been cultivated."

Would that such felicity might again overtake our political process!

Now let's jump into the third of the five important facts mentioned in Chapter 33, the knowledge and understanding of which is essential to all Americans: that this great, God-blessed nation is a constitutional republic, not a democracy.

America's "birth certificate," our *Declaration of Independence*, states: "We hold these truths to be self-evident, that all men are created equal, that they are endowed by their Creator with certain unalienable Rights, that among these are Life, Liberty and the pursuit of Happiness. That to secure these rights, governments are instituted among men . . ."

Instituting a government to secure our God-given rights, America's founders had five forms of government to choose from, a political spectrum ranging from left to right, 100 percent government to 0 percent government: Dictatorship, the rule of one; Oligarchy, the rule of a few; Democracy, the rule of the majority; Republic, the rule of law; or Anarchy, nobody's in charge. By the grace of God, they chose Republic.

Article 4, Section 4 of the United States Constitution asserts: "The United States shall guarantee to every State in this Union a Republican Form of Government . . ." So what is a Republic? The word comes from two Latin words: *res* meaning "thing" and *publica* meaning "public"—that is PUBLIC THING, the LAW. The Greeks said, "Without law there can be no freedom."

In a republic, the sovereignty is in each individual person (as confirmed via Duck.ai on 8 August 2025). Said John Adams: "There is no good government but what is republican . . . They define a republic to be a government of laws, and not of men."

Daniel Webster, one of the greatest orators in American history, who served as a US Congressman, US Senator, and Secretary of State under three presidents, stated: "Hold on my friends, to the Constitution and to the Republic for which it stands. Miracles do not cluster and what has happened once in 6000 years may not happen again. Hold on to the Constitution, for if the American Constitution should fail, there will be anarchy throughout the world."

Said Thomas Jefferson: "It is the manners and spirit of a people which preserve a republic in vigor. Degeneracy in these is a canker which soon eats to the heart of its laws and constitution."

The *Military Training Manual* Number 2000–25, published by the War Department on 30 November 1928, said of a republic: "Avoids the dangerous extreme of either tyranny or mobocracy; A greater number of citizens and extent of territory may be brought within its compass; Results in statesmanship, liberty, reason, justice, contentment and progress."

That same manual said of democracy: "A government of the masses; Authority derived through mass meetings . . . Results in mobocracy; Attitude toward property is communistic . . . Attitude toward law is that the will of the majority shall regulate . . . Results in demagoguism, license, agitation, discontent, anarchy."

This manual was withdrawn without explanation about the time Franklin Roosevelt ordered private ownership of US-minted gold coins illegal in 1933. "The military training manual TM 2000-25 was officially withdrawn from circulation in the early 1930s, specifically under orders from President Franklin D Roosevelt. The exact date of its removal is not clearly documented, but it is generally understood that the withdrawal occurred around 1933. The reasons for its withdrawal are not entirely clear, but it is believed that the manual contained material

> Pursuit of happiness is a legal term defined by Blackstone as: "Freedom to obey God as we are led."[15]

---

[15] My knowledge of this definition was gained in 1996. Attempts to verify it have been fruitless, but other facts previously believed seem to elude both ChatGPT and Duck.ai as well.

that some lawmakers found controversial." (Duck.ai, 17 June 2025)

My thought in church Sunday, 26 October 2014, was this: Silence at the pulpit keeps the sheep relying upon a corrupted media. We need help to make righteous choices. Is abortion not murder? Is homosexual marriage not a justification of the wicked (see Proverbs 17:15 NASB)? We need to be equipped to represent Christ as citizens.

THREE BIBLICAL PERSPECTIVES CONCERNING CULTURAL CORRUPTION IN AMERICA AND RELATED THOUGHTS

1. "An evil doer listens to wicked lips; a liar pays attention to a destructive tongue." (Proverbs 17:4 NASB)
2. "He who justifies the wicked and he who condemns the righteous, both alike are an abomination to God." (Proverbs 17:15 NASB)
3. "He who says to the wicked, 'You are righteous,' peoples will curse him, nations will abhor him; but to those who rebuke the wicked will be delight, and a good blessing will come upon them." (Proverbs 24: 24–25 NASB)
4. "The Good News, not breaking news, must set our attitude." (John Sagherian, YFC friend of Jay Kesler)
5. "Ignorance never settles a question." (From a fortune cookie received April 2025 at the Oriental Pearl, Gas City, IN)

The LGBTQI+ crowd and the rabid leftists characterized by Linda Bowles, my favorite columnist of the 1990s, who left her very effective work to care for an ailing husband: "Two basic reasons underlie the attempt to separate America from its spiritual roots. First, the liberal goal of state socialism is incompatible with a citizenry who look to themselves and to God, rather than the state, for the satisfaction of their needs. Socialism requires that citizens do obeisance to the state as the Source from which all blessings flow. The supreme State can have no other God before it. The second reason for outlawing religion derives from the lobbying of those who wish their sins declared virtues. They seek the validation of the law, in the futile belief that the legal right to be wrong makes wrong right." (*Conservative Chronicle*, October 1999)

The church is under a full-scale political attack. Ought we not organize a political defense? "First they came for the Socialists, and I did not speak out—because I was not a Socialist. Then they came for the Trade Unionists, and I did not speak out—because I was not a Trade Unionist. Then they came for the Jews, and I did not speak out—because I was not a Jew. Then they came for me—and there was no one left to speak for me." Martin Niemöller's point was "that Germans—in particular . . . the leaders of the Protestant churches—had been complicit through their silence in the Nazi imprisonment, persecution, and murder of millions of people."

Is there any part of our lives for which Christ does not care? Is not the Church responsible to help stop the bleeding? Some 65 million innocent, defenseless Americans have been brutally slain in the wake of a political process for which we the people are politically responsible. Some 31 million (worldwide) have died of AIDS, while another 36 million are infected. Abortion and homosexual conduct have killed more people than all the 20th-century atheists combined. Is this issue not yet big enough to earn the attention of the Church? Does logic not apply here?

Politics is policy—and policy is the grease that enables evil, or good, to prosper in our Republic. Policy is made permanent when it is written into our constitutions. Even then it must be carefully monitored and enforced else the jackals of evil purloin it in the dark of night—look at how our US Constitution is abused. What better watchdog for the government that He installed to secure His gifts of life, liberty, and property than His Church that He also installed?

"The church must take right ground with regard to politics," said Charles Finney. "The time has come for Christians to vote for honest men, and take consistent ground in politics or the Lord will curse them. God cannot sustain this free and blessed country, which we love and pray for, unless the Church will take right ground. Politics are a part of a religion in such a country as this, and Christians must do their duty to their country as a part of their duty to God . . . God will bless or curse this nation according to the course Christians take in politics."

NOTES: THE 1994 NAE INSIGHT BRIEFING, WASHINGTON, DC

In Washington, DC, with the National Association of Evangelicals (NAE) back in 1994, God presented me the opportunity to ask, in person, a question of then-President Bill Clinton. We were gathered in the Old Executive Office Building (renamed the Eisenhower Executive Office Building in 1999) adjacent to the White House. President Clinton was taking questions from our group, and he called on me. I stood, identified myself, and said where I was from, then asked, "Mr. President, in your opinion, what is the greatest problem facing the American people, and what do you intend to do about it?" He worried his lip for a moment or two while thinking, then responded, "[The] breakup of the family, working place, and community are the big ones facing the American people, but there is nothing I can do about them." At least he correctly identified the problems.

Sadly, President Clinton, frequently shown by the media, Bible in hand, attending church, evidently had not been schooled about our vital role as ambassadors of Christ to be salt and light in our community.

My copious notes taken at that NAE insight briefing, on 24–27 April 1994, attended with my then-pastor, Jerry Cline, of the UEMC (now UCC), contain several glimpses of God, if you will—insights into the Christian fabric of American leadership gleaned from remarks made by a variety of America's leaders. As the purpose of this writing is to thank and glorify God, it seems appropriate to include a few of said glimpses, evidence of His grace, as well as personal, historic glimpses of our America through the eyes of some of our leaders at that time.

This 1994 NAE Briefing had been held in the Senate Caucus Room where the *Titanic* investigation (Teapot Dome Scandal, Watergate, and Iran-Contra hearings) had previously been held.

Dick Halverson, former pastor of the Hollywood Presbyterian, then-Chaplin of the US Senate, said he "has a good congregation." He remarked, as he reminded us that the upcoming 5 May was the National Day of Prayer, that "[the] single greatest reason for the failures in America today is the failure of God's people to pray."

Dan Coats, then-US Senator from Indiana, being the next speaker, said when Halverson had asked him if he minded waiting, "I will learn much more from your speaking than you will from mine." Humility was certainly in bloom in DC those long-ago April days.

Coats began by saying, among other things, that evangelicals can make a difference; Congress can change laws, not hearts; and that we need to re-establish the authority of the family, Church, education, and community.

I did get to ask him the same question as I had President Clinton about the greatest problem facing the American people. Coats's response: "The breakdown in moral authority."

Don Nickels, then-US Senator from Oklahoma, an evangelical Catholic, said, "God rewarded Israel when it had righteous leaders and punished Israel when it had evil leaders."

Reverend Tim Crater, a member of the NAE staff, said that "[e]vidence is broad and deep that ours is a Christian nation." He then pointed out that the US Capitol is a shrine to the Christian faith; that we have a burden to keep alive the knowledge of our Christian heritage; and that the US was once overwhelmingly run by Christians. This was the nudge that encouraged me, 10 years later, in 2014, to present David Barton's "American Heritage" series at UCC's Sunday school if permitted. Permission was denied.

Guy Vander Jagt, member of Congress from Michigan (1966–1993), now a lobbyist for the law firm of Baker Hostetler, said: "We've not only turned our backs on God, we've expelled Him. RMS *Titanic* needed to change direction, so do we. The bands were playing, people were sleeping, and danger was not perceived." He then quoted from the New American Standard Bible: ". . . when he came to himself" referencing the Prodigal Son. "America needs to come to itself—we are not really bad, just adrift like the Prodigal."

He continued: "It's not complicated, it's simple—'Jesus loves me this I know, for the Bible tells me so.'" This made me curious because at that time much public pressure was being put to help out Bosnia rather than any of the other 75, as I had heard, national conflicts. I asked him why Bosnia in the face of the 75 wars, per Paul Harvey, presently being waged? He said, "It was the 123 wars per Jimmy Carter last week, and the reason for Bosnia was the media. We as a people are led around by the nose by the media."

Vander Jagt told a story about a congressman from North Carolina with the initials LH being on a junket to Europe on a Sunday. No provision had been made to worship. He begged his colleagues to make time for a service among them. They finally agreed, putting together a very multi-denominational time together, keeping some European bigwigs waiting. But all agreed that it had been a real blessing.

When that congressman was asked why he had been so adamant about having a service, he said it was to keep his Sunday church-attendance record perfect, as it had been for 57 years. His dying mother had attended church with him for 10 years and had asked him to keep up her record as long as he could.

Remembering this story as I wrote today, 9 May 2025, reminds me of how much Sunday, the Christian Sabbath, was culturally respected in the USA during my growing-up years. But upon my return to CONUS, following my discharge from the Army in September 1973, I clearly remember observing a distinct waning of that respect. Most retail stores around my new home, Upland, IN, were now open for business on Sunday.

Orin Hatch, US Senator from Utah (Republican), was proud of the Religious Restoration Act of 16 November 93, which he co-sponsored with Senator Edward Kennedy with whom he disagrees on 98 percent of all things. The religious harassment clause warns to be concerned about federal election standards. Said Hatch: "Washington would foul up a two-car funeral; proclaim the Gospel; we have got to get the message out, we have got to get involved in Politics; America is the last bastion of freedom. We're in danger of losing our liberty if we don't all stand up now!"

Paul Weyrich, National Empowerment TV Network, said: "The biggest national problem—disintegration of our culture." My thought on hearing this was that we at LtR are fighting the most critical battle, bar none, facing this nation: the disintegration of the culture.

Weyrich continued: "DC [is] more void of truth than at any time in my 28 years in it; we are created in the image of God, God is trinity, trinity is community, hence family is essential; in America we have made I, god; no question we are at war, a spiritual war. No one sends men into war without training. We need to train our people if we are to fight effectively." My thought: the Church being on the front line of that war ought to at least be providing that training!

Phil Gosten, Clinton's Deputy Assistant for Public Policy, fielded my question: "Daniel Webster said, 'What ever makes a man a good Christian also makes him a good citizen.' Is that true?" Gosten agreed.

Carroll Campbell, then-Republican governor of South Carolina, started with a joke: A little boy asks his dad, "Do men really start out and end up as dust?" "Yes," replied the dad. "Why do you ask?" "Well," the boy said, "I looked under my bed and there's somebody coming or going."

Campbell followed with another joke: A preacher delivered a sermon highlighting all the virtues of a good husband, then challenged any to stand who exemplified these qualities. One man stood, finally, and the preacher said: "You don't have these virtues." And the man replied, "I'm standing up for my wife's first husband."

Then Campbell got serious, saying much, the following being just a few points he made: "We in America have traded a do-good attitude for a feel-good attitude; when Washington promises me something, I hold on to my wallet; keep dollars in the hands of families—they raise kids, government cannot; we have a pluralistic nation, but still have a consensus on what's right and wrong." Later, at the '96 NAE briefing, Robert Woodson, Sr., founder and president of the National Center for Neighborhood Enterprise, remarked of DC: "Others came to clean up this cesspool, special interests appeared, and now it's a hot tub."

In October 1993 there was that tragic incident known as Blackhawk Down. Campbell commented on it: "Those boys in Somalia weren't overrun and killed. They ran out of ammo, surrendered, and were murdered. They asked for armor, and their commander asked Colin Powell in the US, he asked the Sec Def [then Les Aspin] and the request was refused."

Some of Campbell's concluding remarks, made after quoting Timothy, include "Fight the good fight" and "You can't win if you don't fight; balanced budget and line-item veto [are] necessary for the Executive." Condensing 75 agencies in South Carolina down to 17, he said, "A job is the best welfare program going; parents should be first teachers; we have abandoned our foundation." Speaking in general about government lottery, he stated: "Gambling is fool's gold. It looks great at first, but the increased revenue causes people to lose jobs, go on welfare, and revenue is then spent, it's a vicious circle with in the long run diminishing returns."

George Weigel, President of the Ethics and Public Policy Center, a Catholic, spoke of evangelical Protestants and Catholics coming together, creating a document titled *The Christian Mission in the Third Millennium*,

> In 2010, San Antonio pastor John Hagee said, "Symbolism without substance, ritual without righteousness, Hot Tub Christianity—designed to make you feel good without being good."

dated 29 March 1994. It raised the issue of the environment: conservation under Teddy Roosevelt simply means good Christian stewardship; Earth Day, beginnings of government regulations; and Environmentalism, a religion.

Weigel also observed that, since 20 January 1973, a bird in a national forest has more legal protection than does an unborn baby.

You know, as I write today, 9 May 2025, about these comments of our Republic's leaders from that NAE briefing in 1994, how very remarkably relevant they still seem.

NOTES FROM THE 1996 NAE BRIEFING

Lloyd Ogilvie, also a former pastor of Hollywood Presbyterian, then-Chaplain of the US Senate, also spoke to us at the 1996 NAE Insight Briefing in DC. He said that he had been introduced in Darien, CT, by a woman. She had said, "The man you are about to meet will change your life. He will motivate, stimulate, and encourage you—love you. He will cause your life, a river, to stop flowing and start again in another direction. His name, Jesus Christ, and here to tell you about him is Lloyd Ogilvie."

Ogilvie went on to say: Separation of church and state, yes, but not God and state; Sovereign Lord, God, or Master were terms most frequently used in the prayers of our early citizens—they wanted God to rule them in person; they did not want a king. His duty as Chaplain of the US Senate was to bring the sovereignty, judgment, and strength of God into the public leadership arena.

> I recall seeing a TV report on the first Earth Day. A gaggle of clueless college kids buried an internal combustion engine—a six-cylinder Ford engine, as I recall. Then they all, oblivious to their hypocrisy, jumped into their cars and drove away.

He warned of the danger of deifying politics just as we're teaching our leaders that politics isn't the answer. A thought of mine while at this 1996 NAE Briefing: "I hate politics but we should be thankful for it—just look at countries that don't have politics."

Steve Largent, US Congressman (R-OK), former wide receiver for the Seattle Seahawks and member of the budget committee, began his talk saying: "On a visit to DC in a taxi, seeing the dozens of government office buildings and thousands of offices, I asked the cabby, 'How many people work in DC?' 'About half, came the reply.'"

The highlight of Largent's week was a four-hour fellowship, accountability, and prayer meeting with four of his colleagues.

A senior member recommended that he, Largent, as a freshman, change his vote on a particular bill (they have an hour to change their vote after casting it) if he expected to be reelected in 1996. He replied, "I wasn't sent here to be reelected." The senior member went back in and changed his vote.

Largent's three most important decisions were made in his sophomore year in high school: 1) Salvation decision. 2) Stay in football, leading to Seahawks. 3) Taking Latin II (he can't speak Latin but met his wife in that class).

First Corinthians 13 tells us that it is not enough to be right, that we must love, too. Largent is representing Jesus Christ everywhere he goes. His motive in everything must be love! He is an ambassador for Christ.

Largent authored the Parental Rights and Responsibilities Act (HR 96), which has 130 co-sponsors. It defines, for federal purposes, marriage as one man and one woman; that same-sex marriage is wrong, but that we must love those that disagree: tough on the idea, but love the people.

Largent said that we need to apply a moral solution to a moral problem. Compassion means to suffer with you. No government employee is doing that. The Church does. The root problem is moral. We can't legislate an answer, the Church can help.

Robert Woodson Sr., founder and president of the National Center for Neighborhood Enterprise, a black guy, said that he was raised to believe "that any black not a Baptist had been messed with." Primary problem with blacks isn't race, it's grace. He parted company with the Civil Rights Movement when it left Jesus behind. (I thought that this guy was great, I could not keep up with him.)

Woodson desires to empower low-income Americans. He holds an award from the Family Research Council. He complemented our list of speakers.

Woodson went on to say that the value of a society is determined by how they treat the least of their citizens. "If you keep doing what you're doing, you'll keep getting what you've got!"

He noted that the poor have the reverse problem of the Prodigal Son—who had money and family and no character. When no one would give to him, he found himself. What if his dad had given him money at the barn before contrition?

Woodson said that "80 percent of the cost of the war on poverty went not to the poor, but to the poverty industry—$5.3 trillion in the last 30 years." African proverb: "When bull elephants fight, the grass always loses." We need to get the left and the right together.

Woodson shared about Freddy Garcia, a missionary in San Antonio, who said, "Send me your rejects, addicts, and thieves, and I'll get them to Jesus." He spent $50 per person per day, with 80 percent success, whereas government spent $600 per person per day, with 6 percent success. Government tried to shut down Freddy's 75 clinics because his people weren't certified—the issue of certification being synonymous with qualification, which is not always the case. With brain surgeons, there is correlation of certification and qualification.

Woodson went on to say: "Our priority is moral and spiritual reconciliation. Racial reconciliation could happen, but problems would still be here—we are in a moral freefall. If our problems were economic, God would have sent an economist; if our problems were educational, God would have sent an educator; our problems were sin—He sent a savior."

Tom Coburn (a Republican from Oklahoma, freshman congressman, and medical doctor), on this day 23 April 1996, had just returned to DC from Oklahoma where he had spent the weekend delivering six babies. He remarked that he had delivered over 3,000 babies, 40 percent of those to unmarried teens. The best medical advice you can give a teen who has said that they will be sexually active is to abstain! Why are we giving less than our best medical advice to kids? The problem is not abortion—it is unintended pregnancy!

Coburn said that he had not come to Congress to abdicate his convictions. He came because the USA is headed in the wrong direction. Nothing but Christ and medical teaching would influence him in Congress.

Coburn started the family caucus—the largest in Congress, with over 80 members—to revive Judeo-Christian values and is working to: guarantee religious freedom; promote abstinence; eliminate federal funding to Planned Parenthood; promote parents' rights; end doctor-assisted suicide; and confront the dishonest abortion lobby who rationalize one moral mistake with another.

Freshmen in Congress, according to Coburn, have been greatly emboldened by prayer support. We must pray.

John Ashcroft (US Senator, Republican, Missouri) welcomed us to DC, thanking us for coming to choose: life or death; blessings or curse; Jesus or Barabbas. Praying America back to God is a great challenge. We cannot legislate America back to God. Biblical duty of government: punishment of evildoers, praise of good people. Faith in government is governmentalism.

Ashcroft went on to say that we have exchanged discipline for debt, decency for decay, and welfare for work. Remedy for the Republic—he quoted Humpty Dumpty: "Humpty Dumpty sat on the wall, Humpty Dumpty had a great fall, all the king's horses and all the king's men could not put Humpty together again." Government can't do it! Unleash the culture and the Church—government programs provide single-digit percentages of success, at ten times the cost of private efforts with 80 percent success rates. He quoted Mark Twain: "Nothing is quite as embarrassing as a good example."

Jon Christensen (Congressman, Republican, Nebraska, a freshman) said that we cannot change the laws until we change the hearts—and is working on changing the hearts across the aisle (no implication intended that Democrats are not Christians). We need to be about changing hearts for Christ. He has decided to pray for opponents, and says that the best way to tear down walls of partisanship is to raise up friendship.

Christensen's last remark reminded me of Republican President Reagan's legendary friendship with Democrat Speaker of the House Tip O'Neal—often fiery disagreement all day, ceasing at 5 p.m.

Cal Thomas, internationally known columnist, greeted our gathering with: "Welcome fellow, former fetuses. Aren't we glad that our parents were pro-life!" He said that "the Bible is the most banned and least consulted book. You can have God's approval or man's, but not both." He also quoted Chuck Colson: "The Kingdom of God will not arrive on Air Force One, no matter who's on board."

Thomas stated that "our problems are not economic and political, but are moral and spiritual" (which in my mind are both decidedly Church issues). "Revival is all that is left for us. Why is God used as a last resort instead of a first resource?"

On the floor on the evening of 22 April 1996, US House of Representatives Congressman Todd Tiahrt (Republican from Kansas) and his wife shared their testimonies. He said that it's a spiritual battle, therefore the Church's business. Judiciary pursues technicalities instead of justice.

Tiahrt said that America is having a crisis of the soul. Government can't help. Solution of integrity starts in our heart. Integrity, discerning right from wrong, acting on what's right, telling others what you are doing. What's right isn't necessarily what's popular. You can't make right choices with wrong information. Therefore the Church must stand up in the face of corrupted media. We ought to pray for each elected leader in our chain of command—pray for a return of our system to integrity.

Tim Crater, NAE Staff, toured with us in the US Capitol Building, Statuary Hall, and the Rotunda, pointing out 18 specific paintings, quotes, statues, and such commemorating events, Godly men and women, examples of

America's Christian and biblical heritage. So many of the several states' leading citizens, sent to DC as statues, were emphatically Christian.

Crater pointed out a painting of George Washington resigning his commission, and quoted King George III as having said "... that if Washington resigned his commission he would be the greatest man on earth."

US Senator Joe Lieberman (Democrat from Connecticut, an Orthodox Jew and Yale graduate) greeted us at breakfast this 23 April 1996 morning saying, "Blessed be those who come in the name of the Lord."

Lieberman spoke about the Wallingford, CT, Town Council deciding to start their meetings with prayer, the ACLU saying that this was a grave mistake. Lieberman said, "Government cannot, nor should not, do it all. The Church is an ally of Government in solving social problems. Belief in God is the greatest unifying factor in the US." At that time, 94 percent of Americans believed in God. As of 24 June 2022, that belief—down to 81 percent— has reached a new low, according to Gallup News. This includes 54 percent who believe in the God of the Bible.

Joe Lieberman and Dan Coats were honorary co-chairmen of the Center for Jewish and Christian Values. Lieberman hoped to work with Michael Horowitz (columnist and Senior Fellow at the Hudson Institute) and others to stop the persecution of evangelicals worldwide.

Lieberman, while attending a demonstration program of school choice in a DC Seventh-Day Adventist school, asked kids, all black, primary age: "Why did your parents send you here?" The answer from a little girl: "No one would have a gun or knife here." He then asked, "Do you like it here?" "Yes," came the reply, "because our teachers love us." Lieberman told us that we need to focus on why we have schools; for children, not to protect a system (i.e. public schools).

Senator Dan Coats (Republican, Indiana) was introduced to us—at the same breakfast at which Lieberman spoke—by Bob Dugan of the NAE, saying Dan is the "man in DC that I respect the most."

Coats talked about his Project for American Renewal being the culmination of 10 years of work. He asked, "What are the responsibilities of parents and government in social areas concerning kids, like delinquency, abuse, and the like?" We are engaged in a fundamental debate over this. One side is big government solving these problems versus admission that big government has failed; give responsibility back to the states, a decentralized effort.

Coats's Project for American Renewal, a joint project with Bill Bennett, wants to move these problems to other institutions, non-government, which need to be restored—the Church, charities, and faith-based charities. He proposed a $1,000 tax deduction for gifts to, say, Habitat for Humanity. He has seen life-changing transformation of social dysfunction through faith-based charity, but not through government programs.

If we may digress for a minute here . . . Lightrider worked with Habitat for Humanity on a project in Homestead, Florida, following Hurricane Andrew's 1992 devastating rampage that destroyed 25,000 homes and damaged an additional 100,000 homes, doing $26.5 billion in damage in the US.

Taylor University professor Chris Bennett organized relief efforts five Januarys in a row, using LtR and Wheels to make the 2,600-mile round trip with scores of Taylor Business majors, during Taylor's Interterm (a mini semester in January), working on an entire subdivision of Habitat houses. After a full day of work, those students would be lectured on college coursework around a campfire where we'd be camping out for the week.

The first January we'd be pouring concrete slabs and framing in walls on each of two or three houses. The next January we'd see those houses had been completed by other groups of workers, lawns had been grown, and kids would be waiting in the front of their new homes for the school bus. As Lieberman experienced with that Seventh-Day Adventist school, faith-based charity can be used by God to work miracles as His love is recycled through His people, being applied in the form of hard work.

I'm still chewing on the wit and wisdom of the world-class American leaders witnessed at these two NAE Insight Briefings some three decades ago. My unified, definite impression continues to see their acknowledgment of God, His Word, and the need to apply both, in prayer and conduct, to the problems, spiritual and material, continuing to plague our Republic.

My prayer is that you, the reader, may broaden your perspective, as have I, with the points of view of these few political leaders prominent in their day. "There is no safety for republics but in self-government, under the influence of a holy heart, swayed by the government of God." This was said in 1831 by Lyman Beecher, renowned Presbyterian clergyman in New England, father of Henry Ward Beecher, an eloquent preacher of the day, and Harriet Beecher Stowe, author of *Uncle Tom's Cabin*.

HOUSE RESOLUTION 397

111th CONGRESS
1st Session

IN THE HOUSE OF REPRESENTATIVES
May 4, 2009
Mr. Forbes (for himself, Mr. McIntyre, Mr. Lamborn, Mr. McCotter, Mr. Neugebauer, Mr. Akin, Mr. Latta, Mr. Jordan of Ohio, Mr. Franks of Arizona, Mr. Wilson of South Carolina, Mrs. Blackburn, Ms. Foxx, Mr. Gingrey of Georgia, Mr. Jones, Mr. Wolf, Mr. Turner, Mr. Aderholt, Mr. Conaway, Mr. Smith of Texas, Mr. Hoekstra, Mr. Young of Florida, Mr. Wamp, Mr. Kline of Minnesota, Mr. Davis of Tennessee, and Mr. Bishop of Utah) submitted the following resolution, which was referred to the Committee on Oversight and Government Reform:

RESOLUTION

Affirming the rich spiritual and religious history of our Nation's founding and subsequent history and expressing support for designation of the first week in May as "America's Spiritual Heritage Week" for the appreciation of and education on America's history of religious faith.

Whereas religious faith was not only important in official American life during the periods of discovery, exploration, colonization, and growth but has also been acknowledged and incorporated into all three branches of the Federal Government from their very beginning;

Whereas the Supreme Court of the United States affirmed this self-evident fact in a unanimous ruling declaring "This is a religious people . . . From the discovery of this continent to the present hour, there is a single voice making this affirmation";

> The first week of May is still recognized as "America's Spiritual Heritage Week: in some contexts, though it's not an official national holiday." (Google, 8 August 2025)

Whereas political scientists have documented that the most frequently cited source in the political period known as The Founding Era was the Bible;

Whereas the first act of America's first Congress in 1774 was to ask a minister to open with prayer and to lead Congress in the reading of four chapters of the Bible;[16]

Whereas Congress regularly attended church and Divine service together en masse;

Whereas throughout the American Founding, Congress frequently appropriated money for missionaries and for religious instruction, a practice that Congress repeated for decades after the passage of the Constitution and the First Amendment;

Whereas in 1776, Congress approved the Declaration of Independence with its 4 direct religious acknowledgments referring to God as the Creator ("All people are endowed by their Creator with certain unalienable rights, that among these are life, liberty and the pursuit of happiness"), the Lawgiver ("the laws of nature and nature's God"), the Judge ("appealing to the Supreme Judge of the world"), and the Protector ("with a firm reliance on the protection of Divine Providence");

Whereas upon approving the Declaration of Independence, John Adams declared that the Fourth of July "ought to be commemorated as the day of deliverance by solemn acts of devotion to God Almighty";

Whereas four days after approving the Declaration, the Liberty Bell was rung;

Whereas the Liberty Bell was named for the Biblical inscription from Leviticus 25:10 emblazoned around it: "Proclaim liberty throughout the land, to all the inhabitants thereof";

Whereas in 1777, Congress, facing a National shortage of "Bibles for our schools, and families, and for the public worship of God in our churches," announced that they "desired to have a Bible printed under their care and by their encouragement" and therefore ordered 20,000 copies of the Bible to be imported "into the different ports of the States of the Union";

Whereas in 1782, Congress pursued a plan to print a Bible that would be "a neat edition of the Holy Scriptures for the use of schools" and therefore approved the production of the first English language Bible printed in America that contained the congressional endorsement that "the United States in Congress assembled . . . recommend this edition of the Bible to the inhabitants of the United States";

Whereas in 1782, Congress adopted (and has reaffirmed on numerous subsequent occasions) the National Seal with its Latin motto *Annuit Coeptis*, meaning "God has favored our undertakings," along with the eye of Providence in a triangle over a pyramid, the eye and the motto "allude to the many signal interpositions of Providence in favor of the American cause";

Whereas the 1783 Treaty of Paris that officially ended the Revolution and established America as an independent

---

[16] This event is further documented in Chapter 26 of this narrative.

begins with the appellation "In the name of the most holy and undivided Trinity";

Whereas in 1787, at the Constitutional Convention in Philadelphia, Benjamin Franklin declared, "God governs in the affairs of men. And if a sparrow cannot fall to the ground without His notice, is it probable that an empire can rise without His aid? . . . Without His concurring aid, we shall succeed in this political building no better than the builders of Babel";

Whereas the delegates to the Constitutional Convention concluded their work by in effect placing a religious punctuation mark at the end of the Constitution in the Attestation Clause, noting not only that they had completed the work with "the unanimous consent of the States present" but they had done so "in the Year of our Lord one thousand seven hundred and eighty seven";

Whereas James Madison declared that he saw the finished Constitution as a product of "the finger of that Almighty Hand which has been so frequently and signally extended to our relief in the critical stages of the Revolution," and George Washington viewed it as "little short of a miracle," and Benjamin Franklin believed that its writing had been "influenced, guided, and governed by that omnipotent, omnipresent, and beneficent Ruler, in Whom all inferior spirits live, and move, and have their being";

Whereas, from 1787 to 1788, State conventions to ratify the United States Constitution not only began with prayer but even met in church buildings;

Whereas in 1795, during construction of the Capitol, a practice was instituted whereby "public worship is now regularly administered at the Capitol, every Sunday morning, at 11 o'clock";

Whereas in 1789, the first Federal Congress, the Congress that framed the Bill of Rights, including the First Amendment, appropriated Federal funds to pay chaplains to pray at the opening of all sessions, a practice that has continued to this day, with Congress not only funding its congressional chaplains but also the salaries and operations of more than 4,500 military chaplains;

Whereas in 1789, Congress, in the midst of framing the Bill of Rights and the First Amendment, passed the first Federal law touching education, declaring that "Religion, morality, and knowledge, being necessary to good government and the happiness of mankind, schools and the means of education shall forever be encouraged";

Whereas in 1789, on the same day that Congress finished drafting the First Amendment, it requested President Washington to declare a National day of prayer and thanksgiving, resulting in the first Federal official Thanksgiving proclamation that declared "it is the duty of all nations to acknowledge the providence of Almighty God, to obey His will, to be grateful for His benefits, and humbly to implore His protection and favor";

Whereas in 1800, Congress enacted naval regulations requiring that Divine service be performed twice every day aboard "all ships and vessels in the navy," with a sermon preached each Sunday;

Whereas in 1800, Congress approved the use of the just-completed Capitol structure as a church building, with

Divine services to be held each Sunday in the Hall of the House, alternately administered by the House and Senate chaplains;

Whereas in 1853, Congress declared that congressional chaplains have a "duty . . . to conduct religious services weekly in the Hall of the House of Representatives";

Whereas by 1867, the church at the Capitol was the largest church in Washington, DC, with up to 2,000 people a week attending Sunday service in the Hall of the House;

Whereas by 1815, over 2,000 official governmental calls to prayer had been issued at both the State and the Federal levels, with thousands more issued since 1815;

Whereas in 1853, the United States Senate declared that the Founding Fathers "had no fear or jealousy of religion itself, nor did they wish to see us an irreligious people . . . they did not intend to spread over all the public authorities and the whole public action of the nation the dead and revolting spectacle of atheistical apathy";

Whereas in 1854, the United States House of Representatives declared "It [religion] must be considered as the foundation on which the whole structure rests . . . Christianity; in its general principles, is the great conservative element on which we must rely for the purity and permanence of free institutions";

Whereas in 1864, by law Congress added "In God We Trust" to American coinage;

Whereas in 1864, Congress passed an act authorizing each State to display statues of two of its heroes in the United States Capitol, resulting in numerous statues of noted Christian clergymen and leaders at the Capitol, including Gospel ministers such as the Revs. James A Garfield, John Peter Muhlenberg, Jonathan Trumbull, Roger Williams, Jason Lee, Marcus Whitman, and Martin Luther King Jr., Gospel theologians such as Roger Sherman, Catholic priests such as Father Damien, Jacques Marquette, Eusebio Kino, and Junipero Serra, Catholic nuns such as Mother Joseph, and numerous other religious leaders;

Whereas in 1870, the Federal Government made Christmas (a recognition of the birth of Christ, an event described by the US Supreme Court as "acknowledged in the Western World for 20 centuries, and in this country by the people, the Executive Branch, Congress, and the courts for two centuries") and Thanksgiving as official holidays;

Whereas, beginning in 1904 and continuing for the next half-century, the Federal Government printed and distributed *The Life and Morals of Jesus of Nazareth* for the use of Members of Congress because of the important teachings it contained;

Whereas in 1931, Congress by law adopted the Star-Spangled Banner as the official National Anthem, with its phrases such as "may the Heav'n-rescued land Praise the Power that hath made and preserved us a nation," and "this be our motto, 'In God is our trust!'";

Whereas in 1954, Congress by law added the phrase "one nation under God" to the Pledge of Allegiance;

Whereas in 1954, a special Congressional Prayer Room was added to the

Capitol with a kneeling bench, an altar, an open Bible, an inspiring stained-glass window with George Washington kneeling in prayer, the declaration of Psalm 16:1: "Preserve me, O God, for in Thee do I put my trust," and the phrase "This Nation Under God" displayed above the kneeling, prayerful Washington;

Whereas in 1956, Congress by law made "In God We Trust" the National Motto, and added the phrase to American currency;

Whereas the constitutions of each of the 50 States, either in the preamble or body, explicitly recognize or express gratitude to God;

Whereas America's first Presidential Inauguration incorporated 7 specific religious activities, including—

1. the use of the Bible to administer the oath;
2. affirming the religious nature of the oath by the adding the prayer "So help me God!" to the oath;
3. inaugural prayers offered by the President;
4. religious content in the inaugural address;
5. civil leaders calling the people to prayer or acknowledgment of God;
6. inaugural worship services attended en masse by Congress as an official part of congressional activities; and
7. clergy-led inaugural prayers, activities which have been replicated in whole or part by every subsequent President;

Whereas President George Washington declared "Of all the dispositions and habits which lead to political prosperity, religion and morality are indispensable supports";

Whereas President John Adams, one of only two signers of the Bill of Rights and First Amendment, declared "As the safety and prosperity of nations ultimately and essentially depend on the protection and the blessing of Almighty God, and the national acknowledgment of this truth is not only an indispensable duty which the people owe to Him";

Whereas President Jefferson not only attended Divine services at the Capitol throughout his presidency and had the Marine Band play at the services, but during his administration church services were also begun in the War Department and the Treasury Department, thus allowing worshippers on any given Sunday the choice to attend church at either the United States Capitol, the War Department, or the Treasury Department if they so desired;

Whereas Thomas Jefferson urged local governments to make land available specifically for Christian purposes, provided Federal funding for missionary work among Indian tribes, and declared that religious schools would receive "the patronage of the government";

Whereas President Andrew Jackson declared that the Bible "is the rock on which our Republic rests";

Whereas President Abraham Lincoln declared that the Bible "is the best gift God has given to men . . . But for it, we could not know right from wrong";

Whereas President William McKinley declared that "Our faith teaches us that there is no safer reliance than upon the God of our fathers, Who has so singularly favored the American people in every national trial and Who will not forsake us so long as we obey His commandments and walk humbly in His footsteps";

Whereas President Teddy Roosevelt declared "The Decalogue and the Golden Rule must stand as the foundation of every successful effort to better either our social or our political life" [I have anecdotally discovered through personal inquiry of friends and strangers that most Americans, including pastors, though taught in our schools up through the 1950s, don't even know the Golden Rule. "Up in the mornin' and out to school, the teacher is teachin' the Golden Rule . . ." from the song "School Days" (1957) sung by Chuck Berry.];

Whereas President Woodrow Wilson declared that "America was born to exemplify that devotion to the elements of righteousness which are derived from the revelations of Holy Scripture";

Whereas President Herbert Hoover declared that "American life is builded, and can alone survive, upon . . . [the] fundamental philosophy announced by the Savior nineteen centuries ago";

Whereas President Franklin D. Roosevelt not only led the Nation in a prayer including: "The light shineth in darkness, and the darkness comprehendeth it not" (John 1:5), "Wisdom is the principal thing; therefore, get wisdom and with all thy getting, get understanding" (Proverbs 4:7), "What doth the Lord require of thee, but to do justly, and to love mercy, and to walk humbly with thy God" (Micah 6:8), and "The heavens declare the Glory of God, and the firmament showeth His handiwork" (Psalm 19:1);

Whereas numerous other of the most important American government leaders, institutions, monuments, buildings, and landmarks both openly acknowledge and incorporate religious words, symbols, and imagery into official venues;

Whereas such acknowledgments are even more frequent at the State and local level than at the Federal level, where thousands of such acknowledgments exist; and

Whereas the first week in May each year would be an appropriate week to designate as "America's Spiritual Heritage Week": Now, therefore, be it *Resolved*, That the United States House of Representatives—

1. affirms the rich spiritual and diverse religious history of our Nation's founding and subsequent history, including up to the current day;
2. recognizes that the religious foundations of faith on which America was built are critical underpinnings of our Nation's most valuable institutions and form the inseparable foundation for America's representative processes, legal systems, and societal structures;
3. rejects, in the strongest possible terms, any effort to remove, obscure, or purposely omit such history from our Nation's public buildings and educational resources; and
4. expresses support for designation of a "America's Spiritual Heritage Week" every year for the appreciation of and education on America's history of religious faith.

This concludes House Resolution 397.

HOUSE CONCURRENT RESOLUTION 443

106th CONGRESS, 2d Session, December 4, 2000

IN THE HOUSE OF REPRESENTATIVES
Mr. Paul (for himself, Mr. Stump, Mr. Metcalf, and Mr. Sanford) submitted the following concurrent resolution; which was referred to the Committee on the Judiciary:

CONCURRENT RESOLUTION
Expressing the sense of the Congress in reaffirming the United States of America as a republic.

Whereas the form of government secured by the Declaration of Independence, the American Revolution, and the Constitution of the United States is a republic—not a democracy;

Whereas the Nation's founders understood that pure "democracies have ever been spectacles of turbulence and contention; have ever been found incompatible with personal security or the rights of property; and have in general been as short in their lives as they have been violent in their deaths" (Federalist No. 10);

Whereas throughout the 224-year history of the United States as an independent and sovereign nation, the people of the United States have never exercised power as a democracy;

Whereas the people of the United States have always acted by and through the Federal Union of the several States, electing Members of Congress from each of the several States and the President and Vice President by electoral votes proportioned to the number of Members of Congress representing each State;

Whereas in the 2000 election for choosing electors for President and Vice President, it appears that the President-elect and Vice President-elect have won a majority of the State electoral vote, but not a plurality of the nationwide popular vote;

Whereas the prospect of electing to office a President and Vice President who did not win the largest number of popular votes has generated proposals calling for a constitutional amendment to provide for the direct popular election of the President and Vice President;

Whereas such a national popular election for President and Vice President disregards the constitutional integrity and inviolability of the 50 States as independent and sovereign governments;

Whereas in their foresight and wisdom, the people of the United States, meeting by representation in State conventions, adopted a national Constitution preserving the independence and equal standing of the 50 States;

Whereas the Federal system of equal and independent States is an essential safeguard against shifting wills of the majority overriding the unchanging rights of the minority;

Whereas to preserve the rights of the minority from a tyranny of the majority, the Constitution of the United States struck a principled balance between the people of the most populous States and the people of the least populous States;

Whereas to that end, the Constitution of the United States provides that the legislatures of each of the several States, without interference from Congress or any other branch of the Federal Government or State governments, determine the manner of election of the President and the Vice President by State electors from each State;

Whereas the number of electors is distributed in accordance with each State's representation in the House of Representatives and in accordance with each State's equal standing in the Senate, not by a direct nationwide election in accordance with population alone;

Whereas the constitutionally prescribed system in the 2000 election for choosing electors for President and Vice President continues to function as originally designed, protecting minority and States' rights from the exercise of majority power; and

Whereas the electoral college system thereby preserves the diversity of the American people and maintains the United States as a Federal republic—not as a democracy:

Now, therefore, be it Resolved by the House of Representatives (the Senate concurring), That it is the sense of the Congress that the United States is not a democracy—but a republic—and that the present constitutionally prescribed means by which the President and Vice President are selected State by State is essential to preserving the diversity of the citizenry of the United States and to maintaining the United States as a Federal republic composed of independent and sovereign States.

APPENDIX TWO

Details—The H1213 and the H1213 Project

The following is verbiage edited from Chapter 31. (See *Notes: The LowRider* at the end of Appendix 2.)

THE LOWRIDER

The structure[1] (lightweight, corrugated, and cast stainless steel) is half the weight of today's coaches yet strong, durability measured in decades (beet juice in the road salt—no problem[2]). Full-length low-passenger floor configuration yields unique benefits: universal accessibility, including the lavatory and both passenger doors with ramps instead of steps; rear emergency exit; low center of gravity provides world-class handling and stability. Weight: 30,000 lbs. GVW enables use of smaller diameter wheels and tires, reducing mechanical space requirements inside passenger compartment—more room for people; eliminates need for a third axle while making the H1213 the only 45-foot highway coach that meets the federal bridge formula. Stainless steel doesn't need paint or the extremely expensive, intrusive manufacturing process that paint requires; graphics may be wrapped.

All-wheel-drive train with redundant power sources for vehicle motivation maximizes motivational ability in all road conditions, reducing likelihood of stranding.

Diesel engine[3] with automatic transmission and transfer case mechanically drives front wheels; belt drives a generator,[4] which electrically powers the rear wheels while charging batteries. Batteries, pre-charged in station, eliminate local exhaust emissions during hundreds of miles of operation, doubling over all miles per gallon.[5]

Steer axle w/duals, smaller inside dual prevents loss of control if outer dual fails; reduces likelihood of stranding of elderly passengers for whom stranding is a hardship.

Drive axle[6] **w/duals and built-in electric motors** complements low-floor design by permitting access to the rear passenger side entrance and to the rear emergency exit.

Air suspension provides a smooth ride with adjustable height and coach kneeling feature, optimizing the step-less benefits of the H1213 low floor design.

Radiator w/charge air cooler roof mounted[7] **above driver** improves mpg while greatly increasing engine cooling efficiency.

Two passenger doors w/ramp[8] **and handrails**[9] **(or Ramp n' Steps**[10]**)** improve pace of entry and egress enhances safety by easing tight scheduling.

Emergency exit[11] **at rear** (historically the sole undamaged area in fatal coach accidents).

Crew rest compartment[12] located on the driver side of the coach immediately forward of the lavatory.

Luggage system,[13] mechanized overhead, electronically operated and supervised, presents luggage curbside within one minute.

Lavatory, ADA accessible, vacuum operated w/fresh-water flush, positive ventilation, and a door that seals—what happens in the lavatory stays in the lavatory. The semicircular sliding lavatory door closes off the toilet area when the lavatory floor space is being used as an entryway for the aft passenger door during coach loading and unloading; lavatory equipped with the Quantum self-securement system by Q'Straint.

Windows with a tilt-in panel at the top allows ventilation while parked, helping deal with anti-idle ordinances w/out compromising security; enables running down the road regardless of weather or HVAC troubles.

Revolutionary Manufacturing System[14] Coaches are to be created in moving rooms within micro factories. Multiple benefits of this system include minimum start-up costs and the ability to manufacture many different products simultaneously[15] (H1213s, shuttle buses, ambulances, limousines, RVs, and the like).

Made in the USA.

THE H1213 PROJECT

Basically, the H1213 was to be a lightweight, 45-foot, low-floor motor coach with a mechanized overhead luggage-handling system. We believe that God gave us a bigger idea than the H1213 alone, an idea we call the H1213 Project. The specter of actually engineering, manufacturing, and selling a redefined motor coach in the USA to fund Lightrider Ministries while providing these state-of-the-art motor coaches to other ministries serving seniors greatly brightened our vision for the H1213.

Lightrider's H1213 Project took off in earnest with what we consider to be a couple of divine appointments. Denny Johnson, an old friend from my Wandering Wheels days, had introduced us to Randy Redmer, an industrialist working in Michigan. Randy connected us with Bruce Emmons of Autokinetics in Troy, MI. When we took the Lightrider with a group of friends and supporters to Troy to meet Emmons, Tom Crumm, retired after 30 years with General Motors, happened to be visiting Autokinetics that very same day.

Emmons had designed and built, in his micro-factory, a prototype two-axle, electric, 40-foot bus using his patented lightweight, corrugated, stainless-steel structure, that very well might enable the essential as well as innovative design features LtR had envisioned in our H1213. We all took a ride in it.

Crumm, a third-generation auto worker, an industrial engineer with decades of experience, had developed a manufacturing system that replaces the assembly line. A factory using Crumm's system could be started up at a cost of thousands of dollars rather than a cost of millions of dollars. A system that may begin as a single manufacturing bay may then be grown because the product is sold and profits are reinvested.

Once fully grown, this system allows multiple different products to be manufactured simultaneously without the very costly annual need of assembly lines to be shut down for retooling. Of equal importance is that Crum's system dovetails nicely with Emmons' micro-factory concept—building buses in micro-factories located where those buses were to be used, enabling those factories to become maintenance facilities for those buses.

It will be necessary to start Lightrider, LLC, a for-profit company, to establish micro-factories to manufacture, sell and service the H1213, as well as any other vehicles that would benefit from universal accessibility and lightweight structure. All profits not benefiting investors would go to fund the planting of H1213s as mobile retreat ministry tools for other ministries and to support Lightrider Ministries. Our desire is to conduct mobile retreats without charging participants for boarding the Lightrider any more than congregants are charged to enter churches.

THE NORTH AMERICAN MOTOR COACH MARKET

(See *Notes: The North American Motor Coach Market* at the end of Appendix 2.)

Volume—companies, coaches, passengers, miles, fuel, jobs, and dollars: In 2012, 3,954 North American motor coach operators had 39,607 motor coaches in service that carried 637 million passengers a total of 75.7 billion miles, averaging 52,400 miles per motor coach—an industry average of 39.3 passengers on each of that year's 16,100 motor coach trips, achieving (with average fuel efficiency of 6.1 miles per gallon) 222.7 passenger miles per gallon of fuel. The motor coach industry provided 132,900 jobs (71,600 full time and 61,200 part time) at an average of 3.4 employees per coach.[1] The industry contributed about $145.8 billion in economic impact, about .9 percent of US GDP.[2]

New Motor Coach Sales: North American coach sales in 2013—1,510 coaches,[3] up from 2010's total of 1,276 coaches, the lowest since 1992. In 2009, 1,654 coaches were sold. The highest annual sales in recent years were 1998's total of over 3,600 coaches sold. This high was no doubt due to the fact that the 45-foot length had just become available.[4] North America accounts for 1 percent of the worldwide motor coach market. Average annual new coach sales in North America for the five-year period 2009–2013 are 1,581.

Premise: The elderly are the largest traveling people group in America[5]—they have the time and the money to travel. We make specialty vehicles for hauling trash, delivering packages, concrete, and glass. Now we need one for hauling seniors. "In meeting the needs of seniors, we meet the needs of all our riders, especially those who have a disability."[6] "Our future is aging Baby Boomers staying alive for longer periods of time, and whose lives we can make richer and more meaningful by transporting them safely from their dreary parlors and nursing homes to the venues of their remaining hopes and dreams."[7] Want to get out and about? Take the bus.

Green sells: Motor coaches, in 2009, achieved 206.6 passenger miles per gallon (PMG)—over four and a half times as many PMG than the best of the following types of vehicles: light rail, 92.4; transit buses, 31.4; domestic airplanes, 44; personal automobiles, 27.2; hybrid cars, 46.[8] By 2012, motor coach PMG improved to 222.7,[9] a 12.8 percent increase since 2009. Comparing the projected 20–30 mpg of the H1213, PMG (using 25 mpg as one factor and 50 passengers as the other) will be 1,250 PMG. Want to save fuel and keep the air clean? Take the bus . . . or rather the H1213.

Safety sells: Highway coach travel is safer than any other travel mode besides scheduled airlines, according to the National Safety Council. It is by far the safest form of highway travel. The average death rate per 100 million passenger miles between 2006 and 2008 was .03 on intercity motor coaches. It was .6 in passenger automobiles and .06 on railroad passenger trains. Want to arrive alive? Take the bus.

Getting seniors on the coach gets them out of the driver's seat. In 2005, 11% of all fatal car crashes involved drivers aged 65 or older. By 2030, the year Gen Xers (62 million strong) hit 65 and all Baby Boomers are at least 65, safety analysts predict that the Boomers alone could be responsible for 25 percent of all fatal crashes.[10] Just 32 years hence, 2047, the Millennials, 80 million strong, begin to hit age 65.

Falling in the step well is the number-one cause of lawsuits in the motor coach industry.[11] For seniors, falls can be the beginning of their end. Eliminating step wells eliminates a potentially life-threatening danger for senior travelers. ADA has eliminated steps everywhere motor coaches go, so why take steps with you?

Ease of entry and egress eases tight schedules. "I can say with absolute certainty that roughly half of all accidents and incidents are mere symptoms of insufficient running and recovery time."[12] Though this statement refers to city-bus operations, it makes the point that tight schedules lead to mishaps. It takes 18 minutes to unload a highway coach full of seniors, and 12 minutes to reload.[13] That's half an hour just to get on and off the coach. The H1213 will relieve much of this pressure.

Emergency egress located in the only area of a motor coach historically undamaged in fatal motor coach crashes—the rear end (according to John Hill, former Administrator of the National Highway Safety Administration under George W. Bush)—could save lives.

Economic impact—motor coaches spread the wealth: A motor coach on tour greatly impacts local economies when making a stop with an overnight stay. According to a 2005 Peter Pan Bus Lines study, figuring an average of 46 passengers, such a stay nets $5,000 to $7,500 in expenditures for meals, lodging, shopping, admission fees, souvenirs, and local taxes.

Looking at the bigger picture, the motor coach tourism industry employs 1.4 million Americans, drawing $55.7 billion in wages (2012).[14]

Future motor coach outlook: Alternatives to single-occupant vehicles (SOV) will come about through a dramatic shift in our transportation paradigms brought about as we "leverage both technology and the built environment to provide people with mobility options." Further, "the marketplace is likely to shift the transportation paradigm from one based on 'auto mobility' to one based on mobility."[15]

Given the safety issue of seniors behind the wheel, our inability to "pave our way out of congestion," and our stratosphere-bound fuel prices, motor coach travel may be the best alternative to SOVs for seniors wanting to get out and about. "There is little doubt that older people are increasingly placing travel as a higher priority in their retirement years, mainly because they are feeling healthier, wealthier, better educated, more independent, and have an abundance of leisure time and a lessening of social and family obligations compared with younger people."[16]

NOTES: THE LOWRIDER

1. Corrugated and cast stainless steel integral coach body designed and created by Bruce Emmons of Autokinetics, Troy, MI. The full

length of the passenger deck is low-floor—that is the deck is mounted below the center of the wheels supporting the coach, 11 inches above the pavement (about the same ride height as other coaches' first step).

2. Six-year-old, top-of-the-line motor coaches in northern Indiana are requiring structural renovation necessitated by this aggressive road-salt solution.

3. The front of the H1213 is a cutaway truck chassis, including the cab with driver's seat, controls, diesel engine, automatic transmission, transfer case, and steer axle. A large generator is mounted where the passenger seat would have been. The cab has a driver's door, allowing him or her to avoid the crowded main aisle, and so arrive more promptly for outside chores like deploying the overhead luggage-handling system, clearing bystanders from the coach entrances, and such. The cab's passenger door provides access for servicing the generator and getting at emergency equipment stowed in that area, such as flares, reflectors, and the like. A tilt-forward "dog house" provides optimum engine access endearing the H1213 to the truck service world. It also may be easily styled to give the H1213 a retro look. Regenerative exhaust/muffler system, required by EPA, may be mounted as a chrome "stack" on the driver's side, keeping the exhaust fumes and the excessive heat inherent in this system high and out from under the coach.

4. The large generator mounted in place of the passenger seat may be belt- or gear-driven by the same engine powering the front wheels. This dual use of the diesel eliminates the need for a second diesel engine to power the generator.

5. Batteries, charged in station and at overnight stops, will motivate the H1213 for 150 miles before the diesel engine and generator must be employed. When these hundreds of non-fuel-consuming miles are figured into the overall miles traveled, the miles per gallon become most impressive.

6. Drive axle is a ZF AVE 130 Portal Axle. "It is both an advanced low floor axle and a fully-fledged 250-kilowatt electric drive. It considerably reduces consumption in hybrid or purely electric configurations. More over the axle can function very well as the only drive source in buses with absolutely zero local emissions." (*National Bus Trader*, December 2015, page 10) The AVE 130 weighs less than 2,500 pounds, occupies the same space as an unpowered low-floor axle, yet is able to carry AND motivate over 28,000 pounds at highway speeds. It has 321 horsepower available in the short run, and 160 horsepower for continuous operation.

7. The charge air cooler and radiator are mounted above the cab roof, shortening

Model of one iteration of the LowRider/H1213. The roof rack with canvas is actually a fascia, part of the retro look, concealing a mechanized overhead luggage handling system. Note roof mounted all electric AC unit.

the mechanical drive train footprint while, with the use of an air scoop above the windshield, increasing wind velocity across these two heat-exchanging components. Natural airflow at highway speeds greatly reduces or eliminates the use of engine cooling fans. As cooling fans draw about 50 horsepower, this design stops the persistent, parasitic horsepower loss during this, the longest duty cycle of a highway coach.

8. The entrance ramps, made possible at both passenger doors because of the low-floor design, eliminate steps, a barrier for 27 percent (according to Motor Coach Census, ABA Foundation, 11 February 2016) of America's coach ridership—the elderly—increasing coach use by this growing, underserved demographic, reducing per-passenger cost, and increasing profits for coach operators while complying with new ADA requirements. Eliminating steps eliminates the number one cause of lawsuits in the coach travel industry: falling on steps; steps have been removed everywhere coaches go, so why take them with you? Today's high deck coaches take 30 minutes to unload and reload elderly passengers.

   No need for a wheelchair lift—wheelchair users roll right in and tie themselves down using a Quantum self-securement system made by Q'Straint. The driver or escort may see to the luggage or logistics rather than having to assist boarding or departing wheelchair and/or electric cart users.

9. Handrails, on both sides of a ramp, are essential for the safety of walking passengers entering and exiting a coach. Each of the two 52-inch-wide doors on the H1213 is

Another iteration of the LowRider/H1213. Note the electric HVAC unit on the roof, as well as the radiator and charge-air cooler over the driver's area, with an air scoop over the windshield, and the deployed overhead luggage-handling system toward the rear of the coach.

hinged on the forward side of their respective doorways. They open 90 degrees and lock in place. Each has a handrail on the inside, which roughly parallels their deployed ramp. From the opposite side of the doorway, the aft side, a 52-inch handrail swings out simultaneously, mimicking the action of the door, becoming parallel to the rail on the door, and locks in place.

10. Ramp n' Step is a six-foot ramp that may be quickly converted into three four-inch-rise, two-foot-deep steps. Ramps are for wheels. A passenger with a walker, wheeled or not, is safer using short-rise deep steps that accommodate him or her *and* the walker than using a ramp, especially when going downhill as in exiting the coach. At this writing, the inventor of Ramp n' Step, Brian Pierson, is walking those streets of gold.

11. A breakout window, located in the very rear bulkhead of the coach, may be used as an emergency exit should the coach end up

on either of its sides in an accident. If the coach has remained upright, the rear side door would be the easiest and safest exit to use. Tragedies like the fiery semi-truck/motor coach collision in California that took 10 lives, or the horrible situation post-Rita when an evacuation coach loaded with severely mobility challenged passengers caught on fire with the loss of 27 passengers, will be greatly mitigated by this quick, universal exit system.

12. Until an autonomous driving system is perfected, the best hedge against driver fatigue—an almost universal factor in fatal coach accidents—is a second, rested, onboard driver. A crew rest compartment also alleviates much of the expense of getting relief drivers positioned down the road to take the wheel from drivers when their hours of operation expire. It provides a rest haven for drivers to nap during passenger activities off the coach—nothing like a nap to perk up a lethargic mood.

13. Overhead luggage system, locating the greater weight of people and seating below the lesser weight of their luggage, lowers the H1213's center of gravity, significantly increasing vehicle stability. Eight luggage compartment doors and the dangerous, traffic-side luggage handling typical of traditional motor coaches are eliminated; mechanization will reduce workers' comp claims. American drivers are aging just like the passengers and the rest of our population.

14. Crumm, Thomas A. *What is Good for General Motors? Solving America's Industrial Conundrum*, Agora Publishing, 2010 (page 215).

15. Ibid (page 216).

NOTES: THE NORTH AMERICAN MOTOR COACH MARKET

1. Executive Summary, Motor Coach Census 2013, ABA Foundation.
2. Executive Summary, Economic Impact Study, ABA Foundation, 2 January 2013.
3. 2012 Update Motor Coach Safety Action Plan (USDOT), page 3.
4. *National Bus Trader* (*NBT*), March 2011, pages 22–28.
5. *NBT*, March 2007, page 40.
6. *Seniors and Transportation*, Community Transportation Association of America (CTAA) with the Beverly Foundation, page 1.
7. Ned Einstein, President: Transportation Alternatives (www.transalt.com), in *NBT*, March 2007, page 41.
8. Motor Coach Facts 2009, ABA Foundation.
9. Motor Coach Census 2013, ABA Foundation, page 5.
10. "The Dawning of a New Era in Transit: Major Trends," www.nationalrtap.org, February 2010, page 3.
11. *NBT*, January 2006.
12. *NBT*, December 2012, page 40.
13. Anecdotal information—actually the lesser of two egress-and-entry cycles timed by a tour guide and a coach driver in Indiana.
14. The American Bus Association, *Foundation Economic Impact Study: Methodology & Documentation*, 2 January 2013, page 1.
15. Southeastern Institute of Research: White Paper #1—*Mr. Toad's Wild Ride and the Long-Term Impact of the Rising Price of Gas*.
16. *Baby Boomers and Future Seniors: How to Get Them on Motor Coaches*, ABA Foundation, page 9.

www.ingramcontent.com/pod-product-compliance
Lightning Source LLC
Chambersburg PA
CBHW061354010526
44107CB00011B/934